Samuel Timmins

A History of Warwickshire

Samuel Timmins

A History of Warwickshire

ISBN/EAN: 9783337012083

Printed in Europe, USA, Canada, Australia, Japan

Cover: Foto ©ninafisch / pixelio.de

More available books at **www.hansebooks.com**

POPULAR COUNTY HISTORIES.

A
HISTORY OF WARWICKSHIRE.

BY
SAM: TIMMINS, F.S.A.

"That shire which we the heart of England well may call."
MICHAEL DRAYTON'S POLYOLBION XIII.

LONDON:
ELLIOT STOCK, 62, PATERNOSTER ROW, E.C.
1889.

PUBLISHER'S PREFACE.

THE present volume of the POPULAR COUNTY HISTORIES is the fifth of the series in which it appears.

The indulgence of subscribers is craved for the lateness of its appearance; circumstances which need not be particularized have hindered its publication for many months. It is intended that the succeeding volumes shall be issued in more rapid succession: and with greater regularity than has marked the previous ones.

CONTENTS.

CHAPTER	PAGE
I. GENERAL HISTORY	1
II. LEGENDS	17
III. TOPOGRAPHY	23
IV. PHYSIOGRAPHY AND GEOLOGY	29
V. ZOOLOGY AND BOTANY	43
VI. ARCHÆOLOGY	52
VII. BIOGRAPHY	116
VIII. FOLK-LORE AND DIALECT	210
IX. CASTLES, MANSIONS, AND OLD HOUSES	231
X. CITIES, TOWNS, ETC.	252
BIBLIOGRAPHY	288
INDEX	297

HISTORY OF WARWICKSHIRE.

CHAPTER I.

GENERAL HISTORY.

The Forest of Arden.—British and Saxon Times.—Roman Occupation.—Norman Conquest.—Wars of the Roses.—Gunpowder Plot.—Great Civil War.—Battle of Edge Hill.—City of Refuge.—Rupert's Raid on Birmingham.—Sacheverell Rioting.—Birmingham, the 'Hardware Village.'—Reform Bill Agitation.

MICHAEL DRAYTON'S line in his 'Polyolbion' (xiii. 2), 'That shire which we the heart of England well may call,' and his marginal note that 'Warwickshire is the middle shire of England,' fully justify his claim that his native county is the central shire, as a glance at any map will show. A line drawn from Berwick-on-Tweed to the Isle of Wight, from Dover to the Isle of Anglesey, and from the Severn to the Humber, intersect each other in Warwickshire, which is, therefore, fairly entitled to its claim to be the central county. Its comparative isolation from the coast-lines has, however, been modified by the number of great old roads which have traversed its surface, from the old British 'ways' to the Icknield (or Rykenield) Street, and the Watling Street of Roman times. The Icknield Street runs through the county from south to north, and crosses the Watling Street, which forms the north-east boundary of the county, and still retains its name as a great highway. Two roads cross at Etocetum, near Wall and Lichfield, and respectively antedate the Midland and North-Western Railways of our days as to their local direction. The county is surrounded by Leicestershire, Northamptonshire, Oxfordshire, Worcestershire, Staffordshire and Derbyshire. Some of the points of contact are limited as to size, and Birmingham practically extends into Worcestershire and Staffordshire. The name is derived from that of the county town—Warwick, the origin of which is not clearly determined; but it has certainly some connection with a tribe of Wiccii, who, with the Cornavii, occupied this part of England before the Roman invasion. The early history is very obscure, and few definite details are available till the Roman Conquest, when Ostorius Scapula, A.D. 50, the second Roman governor, established a series of military posts on the Severn, and the district was afterwards included in the province known as Flavia Cæsariensis, and in later days as the division called Brittania Secunda. Few traces of Roman occupation have been found, except on the lines of the two great roads, the Ikenield and the Watling Street; and even thereon, as usual, only near the principal 'stations.' The survival of the Roman castrum appears most prominently in the name of Mancetter (Manduessedum) on the north-eastern boundary of the county, but in the next county of Stafford the name Etocetum marks the line of a Roman road. The facts of the Roman occupation of the district are also few. The woodland country evidently gave great security to the various tribes, and the influence of the Roman invaders extended very little beyond their own roads and camps. The successor of Ostorius, however, seems to have made some concessions to the British chieftains of the Wiccii (Venusius), who were allowed to retain some rights and some independence; but Venusius afterwards joined the Silures in opposing the Romans, and under Suetonius Paulinus the Roman domination was completed and secured.

Warwickshire was, in fact, the real 'Arden,' which practically included the whole county, and very little if any beyond its boundaries, and was chiefly inhabited by the Wiccian Ceangi, or herdsmen—so far as the south part of the county was concerned—and this was known as the 'Feldon,' while the county north of the Avon was known as the 'Woodland,' Arden being divided into these two parts. The Woodland is described by Drayton as almost entirely forest, while the Feldon was more open country, partially cleared and cultivated, but still with many patches of forests and woods. The Arden, the common Keltic name for a forest, referred to, is further described by Drayton 'to have been the largest of the British forests,' and it extended from the banks of the Avon to the Trent on the north, and possibly to the Severn on the west, while on the east it had a probable boundary in a line from the High Cross on the Watling Street to Burton-on-Trent. These limits are somewhat doubtful, but it is certain that 'Ardęn' was practically all Warwickshire, and probably included the forest-land of neighbouring counties. On the division of England into shires, the counties of Worcester and Stafford took various portions of the old wild Arden, and the name remains now only in Warwickshire, where Henley-in-Arden in the 'Feldon,' and Hampton-in-Arden in the 'Woodland,' still preserve the old sylvan name.

After the departure of the Romans from Britain the history of Warwickshire is almost blank. Its midland site clearly secured it from the tumults and invasions which troubled the seaboard counties, and left its people in comparative peace. Credda was the first Saxon commander who penetrated into woody Warwickshire, and historians have scarcely any record of the county until the establishment of the Saxon heptarchy, when it became part of the great kingdom of Mercia, and had its share of the rule and rude pomp of the Mercian kings. Tamworth—only a part of which is now in the county—was the seat of several of the Mercian monarchs, and the village of Kingsbury, on the Tame, was once a famous place as a royal residence. A tumulus at Seckington marks the site of the battle and the burial of West Saxons and Danes (when Tamworth had been destroyed by the Danes), and where Ethelbald, the tenth King of Mercia, fought (A.D. 757) Cuthred, King of the West Saxons, and was slain by Barged, one of his own men.

The Norman Conquest begins the first formal record of Warwickshire by the famous survey of lands and landowners in Domesday Book, which not only gives a contemporary report, but a comparative report of the areas, possessions, and valuation of lands in the time of Edward the Confessor, in whose reign a similar but smaller survey had been made. The famous Saxon Chronicle, too, gives many details of names and places, but cannot be compared as to facts and history with the Conqueror's survey. This great national work includes a mass of details, principally territorial or personal, but others of the greatest value as to names of places, condition of cities, towns and villages, and especially as to possessions and values of lands, manors, mills, churches, priests, villeins, ploughs, woods and forests, which are minute and careful enough to enable the student eight centuries later to gain a vivid picture of Warwickshire, as well as of nearly all the English counties. The Norman William may almost be forgiven for his conquest and his confiscations, in consideration of the ample details which his survey affords of the condition of England before and during his reign. The survey, begun in 1081 and completed in 1086, is in every way a wonderful work, and a lasting honour to the Norman scribes, by whose skill and care it was compiled. Its principal Warwickshire interest is in its citation of the names of Saxon landowners and their possessions, and especially of those of Turchill, who, after fortifying Warwick Castle at the command of the King, was then dispossessed, and his vast tracts of land given to Henry de Newburgh, one of the Conqueror's favourites. Also included in the survey is a list of the other Norman followers to whom lands were granted, of the highest historic value, which is increasingly appreciated as the great Survey Record is more fully studied and explored.

The reign of Henry III. owed to Warwickshire some important chapters of the history of those troublous times. The famous Simon de Montfort, Earl of Leicester, who held Kenilworth Castle, had garrisoned the place, and appointed Sir John Giffard governor, and the garrison frequently ravaged the country and destroyed the houses and farms. The Earl of Warwick having taken the side of the King, Sir John Giffard and his troops surprised and attacked Warwick Castle, and took the Earl and Countess prisoners, and became a terror to the neighbourhood by another attack on Brandon Castle, near Coventry, which they demolished. A year after the Battle of Lewes, in which the Earl of Leicester and the Barons gained a victory, and just before the Battle of Evesham—which Prince Edward and his party won—Simon de Montfort, son of the Earl of Leicester, who was proceeding from London with his army to join his father in Wales, was surprised at Kenilworth by Prince Edward, who made a forced and sudden march there, and routed and dispersed De Montfort's troops, and took the Earl of Oxford and many other famous persons prisoners. De Montfort, who had remained in Kenilworth Castle, contrived to escape hurriedly; and Prince Edward felt unable to attack a castle of such enormous strength. In a skirmish, however, the Prince seized 'prodigious booty,' including fifteen standards, which he carried in front of his army on his march to Evesham. They served as a decoy to the Earl of Leicester, who thought his own son was approaching, but soon saw his error, and exclaimed : ' May God then receive our souls, for our bodies are in the power of our enemies.' After the Battle of Evesham, where the Earl of Leicester was slain, his son, De Montfort, who had escaped, returned to Kenilworth, but afterwards fled to France, and Henry de Hastings was left as governor of the Castle. Henry III. approached with a large army, and although the garrison made a brave and memorable defence, famine compelled a surrender after a fierce six months' siege.

The Wars of the Roses contributed another chapter to Warwickshire history. The county was divided in allegiance to the ' Two Roses.' The members of the House of Neville (of which the Earl of Warwick was a distinguished branch) supported the House of York, and his territorial influence made the party extremely strong in the county. The town of Warwick was, therefore, necessarily on the ' York ' side, while the city of Coventry, only twelve miles distant, was thoroughly Lancastrian ; and as Henry and Margaret had won the favour of the citizens by frequent visits, and had made the city and some neighbouring parishes a separate 'county,' the affection and gratitude were increased. In 1460, when a strong force under the Earl of Warwick and the Earl of Marche (afterwards Edward IV.) proceeded to London in search of the royal forces, the Lancastrians were quartered in Coventry; but they quitted the city soon afterwards, and the Battle of Northampton ensued, in which, among the slain on the side of Henry, Sir William Lucie, of Charlecote, was found. In 1470, however, the Earl of Warwick, having quarrelled with Edward, took the Lancastrian side and entered Coventry, where Edward IV. was refused admission, and retired to Warwick, where he found a friendly reception. In the reign of Richard III., when the Earl of Richmond landed at Milford Haven to support his claim to the Crown, the Sheriff of Warwickshire levied troops to assist King Richard; but it is probable that they were not engaged in the decisive battle of Bosworth Field, since Richard Boughton (the Sheriff) was slain two days before that battle, and was probably encountered and overpowered by some of Richmond's troops on his way to help the King.

The Gunpowder Plot next brought Warwickshire into national history, since many of the conspirators, and some of the preparations, were connected with the county. The plot to kill the King, Prince Henry, and other nobles and magnates on the opening of Parliament was principally the work of Robert Catesby, of Lapworth and Bushwood, in Warwickshire. It was further proposed to seize Prince Charles, or the Princess Elizabeth, then living at Combe Abbey, near Coventry, the newly-built house of Lord Harrington, as she was chosen to be the Roman Catholic representative, and to be married to some Roman Catholic peer. Catesby's father had been frequently fined and imprisoned for recusancy, and Robert seems to have been formerly a Protestant, when he married Catherine, the daughter of Sir Thomas Leigh, of Stoneleigh; but his mother was a Roman Catholic, one of the Throckmortons of Coughton Court. He had long brooded over the wrongs done to his religion, and, like some others of his day, would not accept the toleration of the reign, which many of his fellow-believers were disposed to do. He associated himself first with three desperadoes, and afterwards with Guido Fawkes, to arrange the details of the plot, which was discussed and extended chiefly at the old manor-house of Norbrook, at Bushwood, at Clopton, and at Coughton. The Warwickshire part of the plot was arranged to be accomplished by a hunting match at Dunsmore, near Dunchurch, and on receipt of the news of the success of the plot in London, the local conspirators were to ride off to Combe Abbey, and to carry off the Princess Elizabeth. The house at Norbrook was the meeting-place

8   History of Warwickshire.

of the chief conspirators, and they met also at Bushwood and at Clopton, which Rokewood had taken as tenant; but Catesby lived at Ashby St. Ledgers after selling his Warwickshire estates. There was a muster of many people at Dunchurch in the vague hope of some news, and before midnight on the 5th of November, 1605, the news was brought by Catesby, Rokewood and others, who had ridden post-haste from London, that Guido Fawkes had been arrested the night before, and that the plot had failed. The chief culprits fled, seizing what arms they could find, and resolved to make a stand in Staffordshire, near Holbeach. On their way they stopped to dry their powder, which had been damped in fording a stream, and Catesby, Rokewood, Morgan and Grant were blown from their seats, and their faces scorched and blackened. The Sheriff of Worcester arrived and attacked the house, and Percy and Catesby were shot, Rokewood was wounded and taken prisoner, with Winter, Morgan, Grant and others, and the Gunpowder Plot was ended, except as to the trials and punishments which followed, and the hurried retreat of all suspected persons.

The great Civil War supplied some important and exciting incidents to the annals of Warwickshire. The county generally was on the Roundhead side, and Lord Brooke, of Warwick Castle, was one of the fiercest of the enemies of the King. Sir William Dugdale, of Blythe Hall, in the county, was one of the royal heralds, and, as garter king-at-arms, he attended Charles to Nottingham, and made the proclamation when the royal standard was raised and the great Civil War began. The first great battle between the Royalist and Parliamentary forces was fought in October, 1642, near the small town of Kineton, in the south of the county, and on the plain below Edge Hill, from which the battle derives its name. The Royalist troops had arrived from neighbouring villages, and had mustered in large numbers early on the morning of Sunday,

Battle of Edge Hill.

23rd October, on the heights of Edge Hill. The line extended from its right on Bullet Hill to its left at the 'Sun Rising,' and was well protected on flanks and rear, with the plain, then open country, a hundred feet below the cliff. The King rode along the lines 'clad in steel, and with a star and garter on, a black velvet mantle over his armour, and a steel cap covered with velvet on his head;' and addressed his officers in his tent with, 'Come life or death, your King will bear you company.' Lord Lindsay offered up his quaint, brief prayer: 'O Lord, Thou knowest how busy I must be to-day! If I forget Thee, do not Thou forget me! March on, boys!' About two o'clock the royal forces prepared to descend the steep face of the cliff to attack the Parliamentarians on the field below. Prince Rupert led the cavalry on the right, Lord Wilmot on the left, while the centre was entrusted to General Ruthven and Sir Jacob Astley, with the King and his pensioners in the rear. The ground was wet and miry, but the day fair overhead. About three o'clock the sound of two cannon—fired by the Roundheads—rolled and echoed along the lofty cliff, and the battle had begun. The King's left cavalry charged towards Battle Farm (since so called), where Essex had planted some guns, and were repulsed. Prince Rupert, on the right wing, charged down the hill towards Kineton with better success, and drove back Sir James Ramsay and his troops by his impetuous charge, but Rupert, with his characteristic rashness, rushed on to the plunder of the baggage-waggons at Kineton, while the rest of the Royalist troops were losing the day. The Parliamentary left wing was routed, but the right wing stood well, and the centre held its ground and advanced. When Rupert returned it was too late. John Hampden had arrived from Stratford, opened fire on Rupert's troops, drove him to retire in great confusion, and to throw away his beaver and feather that he might cease to be a mark. The royal army was in great danger;

it was severely pressed on its left and its front. The King was within half a musket-shot of the enemy, and the ground from which Rupert had driven Ramsay had been regained. Both armies had suffered severely, but the Parliamentarian troops had held their ground, while the Royalists had retired to their more comfortable quarters. Although the success was doubtful, the Parliamentarians seem on the whole to have had the advantage, for their horse on the field were victorious, and their infantry superior. The slaughter was very great, and has been variously estimated from one thousand to five thousand, but Sir William Dugdale, who was present at the battle, and who, with 'a skilful surveyor,' visited the field in the following February, computes the number to have been less than one thousand men. The Prince of Wales (aged twelve) and the Duke of York (aged ten), afterwards Charles II. and James II., were on the field under the charge of the famous Dr. Harvey (the physician to the King), who is recorded to have forgotten alike his own danger and his royal charges, and to have taken out a book and begun to read, till warned by the whizzing of the bullets around him that it was time to retire. At Alcester, twenty miles away, Richard Baxter was preaching on that eventful Sunday from the text, 'The kingdom of heaven suffereth violence,' little knowing what was doing at Edge Hill, while his audience distinctly heard the solemn booming of cannon during the whole of his discourse.

The site of the battle-field is still well marked and readily traceable, although the lands have long been enclosed, and farms and orchards now flourish on the soil. The 'Sun Rising,' a fine old stone-built house, remains unchanged, and from Edge Hill the details of the first great fight may be clearly made out. On the hills—the Burton Dassett Hills, which join Edge Hill on the east—the old Beacon Tower still remains where the first signal-fire was lighted in the cresset to flash the news to London by way of Ivinghoe, forty miles away. In the year following the battle, Kineton received the King again. His Queen had held her court at New Place, Stratford-on-Avon, where William Shakespeare had lived and died twenty-seven years before. She was on her way to meet the King, who had come from Oxford, and they met at Kineton, where Rupert also came, Prince Charles and the Duke of York, who accompanied the King, 'riding forth with most cheerful countenances to receive the blessings of so deare and renowned a mother.' The meeting was celebrated by a medal struck in honour of the occasion, and by some loyal verses too. Ten months after, the Battle of Edge Hill had wrought some wondrous changes: the King had advanced to London and retired, Essex had taken Reading, Waller had been successful in the West, but his defeat at Devizes and Rupert's capture of Bristol had inspired the Royalists and thrown a gleam of hopefulness over the darkening future of the royal lives.

The great Civil War was largely associated with Warwickshire and its inhabitants in many other ways and on many other occasions, in addition to those connected with the first great fight. Sir William Dugdale had also to summon the garrisons of the castles of Warwick and Banbury to surrender to the King, in August, 1642, and the duties were duly performed in herald's coat-of-arms and with trumpets blowing. The garrison of Banbury surrendered, but that of Warwick refused, and being a place of great strength, and with a large garrison and a more gallant commander, the summons was contemned and the garrison then proclaimed as 'traitors against the King, his crown and dignity.' At Coventry, also, the same anti-Royalist spirit was soon shown, and 'rebels' and 'schismatics' and 'sectaries' assembled there, as a walled city where safety was more certain than in unprotected towns.

On his way from Nottingham to Edge Hill, the King had stopped three nights at Birmingham as the guest of the loyal Sir Thomas Holte, but the Hall had been attacked by the 'men of Birmingham' with a cannonade and partial siege, and the town was afterwards severely punished for its disloyalty. Coventry became a 'city of refuge,' and was in its turn proclaimed, during a short visit of the King to Stoneleigh, some four miles away, when the defenders of the city indignantly refused to surrender to him. Kenilworth Castle, another strong fortress, was at first held by the Royalists, and as the 'rebels' were rapidly increasing, the garrison was secretly withdrawn, but was followed and attacked by troops from Coventry, and a skirmish occurred at Curdworth, near Coleshill, in which the Royalists were victorious, and afterwards present at the Battle of Edge Hill.

One of the most memorable incidents of the Civil War time, next to the Battle of Edge Hill, is found in the year following that contest, when Prince Rupert attacked and burned part of the town of Birmingham, which Clarendon described, as 'of as great fame for hearty, wilful, affected disloyalty to the King as any town in England,' and this disloyalty had taken the most practical form by the alleged supply of 15,000 swords for the use of the Parliamentary troops. As an unwalled town, and without a charter or municipal privileges, the town had long been a 'city of refuge' for those who had been driven by persecutions—religious or political—from other towns. The reward of this civic hospitality had been that a large, ingenious and industrious population was increasing, without any prejudices in favour of sovereigns of the Stuart type. Two months after the first shot had been fired, Charles came to Birmingham with a large force to visit Sir Thomas Holte at Aston Hall; but he found no welcome in the streets of the town, and the troops were received with hootings and groans, and their excesses made the people less loyal than before. On the third day the King had left, but the excited townsfolk hated the surly old baronet who had entertained the King, attacked the Hall, and seized the royal plate from the carriage in which it was being removed, and sent it for safety to Warwick Castle. This was a declaration against the sovereign by force of arms—a declaration of war. Soon bands were formed, drill was practised, arms were provided, and the royal troops as they marched were attacked wherever they were found. Every King's messenger who could be found was seized and 'sent to Coventry,' which, as a walled city, was better able to keep prisoners than a straggling, unfortified town. While ready to supply pikes and swords for the 'rebels,' they refused to supply the Royalists. All the country round looked to Birmingham for help. Coventry was threatened and was in danger, and three hundred men of Birmingham went to aid in its defence. The first great struggle with the Royalists was now imminent. Early in 1643, Prince Rupert had been 'looting' near Henley-in-Arden and Stratford-on-Avon, and rumours came that he would march through Birmingham to the north. On the Sunday before Easter, the news became clearer and the danger greater, and the people resolved to defend their town. Arms were distributed, positions fixed, barricades built across the road which the troops must pass, and all was ready for a serious and brave resistance. On Easter Monday morning great excitement prevailed, but no news came; but soon some of the troopers were seen to be advancing to the town. Rupert had not expected a defence, but relied on his 2,000 horse and foot, his 'four drakes' and his 'two sakers' (as the light field-pieces were called) to secure surrender at discretion. His quartermasters advanced and promised that if the people behaved peaceably and furnished provender all that was past would be forgiven. The reply was a volley of shot. Rupert ordered an immediate attack. The field-pieces were brought to the front and fixed on the rude barricades. The people returned the fire with their guns and shot with deadly effect—rarely missing man or horse. Twice the Cavaliers staggered and retired, but some of the rear had dashed over the hedges around, and were firing the houses behind the brave defenders. There was a wild retreat, and the Cavaliers poured into the town and burned and pillaged all around. The slaughter was general —men, women and children fell under the furious blows of the enraged Cavalier troopers, and among the mortally wounded was the Earl of Denbigh. The fierce Rupert and his troops left hundreds of killed and wounded, and Rupert's 'burning love for Birmingham' became a household word.

Warwickshire has but few historic events during the eighteenth century to record as having occurred in the county as distinguished from those of the general history of the kingdom. The county was generally agricultural, with few places marked by special progress. Warwick, the county town, had no great changes, and remained only as the market-town, with the occasional excitements of Quarter Sessions and Assizes. The ancient and famous city of Coventry had but an uneventful history, and was principally remarkable for its industrial successes in developing the ribbon trade and that of watch-making. Birmingham had not started on its career of industrial progress till the latter half of the century, and 'gentle dulness' was the characteristic of all the district. One class of events, by no means creditable, however, had happened in a series of riots, in which much harm was done. In 1715 the stormy priest, Dr. Sacheverell, had aroused the bigotry and passions of the ignorant people against the Nonconformists, and some serious riots took place in Birmingham, where meeting-houses were burned and destroyed. Still later in the century the evil passions of the people were aroused for 'Church and King,' in 1791, when the town was in the hands of a violent mob for several days, and two chapels and five large houses—one of them Fair Hill, the home of Dr. Priestley from 1780 to

1791, with all its books, papers, laboratory, and philosophical apparatus—were burnt or destroyed by a brutal and furious mob.

Local history in the present century has many triumphs to record. The rapid rise of Birmingham had begun in the latter half of the eighteenth century. The 'hardware village' of those days had begun to expand, the 'freedom' of the town from the fetters of corporate towns had attracted artisans of all trades and classes to a place where they could work and prosper undisturbed by the vexatious restrictions of the older towns. An almost infinite variety of manufactures thus arose, and the town, which had long been a 'city of refuge' for political and religious fugitives, became the seat of various manufactures previously unknown in the district. The gun and sword trade, and the trades connected with iron and brass, had steadily increased; but the great event of the age was when James Watt—practically the inventor of the modern steam-engine—came to Matthew Boulton, at Birmingham, and the Soho Works became more famous for the production of steam-engines than for the steel, jewellery and nicknacks which made the town 'the toy-shop of Europe,' as described by Edmund Burke. From the latter half of the last century to the middle of our own, the increase in population and manufactures in and near Birmingham was enormous and rapid, and even during the disastrous early years of this century the demand for firearms kept that trade flourishing, although the masses of the people suffered terrible distress through the long period of heavy taxation and high prices of food and necessaries inseparable from an age of war.

The Reform Bill agitation for the fair and peaceful revision of the franchise and for the representation in Parliament of large and populous towns instead of the 'pocket boroughs' and places like 'Old Sarum,' had necessarily a great interest for the chief town of Warwickshire.

Birmingham became the most active and earnest of all the unrepresented towns in favour of reform, and its famous 'New Hall Hill meetings' attracted and represented not merely the town itself but the Midland counties generally, and secured the most effective pressure and demand. At one of the great meetings, in the absence of a legal right to a 'member' of Parliament, a 'legislatorial attorney' was elected, and sent to demand admission to the House of Commons, and was, of course, refused; but ultimately, as the result of the energetic and continued agitation, which was full of exciting incidents and indomitable courage, Birmingham was duly included in the Reform Bill to send two members to the Parliament of the realm. The political prominence of Birmingham, so energetically won, has not only been retained, but extended down to our own days, and the town has taken an active part in all the great political events of modern times, and has shown that 'Birmingham will be Birmingham' to the end of the chapter, and that Clarendon's phrase, 'of as great fame for hearty, wilful, affected disloyalty,' no longer describes a town which in 1858 and in 1887 was extremely 'loyal' to the throne, yet still earnest and energetic in all great reforms.

CHAPTER II.

LEGENDS.

Guy of Warwick and the fair Phyllis.—Leofric and Godiva.—Legend of Long Compton.—Wroxall Miracle.—Whispering Knights.—Red Horse Record.

THE Legendary History of Warwickshire is far too widely known to be neglected or despised, even if it must have its corrections in these later days of unbelief. The story of Guy, Earl of Warwick, and his countess, the fair Phyllis; of Lady Godiva and Earl Leofric, of the Legend of Long Compton, and of Hugh of Wroxall, have become portions of English general literature, as well as of local fame. The great fight of Guy with the great Dun Cow on Dunsmore Heath has long been a piece of 'history' in Warwickshire, as well as in the rare early copies of romances of the Middle Ages. The learned and venerable archæologist, Mr. Matthew Holbeche Bloxam, F.S.A., of Rugby, who for sixty years had studied the architecture and antiquities of his own county, had given special care and research to the story of Guy, whose gigantic statue still remains at Guy's Cliff, near Warwick, and whose reputed relics are still shown at Warwick Castle. Sir Guy was certainly a champion of romance, and has a distinctly local fame, and Mr. Bloxam showed that the earliest MS. stories are in Norman-French and in vernacular English of the fourteenth

century, but that none of the earlier MSS., and few even
of the early-printed books, have any reference to the Dun
Cow, the earliest mention of which is in 1570, when Dr.
Caius describes the relics of the animal which he saw at
Guy's Cliff and at Coventry, and of which he gives full
details; and it is only in the seventeenth century that the
story becomes complete, and this in a 'tradegy' (*sic*) published in 1661, and these references, with the fact that there
was a 'Dun Cow' inn at Dunchurch, mentioned in George
Fox's Journal in 1655, sum up the evidence for the legend.
Mr. Bloxam also showed that some diluvial remains of the
mammoth were found in the neighbourhood some forty
years ago, and it may therefore be reasonably supposed
that the legend was founded on some similar remains
discovered before the sixteenth century, which would be
held as proofs, even if they were not really the origin, of
the tales of Guy's killing the Dun Cow. As to the 'relics'
of Guy at Warwick Castle, Mr. Bloxam was more positive,
for they do not agree with the illustrations in the early
MSS. of the romances, or the style of the armour worn at
the supposed date of the story. 'The body and horse
armour shows him to have been no ordinary mortal. We
find a bascinet, or head-piece, of the time of Edward III. to
have formed his helm; a Hungarian "pavois" or shield of
the time of Henry VII. is reputed to be, and does duty
as, his breast-plate, and a vizored wall-shield of the reign
of James I. serves as his back-plate. A two-handed sword
of the era of Henry VIII., five feet six inches long, is
pointed out as wielded by him, while the shaft of a tilting-
lance, the earliest I have met with, served, if you will
believe it, as his walking-staff. His lady, the fair Phyllis,
has a pair of pointed slippered stirrups of iron, of the reign
of Henry VI., ascribed to be her veritable slippers. As to
Guy's horse-armour, an immense chanfron, or head-piece,
a poitrail worn in front of the horse's breast, and a crou-
pière to defend the horse's flanks, are of more than usual

magnitude, and of the reign of Henry VI., whilst his breakfast-cup or porridge-pot, with its fork, is a huge iron caldron of considerable antiquity, used for seething the flesh rations of the garrison.'

The legend of Lady Godiva, made famous by the Laureate's poem (and to some few readers by a brilliant poem in 'The Etonian,' by the former Vicar of Rugby, the Rev. G. M. Moultrie), sadly needs the facts of history as a basis, and Mr. Bloxam shows that Leofric was a powerful noble of the time of Edward the Confessor, and that he died A.D. 1057; that Godiva (or Godgiva) survived him many years, and that she appears as one of the great landowners in Warwickshire in the Domesday Book (A.D. 1086); that the population of Coventry at that date was about three hundred and fifty; that the houses were of a single story, with a door and no windows, mere wooden hovels (as the Bayeux tapestry shows); and that the Saxon chronicle, *sub anno* 1057, records the 'death of Leofric the Earl on the second of the Kalends of October (September 30); he was very wise for God, also for the world, which was a blessing to all this nation. He lies at Coventry.' Mr. Bloxam also cited William of Malmesbury and Florence of Worcester, who praise Leofric and Godiva, but make no mention of the legend. Roger de Wendover (*tempore* John) is the first to mention the legend—at least a century and a half after its alleged occurrence—and his authority is not great, as he tells many strange stories and legends. After all his researches, Mr. Bloxam believed that the 'Peeping Tom' incident did not appear till the latter part of the reign of Charles II., 'if, indeed, so early; for in the reign of Charles I. (1636) a party of excursionists visited the city of Coventry, and one of them wrote an account of what they saw, and alluded to the former part of the legend, but not to the latter' (relating to 'Peeping Tom'); and he then adds that the wooden image long shown at the corner of Hertford Street as representing 'Peeping

Tom,' and on the supposed site of his house, is that of 'an armed man, probably an image of St. George, and taken, as I think, from one of the churches of the city. It is of no greater antiquity than the reign of Henry VII., as is evinced from the broad-toed collerets in which the feet are encased.'

Sir William Dugdale, in his 'History of Warwickshire' (1656), narrates the story from Ingulphus and John of Tynemouth, both very imaginative and credulous chroniclers, and from Matthew of Westminster, who is entitled to rather more credit, as to the ride through the streets of the city, but without any confirmation or contradiction, and leaving the responsibility on the chroniclers themselves. He adds, however, a very significant paragraph, that 'in memory whereof the picture of him (Leofric) and his said Lady were set up in a south window of Trinity Church in this City, about K. R(ichard) II. time, and his right hand holding a Charter with these words written thereon:

' " I Luriche for the love of thee
Doe make Coventre Tol-free." '

There seems little reason to doubt that the legend was 'evolved' from the inscription, and that it grew to its modern form long after the original date. The earl and his countess are clearly shown, by indisputable records, to have been pious and generous benefactors to the church. John Rous, of Warwick, the local chronicler, records that Leofric founded a 'goodly monastery, which was the chief occasion of all the succeeding wealth and honour that accrued to Coventry, and that the earl and countess were the most eminent benefactors that it ever had.' Dugdale adds that Godiva gave her whole treasure thereto, and that she also endowed the monastery of Stow, near Lincoln; so that it may reasonably be assumed that Leofric, having such relations with his wife, was not likely to have imposed upon her so severe and purposeless a shame,

even in those rude days, to induce him to remove any
'tolls' from a city which they together had so lavishly
endowed. Nor is it probable that the record, 'for love of
thee,' could have been deliberately placed as 'a memory'
of so very shameless and unmanly a condition for making
'fair Coventry tol-free.'

The remaining legends of Warwickshire are less important and less generally known. That of Long Compton is one of the earliest, and records that St. Augustine
(A.D. 601) preaching in the church, the priest told him that
the lord of the town refused to pay his tithes, that the
saint immediately excommunicated him, and that he
further said that no excommunicated person should be
present at Mass; whereupon a dead man, buried at the
entrance to the church, rose from his grave and 'went
without the compass of the churchyard, and stood there
during the time of Mass.' The saint questioned him, and
also the priest who had excommunicated him one hundred
and fifty years before for refusing to pay tithes, whereon
the living offender repented of his sin, shaved himself, and
became a follower of the saint during the rest of his life.
This is on the authority of John of Tynemouth, and is a
fair example of his legends. The legend of Polesworth,
near Tamworth, is that St. Edith struck Sir Robert
Marmion, of Tamworth Castle, with her cross, to compel
him to restore the convent of nuns which had been given
to him by William I., and he forthwith confessed and
repented, and restored the nuns, to avoid the fate which St.
Edith had promised him in this world and the next; and
the nunnery—the first 'religious house' founded in
Warwickshire—was fully restored. The priory of Benedictine nuns at Wroxall, near Warwick, had a remarkable
legend, that Hugh de Hatton, a Crusader, was taken
prisoner in the Holy Land and kept there several years.
At last he remembered that the patron saint of Wroxall
was St. Leonard, so he was earnestly entreated to deliver

the captive, whereupon the saint appeared to him in his sleep, bidding him arise and go home and found an abbey for the nuns of St. Benedict. He had no sooner made his vow than he was miraculously removed from his prison to the very site on which the nunnery was afterwards built in Wroxall Wood. His lady would not believe his story till he showed her the broken part of a ring, which being placed with the part she had kept, the two became miraculously united. Among other legends which have a sounder basis than those so popular in the 'ages of faith,' one must be named, although the site is not strictly in Warwickshire, but on the high ground near Long Compton, near the road from Stratford-on-Avon to Oxford. In the old coaching days the traveller's attention was called to some hoary broken stones, which were called traditionally 'The Whispering Knights.' They are found in a circle of about thirty-five yards' diameter, and although originally sixty in number, have been reduced to twenty-two by time and destructiveness. Some of them are still about seven feet high. The largest is known as the king, and the tradition is that some wondrous power turned a king and his knights to stone. They have been known for centuries as the Rollrich Stones, and Camden thought they were probably erected by Rollo as a memorial of some battle; but their form and size, and arrangement and general resemblance to the great circles of Stonehenge and Avebury, probably mark a much earlier date—the Celtic monuments of two thousand years ago. Another remarkable relic, not far away, in the Vale of Kineton, is the famous 'Red Horse,' a great figure cut into the red soil, traditionally reported to be the work of Neville, Earl of Warwick, as a memorial of the battle of Towton, where he is said to have killed his horse so as to share the risks with his soldiers; but some of these details will be best discussed hereafter.

CHAPTER III.

TOPOGRAPHY.

Ancient Roads, Rivers and Towns.—Warwick.—Coventry.—
Stratford-on-Avon.—Rugby.

WARWICKSHIRE, from its place as an inland county, with streams flowing in opposite directions, has necessarily a high level above the sea. Its surface is comparatively flat, but broken up by ranges of hills of considerable height, and some of the high lands of the north of the county have their highest ordinary levels six hundred feet above the mean sea-level at Liverpool. The outline of the county is irregular, and its greatest cross-line lengths are about 50 miles from north to south and 35 miles from east to west, including about 897 square statute miles and 576,271 acres, and a population of 737,339 persons at the last census, in 1881. The divisions of the county are the ancient 'Hundreds' of Barlichway, Hemlingford, Kineton and Knightlow, with a separate 'county' around the city of Coventry. The principal characteristic of the county generally is the large number of woods, parks, etc., and as most of the hedgerows have substantial trees, and the lanes in the country districts have these high hedges, the epithet 'woody Warwickshire' is literally correct. The rivers are only few and small, but often picturesque, as well as famous, and the Avon has long had a world-wide fame.

History of Warwickshire.

The Avon divides the county practically into North and South: Arden, (or Woodland) and Feldon. The classic river, well described as the 'soft-flowing' Avon, has its principal source in a spring at Naseby, in Northamptonshire, not far from the memorable battle-field of the Great Civil War. It enters Warwickshire on the north-east, across the Watling Street, near Rugby, and flows southwest past Stoneleigh and Warwick to Stratford-on-Avon, leaving the county near Bidford, and runs on by Evesham and Pershore to Tewkesbury, where it enters the Severn. The other principal stream of the county is the Tame, which rises near the Lickey Hills in Worcestershire as the Rea, in Staffordshire as the river Tame, and is joined by streams called the Cole and the Blythe, which meet near Whitacre, and also fall into the Tame, which passes to Tamworth and thence on to the Trent and the Humber and the German Ocean or North Sea.

The great roads are of very ancient date—mostly British roads through the forests—improved and re-made during the Roman occupation. The Watling Street, which forms the north-east boundary of the county, runs from near Rugby to Tamworth and thence on to Lichfield, where at Etocetum (now Wall) it crosses the Rykenield, or Icknield Street, which enters the county near Bidford, passes through Alcester and through Sutton Park, near Birmingham, where it still retains its old name Icknield Street in Birmingham, and in the Park of Sutton Coldfield, where several miles of the old road still remain unbroken and unchanged since the Roman days. The Foss-Way, another ancient road, enters the county at Stretton-on-Foss in the south-west, and runs on in a nearly straight line through Stretton-on-Dunsmore to the High-Cross on the Watling Street. The lines of all these roads are generally clearly marked, with very few deviations from their original courses, and many names still remain which show traces of British as well as of Roman occupation. Alcester (Alauna) was certainly a Roman station, and other relics of the Romans have been found from time to time, although no great and important 'stations' have been traced except at Etocetum, Bennones (High-Cross), and Manduessedum (Mancetter), and Atherstone on the line of Watling Street.

The highest levels of the county are near Nuneaton and Atherstone on the north-east, and the Edge Hill range on the south, where Oxfordshire descends suddenly into Warwickshire, and from each of these sites very extensive and picturesque panoramic views of the northern and the southern divisions of the county are obtained. The valleys of the various streams and rivers are singularly beautiful, and the very numerous parks and woods are especially attractive. The county is essentially agricultural, although it includes, in the north especially, several important manufacturing towns. Among these Birmingham stands first for the variety and extent of its manufactures, and Nuneaton and Atherstone are important seats of various trades; and at Nuneaton, Bedworth, Griff and Tamworth very extensive collieries are found. Coventry and Nuneaton have important textile manufactures, and Coventry has long been a famous place not only for ribbons, watches, etc., but is now one of the largest sources of supply of sewing-machines, bicycles and tricycles.

The two cities, Warwick and Coventry, require a passing notice, leaving details for a later page. Warwick, as the county town, has many attractions. Two of its ancient gates remain, with a chapel over each, although few remains of the old walls have survived. St. Mary's Church, with its rich Beauchamp Chapel and its famous tombs, has long been a place of pilgrimage. The quaint Leicester Hospital, founded by the favourite of Elizabeth, is scarcely less interesting than the St. Cross Hospital at Winchester. The great castle on the cliff above the Avon, and the famous park along the riverside, are historically interesting and marvellously picturesque. Various old houses of the sixteenth and seventeenth century give the place an old world look.

Coventry, city and county, would require a volume to give it full justice. Its great St. Michael's Church, now in process of restoration, is the largest parish church in England, except that of Boston. St. Mary's Hall close by is a superb relic of fifteenth-century architecture, and contains a rich and varied collection of charters, deeds, autographs, and sketches illustrating the history of the city, and the visits of the many English monarchs who have been its guests during four hundred years. The remains of the old Cathedral, Trinity Church, and Grey Friars, and numberless old half-timbered houses, combine to form a series of attractions to historians and antiquaries which are comparatively little known to the thousands who rush in a railway train past the famous 'three tall spires' which distinguish the venerable 'city of the spires.'

Next in interest, perhaps, Tamworth, the home of the Marmions, claims a few words. The solid castle on a hill above the Tame has many points of interest, from the Saxon herring-bone masonry to the lordly baronial hall and imposing tower. The church, too, is large and interesting, and worth more attention than it receives. Coleshill, on a lofty hill, with a fine spire, is a landmark for many miles, and its church contains a splendid series of monumental tombs of the Digby family. Alcester is a quaint old town with traces of Roman days, and a pleasant stream—the Alne—from which it takes its name. Henley-in-Arden is a remarkably fine example of an old English small town, with a fine market cross, and a very fine Norman chapel at Beaudesert close by. A near neighbour, Wootton Wawen, has a very ancient church, with Saxon work in its tower and chained books as prisoners in the church. Stratford-on-Avon needs no special mention, for 'the birthplace, the home, and the grave of the bard' is known the wide world over, as thousands (15,000) of visitors prove every year. The birthplace of Shakespeare, the Grammar School where he learned 'his small Latin and less Greek,' the 'great garden' of the house where he passed his later years, the old Gild Chapel overshadowing his garden, the church where his body was buried, are attractions enough and to spare. Around the pleasant little town are the Avon, and many places familiar to him in boyhood and old age, and some places named in his plays. Stratford is a centre of attraction from its pleasant site and quaint old houses, as well as from its direct associations with the life and death of the 'poet of all time.'

One other town remains to be mentioned as among the famous places in the county. Rugby has few relics of the past, but its original name, Rochebury, or Rokebury, goes back to Saxon and Danish days. It was not of much importance at the time of the Conquest, but belonged to Turchill of Warwick. One of the castles which Stephen was always ready to allow during his troublous reign was built near the church, and some traces of its existence have been found. It seems to have been destroyed in the reign of Henry II. The town is mostly modern; it stands on a low hill, but the country around is so flat that Dr. Arnold used to say there 'was nothing between his windows and the Ural Mountains' in Eastern Russia. The great attraction of Rugby is its famous school, which Dr. Arnold raised to such eminence that it had no superior and few equals. His life and influence on this school and the town were beyond praise, and his pupils, many of whom have taken high places in schools and churches and public work, ever honour and venerate his name. The founder of the school, Laurence Sherrif (1569), very wisely gave his endowment in lands, which have so increased in value as to produce five hundred times the income of only one hundred years ago.

This summary includes the principal towns of the county of special interest, but others of minor importance will be at least referred to, if not fully described, in later chapters, whose classifications will include many places of small area and of reduced status, but which still have some connection with the historical or biographical history of Warwickshire.

CHAPTER IV.

PHYSIOGRAPHY AND GEOLOGY.

The Midland Watershed.—Avon, Tame and Smaller Rivers.—New Red Sandstone, Marls, etc.—Forest of Arden.—Physiography.—Coal Formations.—Keuper Red Marls.—Liassic Area.—Rhœtic Series.—Glacial or Post-Tertiary Deposits.

THE geological and physiographical history and condition of a county cannot be fully or clearly described without sections, tabular statements, and full-coloured maps; nor is it the duty of a 'Popular County History' to give a mass of facts and figures which would be as uninteresting to readers generally as they would be imperfect and insufficient for more advanced students. The geology and physiography of the Midland district have, however, very recently been fully described by Professor Dr. Lapworth, of Mason College, Birmingham, for the members of the British Association. The Rev. P. B. Brodie, M.A., has also written many valuable papers from his local as well as general knowledge, and Mr. W. J. Harrison has published some brief handbooks with the results of his researches. A careful abridgment of some of these papers will give the reader the latest records and theories, which often differ materially from the speculations of even fifty years ago.

Warwickshire is practically the great watershed of southern Britain, for Birmingham is practically the topographical centre of England, and is within the basin of the Humber, and is drained by the brooklets which unite to form the Tame, the first of the southern tributaries of the Trent. 'The ground forming the Birmingham plateau rises and falls in an endless succession of heights and hollows, here sinking down into broad, tree-sheltered, stream-cut valleys, there rising into long, low mounds and hills. The subsoil throughout is mainly gravel or sandy clay, and the underground drainage is, as a rule, excellent. The north-western half of the plateau still retains its original forest character, and the primæval aspect of the district is recalled by the wild area of Sutton Park—a picturesque admixture of long, dry, pebbly mounds, covered with thick woods of oak, ash and holly, divided from each other by open glades of gorse patches, with long, flat, treeless expanses, shrouded in dark heather, and picked out here and there with deep, clear-water pools. The central half of the plateau is now covered with the great town of Birmingham and its immediate dependencies. The town stands upon a series of broad rounded knolls, divided from each other by intervening open valleys. The more elevated points are marked by the Church of St. Philip, Newhall Hill, Soho Hill, and the Monument; while the great maze of streets, manufactories and commercial buildings fills up all the space between. Strictly speaking, the town proper lies in the angle included between the river Tame and its little tributary the Rea. The Tame runs in a broad valley round the north-eastern side of the town to the low-lying district of Saltley, and thus takes its course north-eastward across the Midland plain towards the Trent at Burton. The little river Rea, which is the Birmingham river *par excellence*, runs from the Lickey Hills through the south-eastern corner of the town, across the low-lying district of Digbeth, and joins the Tame at Saltley. The south-western portion of the Birmingham plateau is occupied by the fashionable district of Edgbaston and the neighbouring suburbs of Harborne and Moseley. While the original upland character of the plateau is still distinctly apparent, the dwellers in this southern area have, in all other respects, utterly changed its former aspect. The land has been reclaimed and enclosed. In place of the wild oak and ash we have masses of the Elizabethan elm, the fir and the beech; and in place of the wild heather, cultivated lawns and grassy fields. Every advantage has been taken of the natural resources of site and soil, and the result is that Edgbaston and its surroundings form one broad expanse of mansions, woods and fields, well worthy of the town and neighbourhood. . . . To the east of the Birmingham plateau lies the broad plain of Tamworth and Nuneaton, watered by the sluggish stream of the Tame [and Anker]. The plain is continued far to the southward, through the richly wooded district of Warwick, Alcester and the old Forest of Arden, and thence down to the valley of Shakespeare's Avon, to the terrace of the Edge Hills and the northern slopes of the Cotswolds' (Lapworth, pp. 213-216).

'The physiography of the surface is curiously dependent on the geological structure beneath, and every part of the surface is a reflex of the sections beneath. The chief characteristic of the district is the great Mesozoic formation of the Triassic or New Red Sandstone, but its width is greatly reduced compared with its measure in other places. These red rocks must formerly have extended over the whole area, but they now form sheets of red sandstones and marls through which the older Palæozoic rocks protrude, in numerous bands and patches. Although nowhere very steeply inclined, these red beds of the Triassic have been bent into several long, low arches or broad domes, whose longer axes range approximately north and south. The summits of many of these arches have been denuded, and the underlying older rocks have again been bared to day. Four of these arches are especially conspicuous, those of the Wrekin, Malvern, Dudley and Nuneaton. In each of these the underlying coal measures are laid bare, forming the four coal-fields of Coalbrookdale, Forest of Wyre, and Eastern Warwick, all of which show, round their outer margins, a narrow band of the intermediate formation of the Permian. In each of these anticlinals, too, the denudation of the core of the arch has been sufficient to wear away the Carboniferous from its centre, and to expose to view yet older formations —the Old Red Sandstone in the Forest of Wyre, the Silurian in South Staffordshire, the Malverns, and Coalbrookdale, and even the Upper Cambrian and its underlying igneous rocks in the Wrekin, the Lickey, and near Nuneaton. [It is only fair to add that this discovery at Nuneaton was made, some four years ago, by the large knowledge and microscopic observations of Dr. Lapworth himself.] With the exception of the Silurian of Abberley and Dudley, and the recently discovered Cambrian of Nuneaton, however, these pre-carboniferous rocks are comparatively inconspicuous, rising up merely in narrow bands in the cores of long, wedge-shaped hills.'

'From the economical, as well as from the structural, point of view, by far the most important of these geological arches is that of South Staffordshire [close to Birmingham on the north and east], which is the southward continuation of the Pennine Chain, and part of the true backbone of southern Britain. The central axis of this arch runs through the Dudley hills [also close to Birmingham on the east], and dies away in the complex of "faults" to the south of the Lickeys [a range of lofty and picturesque hills on the south-west of Birmingham]. On the natural consequences of the rise of this arch, all the physical, scenic, and economic peculiarities of the central parts of the district are essentially dependent. The hills and plains around Birmingham are all more or less related to this grand anticlinal—the hills marking the uplifted

New Red Sandstone and Marls. 33

edges of the harder rocks—the limestones, sandstones, and pebble beds; and the plains, the position of the gently-inclined soft shales and marls. It has brought within workable distance of the surface the coals and ironstones of South Staffordshire, and the valuable limestones of the Dudley hills; and it has had its final effect in bringing together the overflowing population of the town and district.'

'In the great midland plain to the east of Birmingham [to the eastern boundary of Warwickshire] the strata are spread out in broad sheets. The plain is underlain in great part by the comparatively homogeneous flat-lying Keuper marls, with their intercalated bands of harder sandstones. Its scenery is consequently less varied than that of the Severn Valley, but it is rich in that sweet sylvan beauty which is almost peculiar to the English landscape, and it forms one broad expanse of gently rolling farmland and woodland, whose green-crested waves sweep onward to the east and south, mile beyond mile, till they break against the long shore-like scarp of the harder Jurassics' (Lapworth, pp. 218, 219).

Another geologist—a specialist as to Warwickshire—the Rev. P. B. Brodie, F.G.S., further describes the general geological characteristics of the county in these words:

'The physical features of Warwickshire are in great part those due to its geological structure. Indeed, where not obscured by drift deposits, they afford considerable assistance in mapping the out-crop of the various formations. In the northern part of the county the Lower Carboniferous district is distinctly marked out, forming a bold ridge which stretches in a north-westerly direction to near Baddesley. In the middle of this district, to the south of Atherstone, the county attains an elevation of over 500 feet above the sea. The country occupied by the broad-spread Permian rocks, directly to the south of the Carboniferous area, is characterized by an undulating surface, frequently presenting bold hills, and rising to the culminating point at Corley Moor, with an elevation of 625 feet above the level of the sea. From this point streams descend, which, flowing north and south, ultimately find their way, in the one case into the German Ocean, and in the other to the Bristol Channel. The Triassic district in these parts is occupied by the harder beds, very similar to the Permian area; but owing to the greater development of the Keuper marls, the general appearance is that of an undulating plain. The out-crop of the beds of the Lias district, where not obscured by drift, can be very clearly traced, the layers of hard light-coloured limestone found at the base of this formation standing out from the soft Keuper marls as a well-defined escarpment. It is only in portions of its range in this county, however, that it can be so traced, as throughout the greater part of the northern division it is thinly covered with drift. The Inferior Oolite deposit exists as a small patch in the south-eastern corner of the county, on the Burton-Dasset hills, near Kineton, where it attains a thickness of about 80 feet, and rests directly on the upper Lias Clay' (White's 'Warwickshire,' pp. 141, 142).

The local rock formation cannot be fully or clearly described without a coloured map, but the following summary, so far as Warwickshire is concerned, is given from Professor Dr. Lapworth's recent (1886) elaborate paper in the 'Hand-book of Birmingham,' compiled for the members of the British Association. It includes the entire stratigraphical succession between the Cambrian and the Jurassic middle period, except at the Ordovician and the Old Red Sandstone, which are locally wanting. Under the classification of Mesozoic or Secondary Rocks, the Liassic includes (*a*) Middle Lias (marlstone) at Edge Hill and Fenny Compton; (*b*) Lower Lias Clays at Harbury and Rugby. The Rhœtic shows Marls and White Lias at Harbury, Knowle, and Wootton-Wawen. The Triassic

Coal Formations. 35

(I. Upper Trias and Keuper) shows Lower Keuper or Waterstones at Birmingham and Warwick, and the Lower Trias (or Bunter) : (*a*) Upper Mottled Sandstone at Edgbaston, and (*b*) Pebble Beds and Conglomerate at Sutton Park. Under the Palæozoic or Primary Rocks, the Carboniferous include (*a*) Upper Coal Measures, with Spinorbis Limestone, at Arley ; and under Cambrian, the Tremadoc beds at Nuneaton. Many other well-known and important formations in the immediate neighbourhood are described, but they are found in Staffordshire and Worcestershire, and are therefore omitted from this Warwickshire record.

The only traces of the lowest and oldest rocks are those of the Cambrian series, and are found near Nuneaton, in the eastern corner of the county, and in a strip about eight miles long and one mile wide. They consist of volcanic ashes, quartzites, and thin-bedded shales pierced by dioritic dykes, and were till recently mapped as Millstone Grit and Carboniferous Shale. Whether they belong to the Middle or the Lower Cambrian, or to the earlier Archæan, is still an open question, but they seem to be correlated to the Wrekin and the great Igneous Rocks in Charnwood Forest, Leicestershire.

Warwickshire is less known as a coal-county than many of the prolific sources of supply in South Staffordshire, which is the richest mineral area in Britain as to variety, as well as extent. ' Thick coal seams, rich bands of ironstone and great thicknesses of Silurian limestone, all occur within a short distance of each other, and all within easy reach of the miner. The natural result has been that the South Staffordshire coal-field and its immediate neighbourhood has been the great coal and iron mart of Central Britain, and the abundance and cheapness of the material it has afforded have rendered Birmingham and "The Black Country" the hardware workshop of the world ' (Lapworth pp. 233, 234). The East Warwickshire coal-field is, however, of great extent and importance. These coal-bearing rocks form a strip of about fifteen miles long, from Tamworth, on the north, to Bedworth, near Coventry, on the south. The coal-bearing strata rest unconformably upon the Cambrian below, and pass up conformably into the Permian above. In the north of the coal-field five workable seams occur, separated by many feet of barren measures. Dr. Lapworth thinks that these, and the thick coal-beds of South Staffordshire, allowing for possible erosion prior to the deposition of the Triassic, may extend in a continuous sheet under the red rocks of Northern Warwickshire, and may have been part of one area of deposition.

The Permian rocks of Warwickshire show no true limestone, and are formed of red sandstones and marls, and beds of angular breccia. The lowest strata are seen to the west of the East Warwickshire coal-field. Between Tamworth and Kenilworth the Permian strata floor a wide tract of country, and lie almost horizontal. The Triassic rocks form a large part of the Midland counties, and are composed of red sandstone and marls. The town of Birmingham stands upon, and is surrounded by, rocks of this character, which have two divisions, the Upper (or Keuper), chiefly a stiff marl or clay; and the Lower (or Bunter) mainly sandy, the out-crop of the Bunter being usually barren, with much heath and waste land, as in Sherwood Forest, while the Keuper marls afford a rich soil, well fitted for the plough. The Bunter Conglomerate, or pebble-bed, runs south-west to north-east of the surface of the Birmingham area, near Sutton Park and Lichfield, and in a broad band near the western suburbs of Birmingham by Winson Green and Perry Barr to Sutton Park, where the out-crop is three and a half miles wide, and with a vertical section of thirty feet. Each section shows a mass of well-rounded hard pebbles, which have been so pressed together by the earth-movement since their deposition that many are cracked, and all bear white indentations. The Bunter Conglomerate contains no contemporaneous fossils, but many species of shells have been found in the hard rounded lumps of rock of which it is composed. The Lower Keuper Sandstone is found specially near Birmingham, and forms the ridge on which the Town Hall, St. Philip's Church, etc. (475 feet above sea-level), stand, with a probable depth of 200 feet, forming excellent solid and deep foundations. Near Warwick bones and teeth of four species of the Labyrinthodon have been found, with footprints of the feet also. The Keuper red marls form an undulating fertile plain, ten or twelve miles long, near the valley of the Tame, and Castle Bromwich, Coleshill, and Whitacre, and borings show its depth to vary from 400 to 700 feet. The Upper Keuper Sandstone is a thin band, not more than thirty feet in thickness, a small quarry of which exists at Rowington, near Warwick, and lines of strata crop out in various parts of South Warwickshire. Mr. W. Jerome Harrison, from whose recent and elaborate researches this summary is compiled, believes that all these phenomena show that Central England in the Carboniferous epoch alternated as to condition between a low plain and a shallow sea. In the Permian period land conditions prevailed except in the North and North Midland counties, where a brackish sea, somewhat like the Baltic, occupied a shallow depression. In the Triassic times this central sea appears to have been cut off from the other ocean, and to have formed a huge inland lake, comparable to the Caspian or the Dead Sea of our own day. The southern boundary of this inland sea was formed by a ridge of old rocks which extended from Charnwood by Hartshill and the Lickey, and the Wrekin and Malvern Hills. In the basin north of this axial ridge all the subdivisions of the Bunter and the Keuper were in turn deposited, and the cliffs and reefs of the Palæozoic rocks, of which this coast-line was composed, yielded large contributions in the pebble-beds, sands, and marls which constitute the Trias. According to a theory originally advanced by Professor Hull, and supported by Professor Bonney, the pebbles of the Bunter were mostly derived from the Palæozoic rocks of the north-west and north-east, some being probably supplied by the ancient strata of North-west Scotland. 'The waters of the Triassic sea were so overcharged with salts of iron that every grain of sand was encrusted before its deposition with a pellicle of peroxide of iron, and of chloride of sodium (common salt), and sulphate of sodium (gypsum). There was also an excess, so that much was deposited on the sea-floor, producing beds of rock-salt and gypsum of considerable thickness. The presence of these mineral substances in the water was prejudicial to life, so that—as in the Dead Sea and Lake Utah to-day—few living creatures could inhabit the Triassic sea, and fossils are of extreme rarity in the stratum of this age.' The Triassic strata have a great economic value, since being so porous they absorb a large proportion of the rain which falls upon them, and thus form an underground reservoir which, when tapped by wells or bore-holes, is capable of supplying an almost inexhaustible quantity of good, although somewhat hard, water. In this way Birmingham receives three-fourths of its water from three deep wells—two on the north-east of the town at Aston and Bury respectively, and one on the south-west near Selly Oak. 'These wells extend to the depth of 400 feet, passing through the Upper Mottled Sandstone, and piercing the Pebble-beds, and the average supply of water from each is 3,000,000 gallons per day, of a hardness varying from nine to fifteen degrees' (Harrison, pp. 242-244).

'The Liassic area chiefly consists of the middle and lower divisions. The highest appears in the south and south-east, and the middle in spurs of hills on the north-west, while the lower lies at a lower level in the same general direction, to the southern edge of the Trias. The Upper Lias is chiefly shown by a thin bed of clay with some characteristic fossils, on the Fenny Compton hills, with evidence that it formerly capped the range of the adjacent Edge Hills, in its natural position above the Marlstone or Middle Lias, of which the Edge Hills are chiefly composed. The Marlstone or Middle Lias is largely quarried on the Avon and Burton-Dassett Hills, and forms a good building-stone of varying hardness, of a green or yellow-brown colour, and sometimes ferruginous. In Warwickshire the Marlstone affords few fossils, and those chiefly brachiopodous shells of the genus *Terebratula*. The inferior clays and marls are seen only near Fenny Compton, and these are full of fossils, especially in the zone of Ammonites, Jamiesonii and Ibex, nearly one hundred feet thick, and one hard, thick bed, with numerous corals. The Lower Lias is found extensively, north-east, east, south-east, south, and south-west of Warwick. A very fine section was exposed by the railway near Harbury Station, the strata showing beds of blue clay or shale, interstratified with beds of blue rubbles and argillaceous limestone, much quarried for hydraulic lime. Fine lime-beds are found at Stockton and Harbury, at Wilmcot, near Stratford, and near Henley-in-Arden, and Knowle. The thickness of this Lower Lias is above 600 feet; fossils are not very numerous, but bones and teeth of Plesiosaurus and Ichthyosaurus are found, but only few fish at Harbury and near Rugby. Excepting the remains of insects and fragments of plants, the fossils of the Lower Limestones are entirely marine, Ammonites, Planorbis and A. Johnstoni, being abundant and characteristic. Crustacea and small fishes occasionally occur. The larger Enaliosaurians are well represented by some fine specimens of the Ichthyosaurus and Plesiosaurus, the Plesiosaurus Megacephalus in the Museum at Warwick being nearly entire, and measuring 14 feet 4 inches in length. The most remarkable fossils are the insects, of which more than twenty-four families and genera were determined more than twenty years ago, and many important discoveries

have been since made and described. Many of the
Neuroptera were of gigantic proportions, but most of the
insects of small size, and indicating a temperate climate.

'The Rhœtic series consists of certain hard, fine-grained
limestones, which, from their ordinary white colour, have
been termed White Lias. They cover a considerable area
south and south-east of Warwick, and form a purely local
deposit, limited mostly to Warwickshire and Somersetshire. As close-grained and hard limestones they make
good building material and good lime, of a colour mostly
white, but with a yellow tinge and occasionally pink and
gray. Some geologists class them as Rhœtic, some as
intermediate between Lias and Rhœtic, and some as Red
Lias. The undisputed Rhœtic rocks, which lie between
the Lias and the Triassic marls, are rarely exposed in
Warwickshire, but small sections are visible in the railway-
cutting near Harbury, also near Wooton-Wawen and
Knowle, and some characteristic Rhœtic fossils were
found at Summer Hill, between Stratford-on-Avon and
Alcester, on cutting the railway a few years ago' (Brodie,
pp. 245-247).

The Glacial and Post-Tertiary deposits have recently
been very carefully surveyed, studied and described, by
the Rev. H. W. Crosskey, LL.D., F.G.S., and offer many
facts not readily to be explained. He describes the
'finds' under these headings: (I.) Lower Boulder Clays;
(II.) Middle Glacial Clays, Sands and Gravels; (III.)
Upper Boulder Clays; (IV.) Post-Glacial Clays, Sands and
Gravels. The most complete section is at Harborne, near
Birmingham. Erratic boulders of slate, felsite, quartzite,
intermixed with blocks and stones of local origin, are
found in a Lower Boulder Clay, 480 feet above sea-level.
Many of these erratics are angular, and some, especially
the slates, are finely striated. The whole deposit is un-
stratified and compact, and the boulders are roughly pressed
together in every variety of position, without any orderly

Glacial or Post-Tertiary Deposits. 41

arrangement. The Middle Sands and Gravels follow the boulder clay, and are irregularly stratified, and show false bedding, and fragments of coal occur among the pebbles. The Upper Boulder Clay is a compact mass of clay with erratics scattered through it; but they are neither so numerous nor so confusedly pressed together as in the lower bed. Granite has been found, although rarely associated with the travelled felsites and quartzites, together with a few flints, and local stones and blocks are also mixed up with the clay. The series is capped by a mixture of clay, sand and gravel in varying proportions, which fills many hollows that must have been washed out of the upper clay, and must be regarded as Post-Glacial. Glacial striæ have been observed on the rock of a neighbouring quarry. Dr. Crosskey entertains no doubt of the glacial origin of the facts described, and quotes some remarkable examples of the long distances travelled over by erratic blocks. He mentions specially a number and variety of blocks found near Wolverhampton, which came 'without question' from the Lake District and the South of Scotland; of others found recently in a section of Boulder Clay at Icknield Street, Birmingham, of which some, and a large proportion, had been brought from the rocks which occur *in situ* at the Berwyn and Arenig hills in Wales, and shows that the 'sandstone rock against which this boulder clay rested was broken up, and large fragments of it were lifted out of their position and thrust into the middle of the drift.' If brought by land-ice, the whole face of the country must have changed to allow their deposit so high above the sea-level; and if floated in icebergs, the land must have been lower at least 900 feet to have allowed the icebergs to float and their burden to be dropped. The Midland erratics must have travelled from three distinct regions: (1) from Wales, (2) from the western part of the Lake District, (3) or from Kirkcudbrightshire. Boulders from the more easterly part of the Lake District, such as the Shap granite boulders, so abundantly spread over Yorkshire, have not been found in the Midland district, where erratics are peculiar. 'Commencing at Bushbury Hill (a little to the north of Wolverhampton, on the table-land facing to the north-west), the Lake Rocks and the Scotch Rocks—Criffell granites and Eskdale granites—are largely intermingled. Journeying westwards, a stream of boulders from Wales crosses the northern streams. On and around the Clent Hills (1023 feet), south-west of Birmingham, Welsh felsites are the only boulders to be found, Birmingham being protected by its position from the stream of boulders from the north, and only a few fragments of granite being occasionally found' (Crosskey, pp. 248-253).

CHAPTER V.

ZOOLOGY AND BOTANY.

Native Animals.—Beasts, Birds and Reptiles.—Fishes and Molluscs.—Microscopic Fauna.—Flowering Plants, Ferns, Mosses and Lichens.—Algæ.

THESE two important subjects have had very little attention, except in the publications of local societies, until the meeting of the British Association at Birmingham in 1886, when a series of reports on the Midland district was prepared for the local 'Hand-book.' The zoology was under the editorial care of Mr. W. R. Hughes, F.L.S., and the botany was entrusted to Mr. William Mathews, M.A., and in both cases the reports were written by competent specialists. The result has been a brief but excellent summary, of which only the Warwickshire portion need be given here, and in fact many of the details are too scientific and technical for a 'Popular History.' The radius of the survey was twenty miles from Birmingham, so that the area includes parts of Staffordshire and Worcestershire, and not the whole of Warwickshire.

'The district around Birmingham is admirably suited to our native animals, abounding as it does with fertile and well-watered valleys, wild moorlands, and extensive woods; on the other hand, its large population renders the prolonged existence of individual and striking varieties well-nigh impossible.' Among the mammals the great bat is found near Kingsbury and Tamworth ; the hairy-armed bat, with zigzag flight, on the Avon ; the reddish-gray bat, the Daubenton bat, the whiskered bat, the long-eared bat, the Barbutelle bat, and the lesser horseshoe bat, are found in many parts of the county. The hedgehog, the mole, the common and the water shrew, are also well known, but the two last-named are rare. The badger is rare, but fairly well distributed, and the otter is found in the Tame and Anker and their tributaries, and also in the Warwickshire Avon, in which river the largest otter locally known, and weighing twenty-eight pounds, was caught in 1886. The weasel and stoat are plentiful, but the polecat or fitchet is becoming very rare. The fox, being strictly preserved in many parts of the county, is sufficiently abundant. The squirrel is not common, but is found in most of the many large woods, and builds on the forked branches of the trees. The dormouse is rare, the harvest-mouse very common all over the county, and the long-tailed field-mouse and the common mouse are also numerous. The black rat is rarely found except in the cellars of large towns, where it is comparatively secure from its great enemy the brown rat, which is abundant. The water-vole or water-rat is very common in all the Midland streams. The red field or bank vole is plentiful in the meadows, and is constantly found by hay-makers. The hare and the rabbit are both very common, although greatly reduced in numbers since the passing of the Hares and Rabbits Bill in 1881. The red deer is not known in the county, but the fallow deer is found in large numbers in Stoneleigh, Charlcote and other great parks throughout Warwickshire.

Reptiles are not numerous, but the viviparous lizard is found in Sutton Park, and also the blind worm ; the ringed snake and the viper or adder are locally known, but generally rare. A large number were killed in Sutton Park in 1884. The common frog and common toad are plentiful, and the warty newt and the smooth newt are very generally found.

Birds afford no special interest even to the enthusiastic and microscopic ornithologist, but the numerous brooks, rivers, reservoirs and pools form favourite haunts for all sorts of aquatic birds. The local species recorded are large, consisting of about sixty residents, forty-two migrants, and eighty occasional or rare visitants—a total of one hundred and eighty-two species. Although so far inland large numbers of marine or littoral birds are frequently observed, such as the curlew, sandpiper, turnstone, ring dotterill and common and Arctic terns, from whose visits some of the knotty problems of migration may be solved. These species are generally observed in the autumn, and the examples are invariably immature or birds of the year. The large waterworks reservoirs at Shustoke, twelve miles from Birmingham, are regularly visited every year by large numbers of gulls in search of the fish of the reservoirs, but the visitors are summer visitors only, and do not remain long. The osprey, the peregrine falcon, the hobby, the merlin, the kestrel, the kite, the sparrow-hawk, the common buzzard, the rough-legged buzzard, the honey buzzard, the hen harrier and the marsh harrier are also found, but some (like the two last-named) very rarely. The tawny owl, the long-eared owl, the short-eared owl and the barn owl are very generally found in all parts of Warwickshire. The red-backed shrike is generally distributed, and breeds, and the great gray shrike is sometimes found in autumn and winter. The thrush is common, and the blackbird is everywhere and increasing. The nightingale is not very plentiful, but fairly numerous in many localities, where its nests are built and its rich song heard. The whole of Worcestershire, Warwickshire and Leicestershire are within the remarkable line within which only the nightingale is found. The kingfisher is common in the rivers and brooks, the great crested grebe breeds in Sutton Park, and there are several heronries in the county. The bittern, once plentiful, is now rarely found. The stormy petrel has often been found, and some (as the great auk) have been picked up exhausted during stormy weather in the streets of Birmingham and other large towns. Flocks of geese are often seen flying overhead, but too high and too quickly to be identified, and large gulls also are often seen. The visits of such birds, even as birds of passage only, is remarkable, when it is remembered that Warwickshire is a thoroughly Midland county, nearly one hundred miles from the nearest coast-line. The report by Mr. R. W. Chase, from which these details are taken, is a very valuable addition to local ornithology.

Fishes and mollusca may seem to have little connection with any Midland area, but Mr. G. Sherriff Tye has summarised all that are known, and chiefly from his own personal observations. Many excellent 'waters' are within easy reach of Birmingham, and are therefore well known to the naturalist as well as to the practical 'Waltonian.' He says: 'To those who do not incline to the study of fish or fishery, it will probably be a matter of surprise to know the abundance and the variety of species occurring within an hour's walk of the centre of our town.' Of the river Tame, a well-known angler states: 'In my opinion this is a remarkable little river. In three and a half miles it contains in abundance at least ten species of fish—viz., trout, pike, chub, tench, perch, roach, rudd, dace, gudgeon, minnow, all of which—except the pike—attain to a size equal to any in rivers or pools within a hundred miles of Birmingham. Large fish are not so common now as formerly, but probably this river will recover, and attain its wonted excellence when the "Black Country" sewerage works are completed. The river Cole is a fine trout stream. The river Blythe, Coleshill, is an excellent stream, especially for eels. Earlswood and the Corporation Reservoir, the pools at Sutton Coldfield, Great Barr Park, King's Norton, Barnt Green, and many others, are all well stocked with fish, and will render fine examples to all who seek them.' The recorded number of local species is thirty-three. Perch, carp, tench, bream, roach, dace, loach, pike, trout, grayling, lamprey, are commonly found in some localities in the county. Even 'salmon, the king of British fishes,' comes within our radius of twenty miles. It has been taken from eel-traps in the river Tame at Tamworth, in the river Trent at Yoxall, and in the river Severn at Bewdley, where a fish of 40 lb. has been landed. Lochleven trout have been introduced into the new reservoir (90 acres) of the Birmingham Corporation at Shustoke (April, 1884), by 3,000 fish, and another reservoir at Witton had 2,000 more, and the fish now (August, 1886) weigh from 2 to $3\frac{1}{4}$ lb., so that 'these reservoirs will, in a few years, be good places for this species of trout.'

The mollusca, terrestrial and fluviatile, have an excellent field within a twelve-mile radius of Birmingham, and fifty per cent. of the species and varieties enumerated by Dr. J. Gwyn Jeffreys in his 'British Conchology' are found. The details would be interesting only to specialists, and the scientific names of little general interest, as given in a condensed form by Mr. Tye, but they will be found valuable to those who wish to refer to a very complete and elaborate summary of the numbers and varieties of local molluscs. Insects are by no means a characteristic of the Midland counties, but the report of Mr. W. G. Blatch has given a very elaborate account of the genera and species, many of which have only recently been 'discovered' by local naturalists. He gives special attention to the rarer and more interesting species, and to the localities in which they are found. He notes, too, especially, that while there are many curious gaps as compared with other areas, there are some remarkable 'finds' of examples which are unknown, except in districts a hundred miles away.

Microscopic fauna were most minutely and elaborately described by the late Mr. Thomas Bolton, whose whole life was devoted to—but practically shortened and sacrificed by—his generous and unselfish studies, for many years, from love of science only, and without hope or desire of recognition or reward. He spared no labour or time in personal exploration of the canals, rivers, reservoirs, 'swags,' and 'catch-pits,' among the 'spoil-banks' in the 'Black Country,' as well as among the clay-pits on farm-lands; and he has left an honourable name, and a series of observations which have enriched the records of the microscopic researches of modern times as to minute animal life. He found, for example, in Sutton Park, specimens of the diving-bell spider, which Mr. W. Saville Kent found to be new to science. He discovered, locally, in Olton Reservoir, at Solihull, the transparent *Leptodora hyalina*, which has since been found in other localities, and also the *Melicerta janus*, new to England, in June, 1886, although it had been found in Scotland in 1880. His researches into the beautiful Rotifera were especially valuable, because he spared no time or trouble, and modestly contented himself with occasional contributions to the local Natural History Society, and by his ready and willing help to all who sought his aid in their studies of the wonders of the minute world which he delighted to explore and to explain.

Botany has been the special subject of a 'specialist,' Mr. William Matthews, M.A., who not only edited, but contributed to a series of reports on the botany of the Midland districts in the 'Hand-book' already referred to. No similar survey had been previously made, and no such collection of facts had been compiled. His introduction

sums up the previous works on the subject, local or
general, followed by papers by 'specialists,' as flowering
plants, ferns, etc., by J. E. Bagnall, A.L.S.; mosses,
hepatics, and lichens, by J. E. Bagnall; algæ, by A. W.
Wills; and fungi, by W. B. Grove, B.A. The details,
although compactly set forth, are too elaborate for further
condensation, and only a few general facts will be suitable
for these pages. The flowering plants, ferns, etc., of
Warwickshire are described under a very useful classification—the names of the rivers : (I.) Tame, (II.) Blythe,
(III.) Anker, (IV.) Avon, (V.) Sow, (VI.) Alne, and (VII.)
Arrow; and under each of these heads the number is
shown, and the names of the rarer specimens are given,
while brief details of the general character of the district are
prefixed. 'The greatest elevations occur at Hartshill,
Dosthill, Corley, Alne Hills, and Arrow, none of which
exceed 550 feet above the sea. As a whole it is well
wooded, but the woods are usually small and not produc-
tive of the rarer woodland species. Heathlands are
mostly reclaimed, and the more extensive marshes and
bogs drained, hence ericetal and bog plants are rare.' The
sub-districts are thus described :

(I.) Tame.—' The country is generally flat, but is slightly
elevated both on the right and left banks near Arley,
Middleton, Dosthill, and Shustoke. In this district about
750 flowering plants and ferns are recorded.'

(II.) Blythe.—' This is mostly flat, the soils are usually
sand, marl, and clay. Heathlands occur near Earlswood
and Coleshill; bogs and marshes near Coleshill and
Barston. The recorded flora is about 820 flowering
plants and ferns.'

(III.) Anker.—' In this district the Warwickshire coal-
fields occur; and it is possibly due to the great prevalence
of smoke that its flora is meagre, and the plants often
depauperated. The recorded flora is about 680 flowering
plants and ferns.'

(IV.) Avon.—' This valley is beautifully undulating and

well-wooded, watered by many minor streams, with very varied soils, and usually highly cultivated. Its flora is peculiar from the absence of bog and heath plants, the records comprising about 970 flowering plants and ferns.'

(V.) Sow.—'The flora of this sub-district is about 691 flowering plants and ferns.'

(VI.) Alne.—'Is somewhat hilly. The Lias soils prevail in southern part of the district. The flora is about 745 flowering plants and ferns.'

(VII.) Arrow.—'Is well wooded. The soils are mostly Keuper Marls and sand, with Lias soils prevailing about Wixford. The flora has not been fully worked out, but the record is now about 706 flowering plants and ferns.'

Algæ have been neglected till Mr. A. W. Wills undertook the work, but his care and skill have already made a valuable record. He says: 'Hence, as the neighbourhood of Birmingham is mostly characterized by light and porous soils, the habitats in which algæ are to be found are somewhat restricted. There are, however, two conspicuous exceptions. The tract of land about seven miles from Birmingham, known as Sutton Park, embraces a singular variety of scenery and presents conditions highly favourable to algoid growth in the shape of clear springs and streams, large sheets of water, and a considerable area of peaty bogs,' and the marshy districts of the neighbourhood afford among their 'pit-banks' a 'number of pools which are seldom dried up, even in the hottest summer, and many of which are partially fed by water from adjacent mines or engines,' and thus form a 'rich hunting-ground for students of fresh-water algæ.' Minute details are given of local examples of algæ, and one remarkable 'find' is well worth quotation: 'The Diatomaceæ of the neighbourhood do not appear to have been the objects of systematic study, and the only species of special interest which we remember to have found is the wonderful *Bacillaria Paradoxa*, well known as a remarkable microscopic object, from the strange manner in which its linear frustules slide over one another, so that the whole plant is incessantly assuming a different form. It has been found by [the late] Mr. Bolton, along with many other species, in a disused arm of the canal near Albion Station, and by the writer in a small stream near the same spot.'

Fungi have a literary as well as scientific interest in Warwickshire, since one of the early and able fungologists was long resident in the county, and since he not only first gave fungi their due place in the British flora, but because he also discovered and classified a large number of species and varieties new to Britain and to science. At his residence, Edgbaston Hall, where a large park was at his service, and wherein some of his favourite fungi may still be found, Dr. William Withering pursued his botanical researches and wrote his famous 'Arrangement of British Plants.' Mr. W. B. Grove, B.A., has given a brief but careful account not only of Dr. Withering and his works, but of Thomas Purton, of Alcester, whose 'Midland Flora' (1817-1821) was, and still is, a valuable work, in which were coloured engravings of thirty-five species of fungi; but the study had been neglected for some years till Mr. Grove and Mr. J. E. Bagnall undertook the work, and have now recorded considerably more than nine hundred in the 'district twenty miles round Birmingham,' of which Warwickshire takes a very large share. Mrs. Russell, of Kenilworth, some years ago made a special study of the Hymenomycetes of the limited area of Kenilworth, Stoneleigh and Warwick, and bequeathed to the British Museum more than three hundred coloured illustrations of the examples she had collected. Mr. Grove gives an extensive list of the local varieties of the various species, with the places where they have been found, and notes some remarkable examples which, if not unique in the neighbourhood, have their only resemblances very many miles away. Mr. Grove's paper is a very useful index and record, and he hopes it may reach to still further studies of microscopic mycology.

CHAPTER VI.

ARCHÆOLOGY.

British and Roman Roads.—Tumuli.—Icknield Street.—Fosse-Way, Watling Street.—Anglo-Saxon and Roman Remains.—British Keltic, and Saxon Place-names. — Earthworks and Camps. — Danish Traces.—Norman Surveys and Castles.—Military and Civil Architecture.—Early Churches.—Dissolution of Monasteries. —Sepulchral Monuments. — Sepulchral Brasses. — Effigies and Altar Tombs.—Beauchamp Chapel at Warwick.—Shakespearian and Contemporary Monuments at Stratford-on-Avon.—Ruined or deserted Churches.

'ARCHÆOLOGICAL' has not only superseded the old word 'antiquarian,' but has, during the last forty years, marked a more definite and scientific study of the relics of the past. The present use of the word involves a scientific study and not a mere *dilettante* record of antiquities of all ages. In the last century, even, as shown by the contributions to the *Gentleman's Magazine*, and even by the more careful papers in the *Archæologia* of the Society of Antiquaries, the faculty of observation and the power of description were limited and untrustworthy. The art of drawing, too, was often amusingly faulty; and the engravings of antiquities which still remain almost unaltered, afford ludicrous examples of mis-observation, and so far distort the objects, that they can scarcely be identified unless the names are given. In no cases are these differences more marked than in the representation of architectural remains; and it is especially curious to see how carelessly the artists of the past copied what was before their eyes, as compared with the finished, careful and accurate drawings of the past forty years. The love of antiquities has rapidly increased with the better knowledge of their interest and value, and far more care is given to their preservation, although the 'modern Goth' is still too busy in destroying or 'restoring' the memorials of old times. The principal and popular societies have not only done much to educate the public taste, but have by their visits and papers by competent observers done far more by explaining and illustrating archæological remains. The Ancient Monuments Act of Sir John Lubbock, although far too limited in powers of survey and purchase, has saved many historic relics from destruction, and if Great Britain were as civilized as France and some other states, ample national grants would be given for the preservation of national monuments from neglect and destruction. The 'Society for the Protection of Ancient Buildings' and the 'Society for Preserving the Memorials of the Dead,' well deserve far more support than they receive for their careful surveys and real restoration of places and buildings of historic interest, and of the monuments of the dead which are supposed to be 'sacred to the memory,' but are too often imperilled or destroyed by some 'restorer'—clerical or lay. The English people are notoriously 'conservative,' and even the ignorant and illiterate regard the relics of the past with respect and reverence, while the cultured people profess to admire the quaint old houses, venerable churches, grand cathedrals and picturesque castles; but no adequate organization has yet been formed for the preservation of the memorials which Americans come in crowds to see, and which are, in many senses, a sacred trust for future generations.

ROMAN.—Archæology was originally held to refer

chiefly to prehistoric monuments, but now includes all relics of antiquity, from the dawn of history down almost to our own times. Warwickshire may not be so rich in remains as many other counties, but it has many remains of exceptional interest—far too many to be fully described. In the strict sense of the word 'prehistoric,' no remains are known, except, of course, in the case of early camps and tumuli and ancient roads which are within the limits of written history, but of which little or nothing is definitely known. The antiquities as well as the history of the far-distant periods are necessarily only imperfectly known, and a difference, often of several centuries, may occur as to the date of a stone memorial, or a grassy tumulus, or the age of an ancient road. For example, the Rollright Stones, already referred to, may be prehistoric, or of the time of Alfred and the Danes. The roads which bear Roman names and run past Roman camps may have been originally old British ways through Arden long before even Julius Cæsar's days. The numerous tumuli scattered throughout the county may be of Anglo-Saxon, or early British, or of prehistoric date. The names of Roman stations may, and sometimes do, include the names of earlier British villages or camps; while the names of places are often so ancient as to puzzle philologists to find their origin and meaning.

The 'Commentaries' of Julius Cæsar, as records of his invasion, give a clear and graphic account of what he saw and heard of eighteen hundred years ago; but as he penetrated little further than the Thames, his descriptions throw only a side-light on the Midland counties. The only relics of the Roman occupation to be found in Warwickshire are in the names of the great roads and stations. The Ryknield Street and the Watling Street have long runs through or near the county. The Ryknield or Icknield Street enters the county on the south of Bidford-on-Avon, and runs nearly due north through Birmingham, and meets the Watling Street from the south-east at Etocetum (or Wall), near Lichfield, thus passing through part of South-East Warwickshire, East Worcestershire, the outlying peninsular part of Warwickshire in which Birmingham stands, and thence through part of Staffordshire. The line of the road is singularly well marked, except that near Birmingham; but one part through that town still bears the name 'Icknield Street.' The line through Sutton Park, for nearly three miles, is most distinct, and really unaltered in line and width and level, except that it is grass-grown. No Roman remains, except a few coins, have been found, and Stukeley's guess that the Roman 'Bremenium' denoted Birmingham has long ago been found to be wrong. The little town of Alcester (on the Alne and Arrow) is doubtless the Roman 'Alauna,' and Roman bricks, urns, and gold and silver coins have been found; but no clear traces of a 'station,' although the line of road, the local indications, and the name clearly show traces of Roman occupation. No other 'station' is known between Alcester and Etocetum, for a small square camp at Harborne, near Birmingham, cannot be identified as a Roman work. The whole of the line of road is less solidly constructed than that of Watling Street, and this fact, with the name of the 'Iceni,' an old British tribe of the neighbourhood, is reasonable evidence that Icknield or Ryknield Street was really an old British road from the Severn to the Mersey and the Tyne when extended and developed during the Roman occupation. The very name of the road and the derivation just mentioned require, however, some explanation, as the Eastern counties line is more truly the Icknield Street, which extended from the Norfolk coast by Cambridge, Old Sarum, and Exeter, to the extremity of Cornwall. The western line, running north and south as above named, is, however, more generally known as 'Icknield Street' (from St. David's, by Gloucester, to the mouth of the Tyne, to vary the description); but the authorities generally agree that it should be known as Ryknield Street to avoid confusion.

The other great line of road—originally British, but practically Roman, since it was paved and improved by the conquerors—extended from Richborough through Canterbury, London, Stony Stratford, etc., to Chester, and thence into Wales, forming the great north-western road. It enters Warwickshire near Rugby, and thence to Atherstone forms the boundary-line between Warwickshire and Leicestershire. Although the line of the road has remained unaltered, very few remains of Roman occupation have been found. The first station, Tripontium, is said to be at Cave's Inn, near Rugby, where some glazed Samian ware, a bronze stylus, and some fibulæ and keys of Roman date were dug up some years ago; and similar relics have been unearthed at other places near the line of road. 'High Cross,' about half-way between Rugby and Atherstone, was a place of great importance as the point at which another ancient road enters the Watling Street from the south-west. A few miles further the village of Mancetter marks the site and preserves the name of the Roman station Manduessedum, one of the highest points in the county, and the name of which is held by Keltic etymologists to include the ancient British 'maen,' as a lofty mound, still called Oldbury, is near. No exact site of any Roman camp or station has been found, but the importance of the place and the occasional discovery of gold and silver coins clearly show that Manduessedum was occupied as a Roman station, and Atherstone, very near, was also an important place. On the summit of Oldbury, however, there are traces of a quadrangular camp, which some have supposed to be the 'summer camp' (*campus æstiva*) to the Roman station near, and this is probable; but as many flint 'celts' and other stone weapons have been found, there can be no doubt that an old British stronghold had been extended and fortified by the Romans during their occupation. The line of road continues through Atherstone (which has been absurdly supposed to have been originally Hitherstone, as marking the nearest 'milliarium' to Manduessedum, but which is certainly derived from some Saxon Edric or Aldred). The town shows several marks of Roman occupation, and some fragments of Roman work have been found. A few miles further the Watling Street leaves Warwickshire near Wilnecote (south of Tamworth), and continues to Etocetum (or Wall), where it meets the Ryknield Street, as already shown.

Another of the great old roads through Warwickshire is known by its older name, 'The Fosse-Way,' but is generally called the 'Roman Fosse-Way,' as it was also used by those conquerors in the later times of their occupation of Mid-England. The other two roads only skirted the county, and avoided, with true tactical skill, the dense Forest of Arden, in which the enemy had a secure retreat from any attack on the Roman legions on their marches across the country. The Fosse-Way is now seen to be an inferior roadway as compared with the Watling and the Ryknield Streets, but there is little doubt that it was largely used by the Romans when their power had been more fully assured. It enters the county on the southwest at Stretton-under-Fosse, and runs north-east to High Cross, which was thus an important 'junction,' and where in 1712 a cross was erected to record that this was the centre of Roman Britain, 'whence their celebrated military ways, crossing one another, extend to the utmost boundaries of Britain.' The inscription adds, 'Here the Vennones kept their quarter, and at the distance of one mile from hence, Claudius, a certain commander of a cohort, seems to have had a camp towards the Street, and towards the Foss, a tomb.' The cross and its inscription have long disappeared, but a tumulus near is supposed to cover the remains of some Roman hero, and the site is known as 'Cloudsley' Bush. The line of the Fosse-Way runs nearly parallel with the main road of modern times from Stratford-on-Avon to Nuneaton, which is itself a very ancient road, running through Coventry and Warwick and Kenilworth, but probably not so generally used in Roman times as the other Roman stations which are nearer the Fosse-Way line. The direction of the Fosse-way is even now nearly a straight line between Stretton-on-the-Fosse and Nuneaton, and along the larger part of its course of forty miles it rises and falls with the surface of the country generally, but has some deep cuttings and many picturesque views—really, an 'old-world' road. The principal traces of Roman occupation are found at Chesterton, near Harbury Station and Southam, with remains of a large rectangular camp, evidently Roman; and many Roman coins have been found on the site. Warwick is six miles westward, and as it is considered on good authority to have been the 'Præsidium' of the Romans, it was probably held as one of the old British forts commanding the larger part of Warwickshire. Still further north-eastwards, as Watling Street is approached, the traces of Roman occupation increase, but it is remarkable that Warwickshire is not known to have any cemeteries of Roman date, nor even any cinerary urns. At Brinklow, through which the Fosse-Way passes, there is a large tumulus of uncertain date, and there are some few traces of a camp. At Monk's Kirby remains of old walls and bricks, clearly Roman, had been found, which induced Camden and Dugdale to suppose that the Romans had a station there, but no thorough exploration has been made, and probably, according to Camden, the 'foundations' have been used for other buildings, and are now lost. Near Wibtoft, a short distance from Monk's Kirby, and on the county border, in the angle between the Fosse-Way and Watling Street, at High-Cross, a flourishing Roman city is said to have stood, with the name of Cleychester, which Dugdale describes as having left scarcely any vestiges in his time (c. 1650), 'the very foundations having been for the most part turned up by the plough and the spade, and large stones, Roman bricks, with ovens and wells—nay, coins of silver and brass mixed with its ruins—frequently discovered.' It is certainly unfortunate that no traces remain of one of the most important of all the Roman 'stations' in Britain, whose central position must have brought together all sorts of people, and whose relics might have been more important than those found at Chester or Wroxeter or York.

In some few other parts of the county other Roman remains are said to have been found—for example, at Willoughby, six miles south-east of Rugby, and three miles from Dunchurch, and some at Brownsover and Princethorpe; but the knowledge and vigilance of Mr. M. H. Bloxam, F.S.A., of Rugby, during more than sixty years, has rarely been rewarded by any important discovery of relics of the period of the Roman occupation of Britain, or of any detailed survey of the sites of their numerous camps in or near Warwickshire during the centuries of their imperial rule.

ANGLO-SAXON.—Although this form has long been used to describe generally the influx and influence of successive generations of invaders after the departure of the Romans and before the arrival of the Normans, many modern historians have long held that it would be wiser and more correct to write of 'Saxons' only than to modify the word by the use of the word 'Anglo-,' whose exact extent cannot well be defined. The three great sorts of invaders (or, as compared with the Romans and the Normans, practically and finally 'colonists') were Jutes, who peopled Kent and some of the south-western counties; Saxons, who covered Essex, Middlesex and Wessex; and Angles, who occupied East Anglia and the northern parts of Britain. The exact divisions and descriptions are somewhat arbitrary and uncertain; the lines often overlapped, and the three tribes were very slowly blended in the course of years, although ethnologically and physically the differences in type and race are often strongly marked. Examples numerous enough to be authoritative, or at least puzzling, are found of distinct South-Saxon physique even in Mid-England. The generic name of 'Saxon,' irrespective of shades of difference, will, therefore, be used to describe the monumental remains in Warwickshire. These are not numerous nor remarkable, and in very few instances can definite or even approximate dates be assigned. Many of the tumuli, for example, have had their external lines so changed by time and weather, or by farming operations, that they cannot be positively identified, except in the instances in which they have been opened and some remains found with articles of personal or official forms to show whether the mounds are British or Saxon graves. A considerable number have yet to be opened and examined, but the result is not likely to affect the general record. Another characteristic of some of the Warwickshire mounds increases the difficulties of determining their date and use. Some of the larger and loftier have evidently been used as beacons, but whether they are burial-places as well as beacons could only be discovered by the results of careful searches for any funeral remains. 'Two tumuli near Rugby,' Mr. Bloxam says, not only 'served as sepulchral monuments, but formed links in the telegraphic communications between the two great British trackways, the Watling Street and the Fosse-Road, along the northern boundary of the Dobuni; that on the Lawford road communicating, either directly or through the mound in the village of Church Lawford, to a tumulus at Wolston on the high ground near the Fosse-Road; whilst the tumulus in the [Rugby] School Close was in connection with that at Hillmorton, in a field adjoining the vicarage, which communicates with the small British post near the Watling Street at Lilbourne, from which the communication was again carried on southwards by tumuli on or near the Watling Street.' He also adds that this plan of signalling among the Gauls is alluded to by Cæsar, that smoke from fires by day and the light of fires by night were the means employed; and further adds that 'so late as the Civil Wars of the seventeenth century one of the Warwickshire fire-beacons was erected on one of the ancient British tumuli, that known as Cloudsley Bush, in the parish of Monk's Kirby.' The great tumulus at Brinklow, and the larger one at Seckington, near Tamworth, probably served in their time the double purpose, and although the Seckington mound is definitely assigned to A.D. 757, and the battle between Cuthred, king of the West Saxons, and Ethelwold, king of the Mercians, in which the latter fell by a traitor's hand, there is little room for doubt that it was originally a British work, as the remains of a large circular camp help to prove. As Tamworth and Kingsbury were nearly in the centre of the Mercian kingdom, and the latter is said to have been one of the halls of the Mercian kings, and the place where Burtulphus resided and held a grand council of his prelates and nobles A.D. 851, and as Tamworth was another of the royal seats, and traces of 'herring-bone' masonry are still visible in the base of the lower walls, these two places merit special notice as famous in Saxon times. At Offchurch, near Leamington, Offa, the eleventh of the Mercian kings, built a stately palace, and Dugdale states that first the church and afterwards the village took Offa's name; but the glories have departed, and only a few houses and a few foundations mark the site. At Walton, near Wellesbourne, one of the largest discoveries of Saxon relics was made in 1774, according to Gough's 'Addition to Camden,' when 'three skulls lying in a row, with two Saxon jewels set in gold, one with an opal and two rubies, and the other adorned on both sides with a cross, between two rude human figures, with a sword or lance at the outer hand of each,' were found.

Although the monumental and material remains of the Saxon period are rare in Warwickshire, philology has discovered and explained the origin and meaning of many words which, after many changes, very curiously indicate the extent and influence of Saxon rule. The general forest area of Warwickshire made wholesale invasion and absolute conquest difficult, and changes in population necessarily slow. There can be little doubt that the ancients, Kelts or Britons, 'held their own,' and were only slowly and partially influenced by the invasions of Saxons. The Romans were a military and conquering people, whose power was principally on the lines of the great roads—at any rate, so far as Mid-England was concerned. The Saxons were more like colonists and settlers, and slowly but surely blended with the older tribes. This, in the absence of written history and records of changes which were slow and silent, may reasonably be examined by the light which philology affords as to names and places. The names of rivers and hills still remain distinctly Keltic— Arden, Lickey, Avon, Alne, Arrow and Rea—while many affixes, like 'cote' and 'combe,' are clearly Keltic. The name of the county, although it has had many changes, is, beyond all doubt, of Keltic origin, and is given by Nennius as 'Guoricon, Guorichon and Guerican,' a plural form of which Guorich is the singular; and the root remains in all the twenty-four variations of ancient records from Nennius down to Domesday Book. Some of these will serve to show the links in the chain and the survival of the Keltic root, *e.g.*, Caer Guaric, Caer Gwar, Guarewic, followed by the softer sounds of Waring-wicon, Waerincwic, Werewic, Wareing-wicscire, Weric, down to the Warwic of Domesday Book. All these examples may be accepted as cumulative evidence (although Keltic etymologies are proverbially treacherous), and are supported by the records of John Rous, of Warwick, that the name Gwayr was that of an ancient British prince, and that the softer form

Waring-wicon (which first appears in the Saxon Chronicle) came from Warmund, an ancestor of Offa, King of Mercia. The late Mr. George Jabet ('Eden Warwick'), who was a specialist, but a careful 'Keltist,' and not a mere enthusiastic guesser, held that the original name was 'Gawr' only, and quoted the word as descriptive of many fortified places, always on heights, and especially in Wales. The second syllable, 'wick' or 'wich,' is still a puzzle, but is probably from the Keltic 'gwic,' a fort, while the familiar 'wich,' generally associated with salt-producing places, is supposed to come from the ancient Huiccii, in whose territory, Worcestershire and Gloucestershire, salt-springs were found. The common terminations, like 'ton,' 'ham,' 'ley,' 'stoke,' 'combe,' etc., are numerous in Warwickshire, and Mr. Jabet further noted that while Dugdale's Warwickshire includes 570 names of places, and Domesday Book 300 in Warwickshire, the latter has 113 'ton' and only 4 'ham' terminations, and the former 167 'ton' or 'don,' 55 'ley,' and only 6 'ham,' and he holds this to indicate 'a prolonged intermixture between the Saxon invaders and the native British,' since 'ham' is always home, and 'ton' an enclosed place or fort. He concludes thus: 'The Saxon settlements in Warwickshire were evidently made among a hostile population; while those in the eastern counties, where 'ham' prevails, were made among a friendly people, those counties having been almost entirely Saxonised many years before the departure of the Romans.' Whether this theory is sound or not, it is certainly clear from other words, like 'stoke,' 'worth,' 'cote,' 'thorpe,' 'bury,' etc., that the Saxon influences in Warwickshire were remarkably wide, continuous and permanent, but that large numbers of old Keltic names remained almost unchanged down to our own times.

Although Saxon (or Anglo-Saxon) remains are rare in Warwickshire, their scarcity may be owing principally to the facts that only recently have such remains been historically and scientifically studied, and also that Warwickshire has never been thoroughly surveyed since the importance of earthworks, tumuli, and funeral remains has been recognised. In many parts of England surveys carefully made have brought many important facts to light, and the opening of tumuli has unearthed relics of rare importance as historic evidences for facts and dates. The late Mr. J. Tom Burgess, F.S.A., during his residence at Leamington, continued the researches of his friend Mr. M. H. Bloxam, F.S.A., many years before, and personally visited and examined and measured earthworths and tumuli in all parts of the county. He has left no formal record of his discoveries, except in a brief paper in an obscure and forgotten serial, *Long Ago* (1873); some details of which are worthy of preservation, and especially as they show that further researches might and should be made. He found, in preparing a sketch-map, that there were several blanks left in former records, and especially as to the neighbourhood of the Avon. He remarked that 'along the ancient trackways and Roman military roads, which can yet be traced along the boundary of the county, tumuli, earthworks, and traces of Roman occupation have long been noted and described. Along the course of the Avon until it crosses the Fosse-Way, in the neighbourhood of Wappenbury [north-east of Leamington], where there are considerable Roman remains, there are abundant signs of a large population. The Fosse-Way thence continues its course in a south-westerly direction to Moreton-in-the-Marsh, a distance of about twenty miles. The intrenchments of the Roman camp at Chesterton alone show the footprints of Roman settlers, whilst the remains of British settlements have not been noted. On the verge of the county Roman remains can be again discerned. Throughout this portion of its route the Fosse crosses the champaign country known as the Feldon, which appears for a long period to have been the debatable ground between the ancient tribes—the Roman, and still later the Saxon settlers. There is no station marked on any of the Roman itineraries along this route, though there appear to have been communications between the Roman station at Tripontium (Lilbourne), Benones (High-Cross) on the east [near Rugby], and the settlement at Alauna (Alcester) on the [south-]west. There must, therefore, have been a road or trackway from Wappenbury along the northern bank of the Avon; and this, there is abundant evidence to prove, was the more ancient trackway, for it appears to have connected a series of British forts with each other. These forts were either connected with, or were in the immediate neighbourhood and within sight of, tumuli along the entire route. These forts appear to have been the frontier fortresses of the Cornavii, and before which Ostorius Scapula paused in his course northwards. The frontier fortresses of their southern neighbours can be as easily traced on the bluff headlands on the southern side of the Feldon, some ten to twelve miles distant. Of these northern strongholds only two or three are marked on the Ordnance Map; indeed, the existence of some of them was unknown a few months ago [1873]. In the course of the autumn an agricultural friend, Mr. Cook, of Snitterfield [near Stratford], directed my attention to some earthworks, which he stated were in Barmoor Wood, about midway between Claverdon and Henley-in-Arden; and may be found on the Ordnance Map between the Crab Mill and Cherry Pool. I took an early opportunity of visiting the spot, and by the courtesy of the occupier of the farm was enabled to inspect the wood at my leisure. I was accompanied by Mr. Thomas Gibbs, whose knowledge of that neighbourhood is very minute, and we had literally to force our way through the thick brushwood and round the mound and entrenchments which we found within Barmoor Wood, which appears to have formed a part of the ancient Forest of Arden. We estimated the extent of the earthworks at between three and four acres. They are strongly marked, but what appears to be the outer vallum is considerably altered and modified by the fence which surrounds it. The plan and arrangement closely resemble a similar camp at Beausall, some six miles eastward. On the north there is a well-defined causeway across the fosse which is twenty feet wide and some twelve feet deep, and this causeway connects the enclosure with an open plateau which commands an extensive view in every direction. The plan of the camp is slightly oval, and at its broadest part is 150 paces. We could not secure a more accurate survey in consequence of the thicket. On the southern side the hill was sharply escarped, and this had been increased by excavations for marl. This camp completes the line of fortresses between Alcester and Lilbourne. In all probability the great stronghold of the tribes who occupied these fortified mounds was the mound at Henley-in-Arden, the ancient name of which was Donnilee, but was changed by the De Montforts to Beaudesert. This mound is only two miles distant from Barmoor Wood.

'Encouraged by this discovery, I turned my attention to the south side of the Avon. My first discovery was a tumulus close by an ancient ford in the parish of Tachbrook, midway between Chesterton Camp and Warwick Castle. About one mile to the east of Chesterton is a huge mound bearing the name of Frismore Hill, adjoining the Fosse-Way. Seven miles to the west, on the same road, is Friz Hill, where many Saxon remains have been found. The hill opposite on the north is Red Hill, and within the wood which crowns its summit I found a well-defined large intrenchment which has not yet been accurately surveyed. This opened up a new field, for this was in a line with Meon Hill in Worcestershire, and seemed to indicate that there were the remains of old settlements between Meon Hill and Napton. At Hodnell, about a mile from a Roman intrenchment marked on the Ordnance Map, the sites of two deserted and abandoned villages can be traced ; and on the summit of the hill, towards the north, I found a small tumulus and two parallel banks of earth 50 yards apart and from 100 to 150 yards long. The northern valla fell away on the hillside so as to form a terrace of terraced steps with intervening fosses. A well was found in a hollow to the east. On the opposite hill there are further remains which appear to indicate the existence of a village. The Hodnell tumulus is within sight of the Roman intrenchment, and of the hill at Chesterton, Napton, and the bluff frontier of North Hants. Thus the map of ancient Warwickshire is gradually filled up' (J. T. Burgess).

After all allowances for the enthusiasm of a discoverer, and for possible errors of observation, there need be little doubt that these discoveries are substantially correct. He was an 'expert' in earthworks, and was not likely to be mistaken in his series of observations, which, even if somewhat overrated, certainly greatly help to clear up some of the obscurities of the topography of Warwickshire in the British, Saxon and Roman times. His knowledge of similar remains in many parts of England was extensive, as he was a constant attendant at the archæological excursions of the 'Institute' and 'Association,' and had excellent opportunities of becoming familiar with the early topography and history of England. His references to the Ordnance Map are, of course, only to the 'one-inch' scale, surveyed and printed some forty years ago, and probably not so detailed as would be desirable for archæological researches. The new map, now in course of publication, being on the 'twenty-five-inch' scale to the mile, necessarily gives far more minute and accurate details of all historic and prehistoric remains. On such a basis as is now available, and with the fact that the recent survey has given very special care to all ancient remains, by 'taking

5—2

counsel' with local 'experts' as to names and places, and varied pronunciations and spellings of place-names, the topography not only of Warwickshire, but of the counties generally, will have a stimulus and a reward for further reports on the roads and earthworks of old times.

The Roman remains in Warwickshire are comparatively few and unimportant, and nearly all are limited to what are known as the great Roman roads, but these were always on the lines of the older British or Keltic roads, straightened, widened, improved, and with camps or stations as military posts to secure the communications 'cross country' from the Thames to the Mersey and the Severn to the Humber. These great roads have already been described, but one less known is that which still bears the name of 'the Roman Fosse-Way,' and runs through the county from south-west to north-east, from Stratford-on-Avon to the Watling Street, and whose line still bears the older names of Shirley Street, Street's Brook, Monkspath Street, etc., which clearly indicate an ante-Roman road passing through the heart of 'Arden.' Only one Roman station in Warwickshire is mentioned by the early topographers, Manduessedum (or Mancetter, near Atherstone), but another Alauna, now Alcester, is mentioned by Richard of Cirencester. Other Roman forts and towns are, however, known by casual mention, and Roman remains having been found at Warwick, Coventry, Chesterton, Cesterover, Harborough Banks, Willoughby, Monk's Kirby, Princethorpe, Wappenbury, Beaudesert (near Henley-in-Arden), Nabworth Camp and Vennonæ. Most of these, however, show traces of earlier British names, and after the departure of the Romans these old British names were in many cases restored, and used not only in Saxon, but in Norman and later days. The Saxon affixes 'ceastre,' 'ley,' 'ton,' 'worth,' etc., were really the revivals of the earlier Keltic names, and it seems to be clear that the ancient peoples were not lost but blended with the later invaders age after age. The Roman camps were of three classes: the 'castra exploratoria,' or temporary camps for surveys and short occupation; 'castra æstiva,' for summer or temporary use; and 'castra stativa,' or permanent camps for conquered districts (which were to be held in subjection, and which often included the two previously named), and also the 'castra hiberna,' or winter quarters, which were often formed when more than a summer camp was found necessary. In the Warwickshire examples, and especially the remains at Mancetter and Atherstone, there seem to be remains of the 'castra æstiva' and of the 'castra stativa' respectively. The remains, however, are too few to indicate distinctly the extent of these camps, nor does the Roman Etocetum (near Lichfield) give much help, although, as the meeting-point of the Rykenield and Watling Streets, it must have been an important station. The famous Itinerary of Antoninus (A.D. 320) mentions only the names (and distances) of three places in Warwickshire: 'Etoceto, m.p. xii.; Manduessedo, m.p. xvi.; and Venonius, m.p., xii.,' and no other early and authoritative account is given. The relics found from time to time have been few and unimportant, and no traces of Roman buildings, or mosaic floors, or public buildings, as at Wroxeter and Leicester, and only traces of the famous Roman roads.

SAXON AND DANISH.—It is impossible to use the words 'Anglo-Saxon' or 'Saxon' in any very exact or scientific way, since critics and historians are still discussing how far the 'Angles' and the 'Saxons' influenced the history of England as to their numbers and importance. It will be best, therefore, to use the more comprehensive word 'Saxon' to include the general population and the general history of England between the departure of the Romans and the arrival of the Normans on our shores. This is the more necessary in a mere general summary, and especially in the consideration of archæological remains. The

British (or Keltic), the Saxons, Angles and the Danes soon became irretrievably mixed in Mid-England, and it is difficult, if not impossible, to assign to each element its ethnological value in the complex 'English people.' The comparatively few material remains which have been preserved are rarely marked enough in form or character to be assigned with certainty; and the very plausible but treacherous temptations to find history in words, and to settle historical and ethnological assertions by the mutations or survivals of words—especially as to alleged Keltic etymologies—invariably end in making confusion more confounded, and in leaving doubts and uncertainties more marked than ever. In matters strictly archæological, as to material remains, there is far less risk. British and Saxon tumuli and barrows and camps can be readily and positively distinguished from Roman remains. Saxon and British and Roman coins have marked differences. In architecture the 'herring-bone' Saxon work is clearly different from Norman 'rubble,' but in minor details, and especially those of later dates, it is more difficult to decide as to the age and history of the relics of old times. The isolated position of Warwickshire, the fact that it was really a county to be crossed, rather than a place to dwell in, left it for many centuries almost unchanged and uninfluenced by the busier and more accessible peoples of the counties nearer the coasts. It was like a large town, famous in old coaching days, but deserted and isolated when the nearest railway, some miles away, left it neglected and 'out of the world.' Hence, during nearly a thousand years, from the landing of the Romans to the coming of the Normans, it was but little affected by external events. The Saxons and Danes slowly advanced, rather as colonists than conquerors, and slowly mingled with the people of the woods and forests. Changes of customs occurred slowly and silently. The Saxon element pervaded the whole district. The Mercian kings had their castles, palaces and courts. The Heptarchy slowly welded the scattered elements together. The arts of peace were more favoured than the arts of war. 'The Romans were imperial and centralizing, the Saxons agrarian and domestic; the former built and fortified, the latter appropriated and enclosed.' The new element of Christianity introduced churches and monasteries, and helped to blend the people into a nation with a language and laws which have formed the basis of English life and progress for a thousand years.

Saxon remains are rare in Warwickshire, and only a few examples of metal-work have been found near Warwick—some, jewellery discovered in an Anglo-Saxon grave, and one of early date; but many grave-mounds and tumuli have never been disturbed—at least, in modern times—and probably important relics may yet be found in some undisturbed grave. Among buildings, however, there are at least two with unquestionable Saxon work, but of course only fragments of the bases, the superstructure being of far later date. The first of these is found at Tamworth Castle, forming the base of the long wall leading up to the keep. The castle was built by King Alfred's daughter, Ethelfleda, *circa* 913, but the old 'herring-bone' work is probably of much earlier date, and part of the original fortification. The other example is at Wootton-Wawen, or Wood Town, from Saxon *wudu*, or *wud*, and *tun*, enclosure or town, and Waga, or Wagen, one of the great Saxon lords, who was one of the witnesses to Leofric's foundation charter of the monastery at Coventry, *circa* 1043. The tower of this church, up to a height of three-fifths, is the oldest part of the church, and certainly of Saxon masonry, and the church itself is the only one in Warwickshire in which Saxon work has ever yet been found. Saxon burial-places have been found in Warwickshire (as part of the Mercian and Mid-Angles' kingdom), at Cesterover, Churchover, on the north-east, or Leicestershire border of the county; and also at Warwick, near the castle and the Church of St. Nicholas, but none of any historic or artistic value. As there are so many proofs of the Saxon people and influence in Warwickshire, more relics might be expected, and probably more may be found.

The immigrations and presence of the Danes are but little marked in Warwickshire, but generally the Danes seem to have left few remains in Mid-England. There is a popular belief that while they certainly advanced into Warwickshire, it was practically their boundary, as the affix 'by' (as in Rugby), and said to be Danish, is rarely found south of that ancient town. Their camps were supposed to be circular or oval, but it would be difficult to distinguish them from old British camps (which are numerous in Warwickshire), and probably 'names' are the safest guide, as where 'Danes' camp' and 'Danbury camp' sometimes occur, but no such traces are found in Warwickshire. Much, however, may yet be discovered by more careful surveys of the numerous woods in many parts of the county, which have never been thoroughly explored, and in whose untrodden recesses many mounds —even of prehistoric date—may yet be found to reveal the secrets of ancient dwellers in the Forest of Arden.

ANGLO-SAXON AND NORMAN.—The later half of the tenth and the earlier half of the eleventh centuries (966 to 1066) afford but few direct evidences of the changes in the condition of England, from the reigns of the Anglo-Saxon and Danish kings of the Heptarchy to the Battle of Hastings and the beginning of the Norman rule. There is, however, a great light thrown back on the past by the great survey known as Domesday Book (1083—1086), which gives a graphic picture of Anglo-Saxon England a hundred years before. With the ever-notable Saxon Chronicle, compiled under Alfred (872), but begun at least as early as 849, and forming a most valuable historic record, and the territorial valuation of lands under Edward the Confessor (1041), which were afterwards a chief basis of the Norman survey in 1083, a curiously careful and detailed summary of the 'condition of England' for more than a century of comparative darkness has been preserved. Neither the Saxon Chronicle, nor the Edwardian valuation, nor the Domesday Book, throw much light on the details most interesting in our modern tastes and studies. The Saxon Chronicle was chiefly a chronology of historic facts, as history was then regarded. The Edwardian survey and Domesday Book were principally territorial, chiefly as records of landed property for the purposes of taxation; but fortunately Domesday Book mentions churches, mills, ploughs, oxen, priests, villeins, etc., which materially help to form a picture of Saxon England. The details of the limits of land and of the various owners, the comparisons of the value of land with the estimates of King Edward's time, and the numerous minor incidental facts recorded, make this famous survey of incalculable value and interest in all researches into the history of England from eight hundred to nine hundred years ago. As an archæological record, it remains quite unrivalled in the history of Europe, and the great treasury of otherwise unrecorded facts. 'Castles,' says Grose, 'walled with stone, and designed for residence as well as defence, were not of earlier days than the Conquest,' so that few remains of 'castles' in our modern sense of the word have left any traces. Forty-nine castles are mentioned in Domesday Book, and only one of them (Arundel Castle) is noticed as having existed in Edward the Confessor's time; but Warwick Castle is mentioned, although probably only a fortified mound like those at Dudley and Tutbury, and similar places in the Midland counties. Forests, parks manors, mills, fortified towns, and even vineyards, are frequently mentioned, and Warwick Castle, like that of

Tamworth, is reputed to have been built by Alfred's daughter, Ethelfleda, *circa* 913. The castle-building fashion, however, was the work of Norman influence, and necessary to keep the conquered country in subjection, and in the twelfth, thirteenth and fourteenth centuries most of the famous English castles were built.

The Saxon style of architecture was chiefly based on Roman example, and in a ruder and rougher style. The masonry was irregular 'long and short,' the arches semicircular, and even triangular, the columns low and broad, and the sculpture rude in design and unfinished in style. The Norman buildings, military as well as ecclesiastical, were solid and substantial, but more graceful in form and more decorated in style. Many examples of such works have been preserved with comparatively few changes down to our day. Numerous additions in later fashions have been made, but in many of the oldest buildings which have escaped the ravages of the 'restorer,' some very fine examples of Norman work have been preserved. Even in those early times Norman architecture had its 'periods' and 'stages,' described as early, later, and transition, and the Warwickshire examples under these headings will be worthy of a brief review. Under the 'early Norman' (1066-1087) Wootton-Wawen is the only example, and that only as to the later portions of the church, for the larger part of the base of the tower is unquestionably Saxon, as already shown; and the 'early Norman' has long been covered with a coat of stucco. Another and very beautiful example is the porch of the Priory Church of Kenilworth, built by Geoffrey de Clinton in 1122. Of the 'later Norman' (1135-1154) there are several examples in Warwickshire, as in the beautiful Norman work in the little church at Beaudesert or Beldesert (originally Donnellie), at Henley-in-Arden, and at Packington Church, built by the younger Geoffrey de Clinton in 1150; Wormleighton Church, the same donor and date, and also at

Radford Church, also the gift of De Clinton, and thus connected and similar as the work of the same artist. No example of 'transition Norman' has been found, nor of the next division—the 'early English' (1189-1272)—of which there are, however, many renowned examples on the borders of Warwickshire, at Pershore, Halesowen, Dunstable, and the choir of Worcester Cathedral; nor is any Warwickshire example identified of the 'transition early English' (1272-1307), the age of the famous Eleanor Crosses and of most of the grandest of English cathedral work. The 'Decorated' (1307-1326) is not represented, nor the 'Later' (1327-1377), but the 'Transition' (1377-1399) has still some fine examples in St. Mary's Church at Warwick. The 'Perpendicular' style (1319-1547) has the very fine example—unrepaired and unrestored—of St. Mary's Hall at Coventry (1401); the rich and graceful Beauchamp Chapel, and the tomb of Richard de Beauchamp, in St. Mary's, Warwick (1439); the grand chancel of the church of Stratford-on-Avon, built by Thomas Balsall (1463-1491), with his own sadly-mutilated monument, next to Shakespeare's grave; the Bablake Hospital, Coventry, built by Thomas Bond (1506), and the picturesque and secluded old house, Compton Wynyates, near Banbury (1520), the home of the Comptons, and famous for its siege during the great civil war.

The dissolution of the minor monasteries by Henry VIII. soon led to the destruction, or at least the desecration, of many fine old buildings in Warwickshire, but some still remain, more or less 'restored.' As most of these were founded in the period under consideration, some notes on them are necessary as to their existence, date, and fate. Alcester Abbey (Ralph Boteler, of Oversley, 1154) has few traces left. Coventry Cathedral and the Priory of St. Mary's (founded by Leofric, Earl of Mercia, and his wife, Godiva, 1043), are represented by little more than foundation walls. Henwood (formerly Estwell) Nunnery (founded by Kettleberne, Lord of Langdon, about 1154) has but few traces of its site. Pinley Priory, or Nunnery (Robert de Pillardinton, *circa* 1135), near Henley-in-Arden, has only some walls left. Polesworth Nunnery, near Tamworth (founded by King Egbert in the ninth century), is now a picturesque half-ruin, with some rooms devoted to baser purposes; and Wroxall Priory (founded by Hugh de Hatton, 1141, in accordance with the legend already described, has the principal lines of its buildings left standing, and its chapel restored beyond the recognition of Sir Christopher Wren, to whom it once belonged, and who left the ruins merely as he found them), complete the list of the Benedictine monasteries. The Cluniacs had no house in Warwickshire, but one at Dudley, near Birmingham, founded by Gervase Paganell, in or before 1161, and of which some ruins remain. The Cistercians had Merevale Abbey, near Atherstone, founded by Robert, Earl of Ferrers, in 1148, and the church still remains for services, and with some fine fragments of old glass in its ancient windows; also Stoneleigh Priory, near Kenilworth, founded by Henry II. in 1154, and with the basement story and the gatehouse, well preserved by Lord Leigh, but the rest of the priory was long since removed or covered by a mansion of the Georgian style.

The Carthusians had St. Anne's Monastery at Coventry (founded by Lord Zouch in 1381, and Richard II. laid the first stone in 1385), which retains many of its old features, although greatly changed. The Austin (or Augustine) Canons held the Priory of Kenilworth (afterwards an abbey), founded by Geoffrey de Clinton, *circa* 1122, and also Maxtoke Priory (founded by Sir William de Clinton in 1336), and a large part of whose fine ruins still remains; and also the St. Sepulchre Priory at Warwick, founded by Henry de Newburgh, Earl of Warwick, before 1135, and with some of its original rooms little changed since the Dissolution. One of the 'preceptories' of the Knights

Templars passed to the Knights Hospitallers of St. John of Jerusalem, which Order was founded by Jordan Briset in 1100, and this is at Temple-Balsall (or Balsall Temple), near Knowle. The church (one large interior without aisles or columns) is in singularly fine preservation—indeed, so little changed that it is generally looked upon as recently restored. The neighbouring buildings, used as almshouses, are singularly interesting from their old-world appearance. Another 'preceptory' is recorded at Warwick, but it seems to have disappeared. The Grey or Franciscan Friars had a house at Coventry, and a church still bears their name. The White Friars, or Carmelites, also had a house at Coventry. The Austin Friars, or Friars Eremites, had a house at Atherstone; and the Maturins, or Friars of the Holy Trinity, had a cell at Thelesford, near Hatton. In addition to these there were some houses of minor importance and interest, as, for example, the Priory of St. Thomas, in the present centre of Birmingham, nearly all traces of which have been lost. The names given to some streets and various legal deeds show the boundaries of the lands around the Priory; but, although recent rebuildings have opened most of the area, the exact site of the building itself still remains doubtful. As late as the last century some remains were found—'carved stones well chiselled,' which William Hutton, the amusing historian of Birmingham (who professed to be an antiquary), writes down that he used for some cellars, etc., without supposing that it was his duty to preserve them as relics of a place once famous in the history of the town of his adoption.

The MILITARY ARCHITECTURAL remains in Warwickshire are more numerous and remarkable as to antiquity and interest than is generally supposed. Not only castles of great size and importance, but fortified houses are numerous, and deserve some record. Many are singularly picturesque, as well as historically interesting; and some, like Warwick Castle, have seen so many changes that they may be accepted as practically the history of the county in stone. During the reign of Stephen (1135-1154) so many castles had been built by the Normans who had followed the fortunes of William that 1,150 were destroyed by Stephen's successor, Henry II. (1154-1189), and after his reign no castle could be built and no house fortified without a license to 'crenellate,' or fortify, where necessary. This precaution against the increasing power of the barons and others was also recognised in later times by inquisitions under Edward III. and Henry VIII., and as to the demolition of many by the Parliament under Cromwell. Castle-building had, indeed, become a great and progressive art, the history of which (as given in Mr. C. F. Clarke's two volumes on English castles, with numerous plans and views) is singularly interesting, and an important and valuable contribution to English history.

Castles may be generally classed under four descriptions: (1) Norman castles, mostly built on a mound, and being one large 'keep' or tower, chiefly square, and often popularly called a 'Cæsar's tower,' with only one entrance, defended by one portcullis, and various other means of defence from the upper stories. (2) Edwardian castles, principally built in the reign of Edward I., and having more than one tower, with overhanging turrets and one large hall, and more numerous portcullises to the entrances. (3) Palatial castles, where still more numerous rooms were provided for residence, while full protection was secured against any sudden attack, or even any prolonged siege; and of this class Warwick Castle formed one of the best examples in the fourteenth century. (4) Castellated mansions, in which more peaceful times allowed the residence to predominate over the fortress, and yet to be ready for defence in case of need. These four classes of castles were necessarily modified according to local circumstances, and were all more or less secure until the invention and improvements of artillery had made even the stoutest stone walls insecure against a cannonade.

The principal castles in Warwickshire may thus be described from Mr. Henry Godwin's 'Archæologist's Handbook,' from which excellent summary most of the facts in the descriptions are derived. Kenilworth necessarily comes first, from Mr. Godwin's brief description, but the elaborate history in the handsome and fully illustrated quarto of the Rev. E. H. Knowles gives a mass of most interesting details, derived from several years' residence at Kenilworth, and long and patient researches among old records.

'Kenilworth Castle was built by Geoffrey de Clinton, *circa* 1120, with walls of the tower 16 feet thick. It was enlarged and fortified by Simon de Montfort, *ante* 1265, and again enlarged by Edward III., and with many additions by John of Gaunt between 1340 and 1399. The gatehouse gallery and two towers were added by the Earl of Leicester between 1563 and 1588. The Castle was sold by the founder's grandson to Henry III., who gave it as a marriage-portion with his sister Eleanor. Montfort's son surrendered it, compelled by famine, to Edward I., by whom it was given to Edmund, Earl of Leicester, on which occasion the "Dictum de Kenilworth" was enacted. Edmund Earl of Leicester held a tournament in it, which was attended by one hundred ladies and knights, in 1268. Edward II. was confined here previous to his removal to Berkley in 1326. On John of Gaunt's son becoming king the Castle became Crown property in 1399. It was given up by Elizabeth to Robert Dudley, Earl of Leicester, who magnificently entertained her and her court for seventeen days in 1562. Cromwell took possession of it and gave it up to his soldiers to pillage and destroy in 1646.'

The castle and lands afterwards passed into the hands of the Hyde family, and have been inherited by the present Earl of Clarendon, who has always reverently preserved, without attempting to restore, the ruins. Even in their present dilapidated state they are wonderfully interesting and charmingly picturesque. The Norman tower is almost unchanged, except that its narrow 'lights' were made into windows centuries ago. The interior has been cleared of rubbish, and the old well of the Norman garrison opened.

The roof and the floors are long ago gone, but the massive walls remain unshaken, and the interior of a Norman fortress can be fully understood from the walls and 'œillets' which remain. The magnificent John of Gaunt 'great hall' is floorless, but its grand proportions can be fully realized; and the Leicester buildings, although mere ruins, recall the scenes which the 'favourite' Leicester presented to his Queen. One romance of that period, immortalized by Sir Walter Scott, must be dispelled. His 'Amy Robsart' never did and never could have stood within those walls to meet Leicester and the Queen. The story must remain a romance, for all the facts of history are against it in all its details. 'The tall old gentleman who leaned on his stick, and asked all sorts of questions about the ruins,' was well remembered by the old custodian of the grounds and castle, who died a few years ago, and the 'Wizard of the North' went back to Scotland and gave the world the pathetic story of poor Amy Robsart, and cast a glamour of romance over the old crumbling walls of Kenilworth and the visit of 'good Queen Bess.'

WARWICK CASTLE is only six miles from Kenilworth, from the walls of which St. Mary's Church at Warwick may be seen. If it has not the picturesqueness and romance of Kenilworth, it has more real history and more striking attractions, for it is not a ruin, but in perhaps a fuller splendour than in any of its ancient days. It is traditionally said to have been built by Alfred's daughter Ethelfleda; but if this is doubtful, it may certainly claim the greater distinction of having been originally an old British fort overhanging the Avon, far below the ancient mound and the rock on which the present castle stands. Whatever the first castle may have been, it was 'rebuilt or enlarged by Edward the Confessor and by William the Conqueror. Parts of the walls were pulled down in 1265, but much was rebuilt, and Guy's Tower erected by Guy de Beauchamp, afterwards Earl of Warwick, in 1394.

It passed, by the marriage of Ann, daughter of Warwick, the king-maker, to the Duke of Clarence, by the judicial murder of whose son it vested in the Crown. Edward VI. granted it to John Dudley, Earl of Warwick, and James I. to Fulke Greville, Lord Brooke, and it was visited by Queen Elizabeth in 1572.' Nearly every part of the castle has some special interest. The entrance gate, only a few years ago, had some of the hooks from which wool-sacks were said to have been suspended to protect the wall from attacks during the great Civil War. The porter's lodge used to contain the marvellous relics of the great giant Guy and his armour, and of the Great Cow of Dunsmore Heath, which, however, have now been removed, as the tales of their genuineness have long been disbelieved. The great inner gateway, with its double portcullis and machicolated tower, is an excellent object-lesson of the art of war four centuries ago. The courtyard, with the Guy Tower, the old grassy mound, the splendid Great Hall and series of state-rooms, with their numerous rich and rare treasures, and the fine view over the cedars on to the broken bridge, and the Avon far below, are too well known to need any further description. The great park sloping down to the Avon, the conservatory with the far-famed vase from Tivoli, are all well known, and all help to make a visit to Warwick Castle one of the pleasantest of the memories of travel. Warwickshire may well be proud of having amongst its attractions a place so famous and so fully illustrating the history of England for so many centuries.

MAXTOKE CASTLE is another fine example of the Edwardian castles, and from its secluded situation is comparatively little known. It was built by William de Clinton, at the end of the fourteenth century, in the reign of Edward III., and remained as the seat of that powerful family till the sixteenth year of Henry IV., when Sir William de Clinton exchanged it with Humphrey, Earl of Stafford, afterwards Duke of Buckingham. In 1483 his grandson was attainted and executed, and the castle was committed to an officer appointed by the Crown. Richard III. visited this castle on his way to oppose the Earl of Richmond at Bosworth Field, and ordered all the inner fittings of Kenilworth Castle to be taken to Maxtoke; but as he lost his life at Bosworth, this order was not carried out; and Henry VII. granted the castle to William Compton and his heirs, and the family in 39 Elizabeth disposed of the castle and lands to the Lord Keeper Egerton, who soon after sold the place to Thomas Dilke, Esq., in whose family it still remains. The castle has remained almost unchanged externally, but the interior has been modernized from time to time. Some of the old rooms still remain—a noble hall, a dining-room with carved door and chimney, a spacious kitchen and a fine chapel. The walls of the Great Court still show the old means of defence, and the 'casernes' for the soldiers and the rooms of the two principal towers have suffered scarcely any change. The exterior of the castle is singularly picturesque. A broad moat still surrounds the outer walls. The one entrance is between two lofty hexagonal towers, and through a venerable gate-house with double gates; and the line of wall all round is unbroken, except by four low towers and battlements, and the gables of the later buildings in the Great Court. The form of the mural enclosure is that of a parallelogram, with hexagonal towers at each corner, and the gateway is between the two principal towers, with lofty machicolations for defence. The old drawbridge has long ago been replaced by a stone bridge, but the wrought-iron gates remain almost unaltered since they were erected (1444-59) by Humphrey, Duke of Buckingham, and are still covered with plates of iron, with his arms embossed on the plates. The castle stands in a fine park, on so low a level among the trees that it is almost hidden, except from a footpath through the park, from Coleshill, two miles away.

TAMWORTH CASTLE, another example with comparatively few changes, stands on a lofty mound by the side of the Tame, from which the town takes its name. In prehistoric times it must have been an important fort—British or Keltic—and was later a Mercian palace and fortress, between the Anker and the Tame. Tradition reports that the castle and a large part of the town, after the ravages of the Danes, were rebuilt in the tenth century by Ethelfleda, the daughter of Alfred. After the Conquest it was given to Robert Marmion, in whose line it remained till 20 Edward I., when it passed by marriage to William Mortein, and afterwards to the Freville, Ferrers, and Compton families. The castle as it now remains is very picturesque, a solid square low block rising from the trees and overlooking the two rivers and extensive views. A winding carriage-road leads up to the great entrance, and to the large old rooms, a great hall, kitchen, and other rooms almost unchanged except by modern furniture and subdivision of larger rooms. A narrow stone staircase leads to the exterior of the tower. The whole building is extremely interesting as contrasted with the larger areas of Warwick, Kenilworth, and Maxtoke. It is practically a fortified 'keep,' and might be ranged as a 'transition' example between the Norman keep and the Edwardian castle. It is a block of building with no surroundings and no great inner court. The height of the mound, the junction of the two rivers, and the strength of the walls, made it a great 'stronghold' against the attacks of eight centuries ago. A small park now still surrounds the castle, and probably marks the boundaries of an old moat, or other line of defence, for Dugdale mentions the remains, in his time, of a trench forty-five feet wide, which, together with the two rivers, formed the protection of the castle and part of the town.

Other castles of minor importance are found in Warwickshire, which have, however, considerable interest, as some of them have been little altered by the ravages of time or 'restoration.' One of the best preserved is that of *Astley*, near Nuneaton, which is an example of a small castle, or fortified manor-house, where the exterior walls are quite unbroken, and a moat surrounds the whole. The only entrance is over a bridge—originally a drawbridge—to a large open courtyard, with the house-windows looking on it, and only some small later windows looking over the moat. The exact date of this castle is uncertain, but the moat and the main buildings are probably of the thirteenth or fourteenth century, when the family of Astley held the manor; and one of them—Sir Thomas de Astley (Edward III.)—built the collegiate church, which was pulled down, but partially rebuilt, in 1600. The present castle is singularly picturesque, with its parterre of flowers and its ivy-covered old gray walls. It was probably dismantled in Mary's time, when the Duke of Suffolk, the father of Lady Jane Grey, held it. In the woods near he was concealed for some time, but betrayed by a keeper (or the keeper's dog), and taken to London, where he was beheaded on Tower Hill. His portrait and a table of his are still preserved as 'heirlooms' in the Newdigate family, to whom the Astley estates came by exchange about a century ago. *Caludon Castle*, near Coventry, was another example of a similar building of the same period, but only fragments of the ruins and of the area of the moat remain. The place has, however, some historic as well as archæological interest, since from its walls Thomas Mowbray, Duke of Norfolk, went forth to meet the Duke of Hereford at Gosford Green, Coventry, in mortal combat, as described in Shakespeare's 'Richard II.' (act i., scene 3). Similar ruins of a castle of the same style and date remain at *Fillonghley*, and are probably as early as the reign of Stephen. At *Brandon* also—all near Coventry—some grassy mounds still show the lines of a larger castle, destroyed by the adherents of Simon de Montfort, Earl of Leicester, when its owner, John de Verdon, raised troops to support Henry III. against the De Montfort 'rebels.' The castle was probably rebuilt afterwards by Theobald de Verdon, but only a few walls and mounds now mark the site. At *Hartshill*, near Atherstone, another castle existed, and some embattled walls were extant in Dugdale's time; only a few vestiges of which may still be seen. The history of most of these places is obscure, but the remains are numerous enough to have considerable interest, and if carefully surveyed, planned, and described, the results would throw much light on the mediæval history of the county, which has never yet had the full research which it deserves and would repay.

Licenses to 'crenellate' (or fortify) between the years 1256 and 1478 are given in Godwin's 'Archæologist's Handbook,' and are extremely valuable as records not merely of dates of 'crenellation,' but of facts long forgotten, since in some cases all traces of the buildings have disappeared. These royal licenses to fortify were not only given to owners of secular buildings, but even for the protection of abbeys and other ecclesiastical buildings, although these were supposed to be protected by their sacred purposes. One example is very curious, for in 31 Edward I. Walter de Langdon, Bishop of Coventry and Lichfield, seems to have possessed the royal power of licensing to 'crenellate,' and granted such license to *Beaudesert* (or Donnelei), near Henley-in-Arden, one of the small mound-castles, and apparently for other places: 'Domos per omnia loca quæ idem episcopus habet in Anglia,' etc. Caludon, near Coventry, 'manerium suum,' was fortified by John de Segrave in 33 Edward I. (1358); Coventry, as to the city ('civitatem'), rather than a castle, by the 'mayor and men of honour' ('Maior Ballioi et probi homines') in 1362 and again in 1364; Astley (Esteleye), 'domum suum,' by Warren de Basingburne in 1265; Fillongley (Filumgeleye), 'manerium suum et villam,' by John de Hastings in 1300; Langley (Langele), by Edward de Hereforde in 1340; Maxtoke (or Makstoke), by William de Clinton in 1342; Ragley (Ragele), 'domum super janua manerii sui,' by John Rous in 1381; while Hugh le Despencer, who had various lands and manors in Warwickshire, claimed the more general power to fortify 'omnes domos et cameras in quibuscunque maneriis suis in regno nostro,' under 5 Edward II. (1330).

FORTIFIED MANOR-HOUSES became, in more peaceful times, houses for residence, in which the moat was the principal feature which remained of the old troublous times. The buildings became more decorative in style, and more like modern mansions. One of the most remarkable of these in Warwickshire, if not in all England, is COMPTON WYNYATES House in the south corner of the county, and under the shadow of the Edge Hill cliffs. Its old name was Compton-in-the-Hole, and the house is hidden among the trees of the 'comb' or hollow in which it stands, and can scarcely be seen in summer even from the highroad close by. It is a house of the early years of the sixteenth century, *circa* 1519, and was built by Sir William Compton, to whose family the lands have belonged from 7 Edward I. (1278). The materials are said to have been removed from the old castle (or manor-house) of Fulbrook. Leave was gained to enclose 2,000 acres of land and woods for a park, 11 Henry VIII. (1519). The house has remained almost unaltered to the present day, and is in the hands of the Compton family still. It is a marvellous and artistic combination of stone, wood, and brick. Some of the more important parts are stone; others are stone and brick, and others are brick and old oak timbers in most picturesque arrangement. Most of the chimneys are of brick, moulded and built up into most artistic forms. A grand porch with bullet-battered gate—a record of the Civil War siege, when the house was garrisoned for the Parliament—leads into a noble quadrangle, around which the principal rooms are built. A great hall, of grand proportions, with a min-

strels' gallery, reached by solid oak steps, is wainscoted
with oak and very charming carved work. A long gallery
is also panelled, with hiding-places behind the panels, and
over its ceiling soldiers' 'casernes' are formed under its
tiles. The house contains ninety rooms, mostly unaltered
till some twenty years ago, when the house, which had been
unoccupied for several generations, was repaired (not
restored) by Mr. Digby Wyatt. The ancient chapel has long
been unused, but much of its fine old oak carving remains
more or less in ruin. In the highest room in the great
tower is another chapel of small size, and with three separate,
and secret, staircases, which doubtless suggest the changes
of religion from the 'old' to the 'new.' Almost every part
of the house has some strange interest from its quaintness,
and picturesqueness, and old-world look. Over the principal
porch the royal arms, surmounted by a crown, are placed,
supported by a greyhound and a griffin, and a rose and
crown. The ancient window, of rare workmanship, was
destroyed during the Civil War troubles, and also the little
church near the house, and the monuments of the dead were
broken up or damaged so that scarcely a wreck remains.
Only a small part of the moat has been preserved. After
the mansion was finished, Henry VIII. was a guest for
several days. Oliver Cromwell himself is said to have fired
a few shots at the mansion in 1646. Bishop Compton was
born in the house in 1632. There is considerable doubt as
to the origin and meaning of the word 'Wyngates,' and
even as to the spelling, but the original license is said
to give 'Vinegates' or 'Vineyard'—some affix being
needful to distinguish the place from the 'Long,' 'Murdack,'
and 'Scorfen' Comptons in the same county. Although
Compton Wynyates has so many attractions, archæological
architectural, historical, and artistic, it was almost wholly
unknown till the late William Howitt included it among
the 'Remarkable Places' which he visited some forty years
ago. Since then all lovers of old places and picturesque re-

mains have delighted to procure leave to see one of the historic treasures of Warwickshire.

BADDESLEY CLINTON, another relic of the famous Norman family who 'came over with the Conqueror,' as 'Renegalds,' and who assumed the 'de Clinton,' has almost an equal interest with Compton Wynyates as an 'old moated grange.' It lies near Knowle and Kingswood, in a large secluded park, and has, happily, had no great alterations, internal or external, for several centuries. It is an old stone house, surrounded by a moat, over which a bridge has replaced an ancient drawbridge, and leads to a fine embattled gateway and a small but charming court, with beds of flowers, old half-timber gables, and one side of the quadrangle open to the moat. The interior of the hall has a delightful old-world look. Panelled walls and ceilings, old furniture, quaint old glass and china, tapestry hangings, old oak stairs, low long galleries, pleasant peeps through pretty windows, heraldic arms emblazoned in colours on the glass, or painted on the panels, all conspire to revive the life and surroundings of centuries ago. The general structure is of the latter half of the fifteenth century, and some of the gables, seen only from the inner court on one side of the moat, are of later date, perhaps the middle of the sixteenth century, while the latest portions of the rooms, as to furniture, is probably two centuries old. In the reign of Henry IV. (1399-1412) the manor was bought by John Brome (and the house is possibly as old as that date), and afterwards, in 1517, passed by marriage to the Ferrars (or Ferrers) family, with whom it remains. The hall is a most interesting relic of the old moated-house period as to its external appearance, and as it has been held so long by one family, and has had so few internal changes as to structure or furniture, it is famous as one of the sights of Warwickshire by all who have the good fortune to enter its fortalice-gate.

COMBE ABBEY is another example; a double attraction,

as an old mansion built on the site of an older monastery, and having also some historical interest. In the reign of Stephen (1135-1153) a monastery was built for Cistercian monks by Richard de Camville, and many privileges were granted and many benefactions given, but four hundred years later the monastery was dissolved by Henry VIII. as one of the minor foundations, its revenue being £302 15s. 3d. according to Dugdale, but £303 0s. 5d. according to Speed. Edward VI. granted the site to John Dudley, Earl of Warwick, after whose attainder it was leased to Robert Kelway, surveyor of the court of wards and liveries, and by his daughter's marriage next passed to John, afterwards Lord Harrington. On the death of his son it passed to Lucy, Countess of Bedford, through whose extravagance it was sold to Sir William Craven, Knt. Lord Harrington had the good taste to preserve the ancient cloisters and some other parts of the old foundation. William, Lord Craven, collected a fine gallery of portraits, and took great interest in Elizabeth, Queen of Bohemia, eldest daughter of James I., to whom he devoted his life and a large part of his fortune, and who left him her gallery of pictures as the reward of his romantic gallantry. Elizabeth was at Combe Abbey when the Gunpowder Plot was formed, and the conspirators proposed to seize her to carry her off to London to represent the Roman Catholics, and to marry her to some Roman Catholic peer.

Many other moated houses, generally with the moats drained or filled up and only partially visible, are found in all parts of Warwickshire, but few, if any, have any historic interest, except for their picturesqueness as 'survivals' of old times. Clopton House, near Stratford, and Bushwood and other places, had or have still some historic interest. In many cases the moats only remain as landmarks, as, for example, the site of Park Hall, near Castle Bromwich, and Birmingham, whose grassy lines are the only memorials of the family of the Ardens, who lived there for three hundred years. Almost in the middle of the great town of Birmingham two moats remained till about seventy years ago, one of them around the old half-timber house, the rectory of St. Martin's Church, and the other (near that church) which surrounded the old home of the Lords of Birmingham six hundred years ago.

SEPULCHRAL MONUMENTS are numerous in Warwickshire, and are often important and interesting as memorials of history and art. Fortunately more care has been given to their preservation during the last thirty or forty years. Mr. Matthew Holbeche Bloxam was among the first to call attention to their merit and value, and nearly sixty years ago the publication of his invaluable 'Gothic Ecclesiastical Architecture' greatly helped to form the fashion and to cultivate the taste for the study of the remains which bigotry and ignorance and carelessness have left us. His life-long studies and sketches and notes have given us excellent records, and a brief account of these, almost in his own words, will have a special value.

The earliest monument in Warwickshire is the large unlettered monolith known as the King's Stone, standing near the Rollright Circle, with a cromlech close by on the southern boundary of the county. Mr. Bloxam believed this to be one of the Maen Hir, high or pillar stones found in Wales, the Isle of Man, and many other places—the earliest type of British sepulchral memorials, and probably the lineal descendant of the 'pillar over the grave' of Rachel which Jacob placed in the patriarchal days. Only one Roman tomb or monument has been found in Warwickshire, and that the sarcophagus, now in the museum at Warwick, which was found near the Roman Road at Alcester. 'It is in the shape of a parallelogram, rudely worked, with a plain slab cover, and though uninscribed, it originally stood, I have little doubt, above ground'—a roadside memorial, probably like those on the Appian Way, near Rome. No Anglo-Saxon monument has been found, but Roman and Anglo-Saxon relics have been unearthed at and near Princethorpe and the Fosse-Way, and Anglo-Saxon remains have been found at Marton, Alcester, Chesterton, and an Anglo-Saxon burial-place was disturbed forty years ago between Pilgrim's Low and Bensford Bridge, with a number of interments in regular order, a short distance below the surface. Only one sepulchral urn was found, but that was clearly Anglo-Saxon. Near it were two drinking-cups of rude, imperfectly-baked pottery, an iron sword, and a spear-head with a portion of the wood in the socket. 'With other male interments were found the bosses or umbos of shields and spear-heads; with female interments were found fibulæ (of the cross-bow shape, and circular) of bronze, clasps of silver, tweezers, beads, and other articles,' which have been carefully preserved at Marton, near Rugby. The railway cutting brought to light another Anglo-Saxon burial-place with sepulchral urns, one of the rare 'syphated or saucer-shaped' fibulæ, fragments of iron weapons, and the iron umbo of an Anglo-Saxon shield.

Norman remains are quite unknown in Warwickshire, but one or two plain 'ridge-shape or prismatic' coffin-stones were found some years ago in the cemetery-garth or burial-ground of the Priory at Kenilworth, but these were more probably Anglo-Norman—that is, of the twelfth century. Norman and Saxon remains, non-sepulchral, are often found in rebuilding old churches and old buildings generally, and at any time slabs of Norman or Anglo-Saxon work may be found if proper inquiries are made before such stones are broken up, or buried again in foundations or inside walls.

The earliest monuments known in Warwickshire are of the thirteenth century, and the oldest and finest is that recumbent but much-mutilated effigy of a knight, formerly in the abbey church of Merevale, near Atherstone. This effigy is specially interesting as that of William, fourth Earl

Ferrers, *circa* 1244, and closely resembling the two oldest effigies in the Temple Church, London. The effigy, although little more than a *torso*, is valuable as a record of the defensive armour worn by knights in the great Barons' War.

The remote church of Avon Dassett, on the slope of the Edge Hill range, has a rare effigy of great interest, which was 'discovered' by Mr. Bloxam himself, and its fame secured. It represents a Deacon in a recumbent effigy, and is probably unique, and has not only monumental, but ecclesiological interest. 'The material is dark-coloured forest marble, and the effigy is placed beneath a horizontal canopy composed of a semicircular arch with the representations of buildings above, and this canopy is supported by shafts with bell-shaped caps running up the sides of the tomb.' The vestments are especially interesting, and differ materially from those on the only other known effigy of a deacon, at Furness Abbey. The effigy is sculptured in low-relief, and is of the thirteenth century. The monument is not even mentioned by Sir William Dugdale, and his continuator, Dr. Thomas, dismisses it in a few words as representing a priest with his shaven crown, but no inscription on it—a remarkable example of want of knowledge of ecclesiastical art, even so lately as a century and a half ago. Fortunately the interest of the monument will have now secured it from any negligence, and Mr. Bloxam immediately had careful drawings and measurements made of his important discovery of so valuable a work of Church art.

In Newton Regis Church there is a very fine low-relief slab of a priest of the fourteenth century, and others at Hillmorton, Stoneleigh, and Kineton. Another remarkable effigy of an ecclesiastic is preserved in St. Martin's Church, Birmingham, although somewhat damaged in the shamefully 'Gothic' ravages of a hundred years ago. This also has very special interest and value as a record of the dress of the clergy of the fifteenth century. Only one episcopal effigy is to be found in Warwickshire, that of John Vesey (or Harman), a native of Sutton Coldfield, near Birmingham, once Bishop of Exeter, and a munificent benefactor to his native town. Mr. Bloxam believes that this effigy was executed in the life-time of the Bishop, and long before his death, for it represents a man of middle age, and the Bishop died aged 103 in 1555. A fourteenth century effigy of an Abbess is another important memorial, and is preserved in the Priory of Polesworth, near Tamworth. It represents a Benedictine nun, and is curious, and probably unique.

All through Warwickshire there are 'numerous effigies—scarcely two alike—of laymen, frankleins, lords of manors, etc., but neither warriors nor ecclesiastics. These, as a class, have never been treated of, and so little have they been understood that they have frequently been pronounced to be monks.' One of them is in Cherrington Church, in the south-west of the county. The whole monument, canopy as well as effigy, is remarkably interesting, and the effigy more especially as representing the civil costume or ordinary dress of a franklein, or lord of the manor, or squire of a parish in the fourteenth century. The very name of the original of this recumbent effigy is unknown. The monument is not even mentioned by Dugdale or Dr. Thomas, but Mr. Bloxam had little doubt that it represents William Lucy, born in 1277, Knight of the Shire in five Parliaments, in the reign of Edward II., and who was living in 1326. Mr. Bloxam's elaborate description fully justifies his remark that 'it is one of the most interesting monuments he has ever met with.' Among other sculptured effigies of laymen are: a mutilated fourteenth-century work in Wolston Church; one of Henry VII.'s reign in St. Michael's, Coventry; the fine effigy of Shakespeare's friend John Combe, in Stratford-on-Avon Church; and one of 1618 to William Clarke, in Tysoe Church—which is interesting as showing the dress of Shakespeare's later days—who outlived his own countyman two years. This dress is worth describing: 'William Clarke is represented bare-headed, with a moustache and spade-beard; a short ruff round the neck, a doublet, buttoned in front and belted round the waist, with close sleeves cuffed at the wrists, trunk-hose, stockings and shoes, and the hands bare'—surely Shakespeare in his very 'habit as he lived' and died,—two years before.

Effigies of knights in armour are numerous in Warwickshire, and there are two singularly fine examples of the fourteenth century in Coleshill Church. In Hillmorton Church is a curious and much-mutilated figure of a man in armour, which Hollar engraved very inaccurately, and which Dugdale assigned to Sir Thomas de Astley, who died in 1285, but which Mr. Bloxam, with far more knowledge and experience than Dugdale could have had, assigns to Thomas de Astley, who, in the 9th of Edward III., A D. 1336, 'had a special patent *exempting* him from knighthood.' Effigies in armour of the fifteenth, sixteenth, and seventeenth centuries are common, and only one needs special mention, that in Radway Church, a fine but shockingly-mutilated recumbent figure of Captain Kingmill, who was killed in the Battle of Edge Hill in 1642. The monument is a curious example of art in the seventeenth century. It was erected by the mother in 1678, but one part of the dress is of 1642, another of 1678, and another of the fashion of James I. (1602-24). One effigy of a Judge exists in Middleton Church, commemorating Sir Richard Bingham, Knt., of the Court of King's Bench, who died in 1476, and who is represented in his judicial robes, and with his 'lady' in a graceful dress. Among the effigies of ladies is a fine example in Hillmorton Church, in memory of Dame Margaret de Astley, *circa* 1353, which represents her 'in a wimple and veil, the latter falling in folds on the shoulder, in a gown with ample skirts, belted round the waist, and a mantle attached in front by a cordon: the sleeves of the gown are close-fitting, and the hands are conjoined on the breast and upraised, and at the feet are two whelps,' the figure being surmounted by a rich decorative canopy, in the best style of fourteenth-century art. The decadence of art, from the graceful recumbent memorials of the fourteenth century to the pert, self-complacent, erect figures and hideous busts of the last century, need not be illustrated by examples. The earliest examples of the seventeenth century are those of Shakespeare, a bust to the waist (in sad contrast to the recumbent effigy of his friend John Combe), and others in Stratford and other churches. The monuments to ladies became strange records of the changes of fashions, and the brief prayers for mercy and forgiveness were followed by long laudatory epitaphs on the dead in the Jacobean, Elizabethan, and Georgian days.

The SEPULCHRAL BRASSES of Warwickshire are not very numerous nor very important, but many of them have considerable interest, and those which have survived are generally well preserved. Until very recently no attempt was made to preserve, or discover, or describe them; but the late Mr. Charles Williams, of Birmingham, gave several years of time and labour in order to examine and to get rubbings of all he could find, and the result of his long studies and researches was embodied in an original, exhaustive and valuable paper, read to the Archæological Section of the Birmingham and Midland Institute on the 26th of March, 1884. The paper was fully illustrated by drawings of 'rubbings,' and included a complete catalogue of all known Warwickshire brasses, from which most of the following descriptions are derived.

The origin of monumental brasses has been much discussed, and the great authority, Haines, is probably right in his theory that they are the 'evolution' of the early incised slabs which were sometimes filled with a dark enamel composition, and afterwards with the more solid and permanent material known as 'brass.' 'Brasses' seem to have appeared almost simultaneously in England,

France, and the Low Countries, and were unknown till the thirteenth century, when the fashion soon spread. The earliest English 'brass' known is that to Simon de Beauchamp, in St. Paul's Church, Bedford, who died before 1208. The finest known example is that to Sir John d'Abernon, of Stoke d'Abernon, Surrey, of the year 1277. The second is that of Sir Roger Trumpington (Cambridge), of 1290, a superb specimen of the new art, and one of the finest examples known of any date. The earliest Warwickshire brass is that of a lady, probably of the Astley family, and of the year 1400, at Astley, near Nuneaton, remarkable for its sideless tunic or *cote-hardi* (which remained in fashion from 1340 to 1450), under which was the kirtle, covered by a mantle fastened by a tasselled cord drawn through studs, and itself furred and jewelled. The next in date is that of Thomas de Beauchamp, in 1491—an Earl of Warwick— and his wife. The emblems used on brasses form a very interesting study, and include symbols of the Trinity, the Passion, figures of saints, records of martyrs, badges of honour, armorial bearings, collars of dignities, suns, roses, lions, dogs, chalices, etc. At Coleshill, in Warwickshire, are two very remarkable brasses, each representing a priest—one before and one after the Reformation. The first is that of William Abell, vicar, 1500, and is supposed to be a work of local art. The second is that of Sir John Fenton, vicar, 1566, and he is represented holding an open Bible, with the words 'Verbum Dei.' The first holds a chalice and wafer in his right hand, and supports the vase of the chalice with his left hand. Both have the prayer, 'Whose soul God pardon.' Although the changes of fashion were few, the varying dresses, especially of ladies, generally indicate the period even when the date is not given in the inscription. The brasses to men, whether clerical or secular, whether of 'gentle blood' or mere merchants or tradesmen, are curiously significant, and often quaint, as the latter have generally some symbol to indicate their trade. The earlier inscriptions are always in Latin, about the end of the fourteenth century often in French; and after Edward VI. the old Gothic square letter changed into the Roman round-hand, and the 'Orate pro animâ,' at the commencement of the inscription, was omitted. The variations in the style of armour worn are curiously historical and singularly exact, and form a correct record of the various changes in the order of date. In the earlier brasses there seems to have been no attempt at portraiture, but in the sixteenth and seventeenth centuries the faces are more individual and the brasses more like large engravings in minuteness of detail.

Warwickshire contains about sixty brasses, distributed through forty churches, and may be briefly described in chronological order, beginning with Priests. The earliest is in the Church of St. Nicholas, at Warwick, and represents Robert Willardsey, the first vicar, in 1424. This, curiously, was lost, until in 1847 its absence was noted, and it was replaced. At Tysoe there is a brass to William Auldington, 'parson of Whatcote,' from 1486 to 1511. Another is in Great Packington Church, to John Wright, 1597. At Barcheston, to Hugh Humphray, 1503 to 1540. At Whitnash, one to Richard Bennett, 1531. At Upton, one to Richard Woddomes, 'parson, patron, and vossioner of the church and parish,' 1587. At Whichford, one to Nicholas Ashton, 1582. Brasses to the memory of ladies begin with one at Hillmorton, *circa* 1410, a very fine example, but name unknown. At Tysoe are two small brasses, neglected by Dugdale and Haines, but curious and interesting. of 1598 and 1601. At Coleshill, one to Alice Digby, 1506, holding a pomander or scent-box in her hand. At Middleton, one to a married daughter of Sir Henry Willoughby, 1507. At Coventry, in St. Michael's Church, one to Maria Hilton and four infant children, 1594, with a pathetic inscription and some curious details; another to Ann Sewell, 1609, with remarkable details of dress. At Sutton Coldfield, a figure of Barbara Eliot, wife of the rector, 1606. At Tanworth, one to Margaret Archer, 1614—one of six brasses—five having disappeared. At Preston Bagot, one to Elizabeth Randoll, of which the head is lost, 1606. At Meriden, a quaint brass and inscription, with an anagram of her name, Elizabeth Rotton, as 'I to a blest throne,' 1638.

The Church of St. Mary, Warwick, has in the Beauchamp chapel one of the most magnificent works of art in England, the 'herse' of the great Richard Beauchamp, Earl of Warwick, who died at Rouen in 1439, a monument beyond all praise; but there is also a brass to Thomas Beauchamp, Earl of Warwick, and his wife, who died in 1404, and his Countess in 1406. The brass is a superb work of art, and deserves a further description, but it could not be appreciated without illustrations. At Wixford is one of the finest brasses in Warwickshire, that to Thomas de Crewe and Juliana, his wife, a work admirable alike in design and execution. Its size is 9 feet by 4 feet, and it was erected in his own life-time (in 1611) to the memory of his wife, and he died about 1619. The brass is a magnificent example of the best period of the art. At Merevale is a brass to Robert Lord Ferrers and his wife (of Chartley), of the date of 1412 according to Haines, and of 1425 according to Boutell. At Wellesbourne-Hastings is a neat, small brass to Sir Thomas le Strange, 1426. At Hampton, in Arden, one of a civilian of the end of the fifteenth or beginning of the sixteenth century, name unknown. At Wootton-Wawen, one to John Harewell and a large family, 1503. At Coughton one to Sir George Throckmorton, with the dates of day and of year left blank, but of the sixteenth century. At Compton Verney, one of Edward Odingsell's (Udyngsale's) wife, 1423, and George Verney, 1574. At Aston to Thomas Holte, 1545, and Margaret, his wife. At Solihull to William Hill, 1549, and his wives, Isabel and Agnes, and another to William

Hawes, 1610. At Exhall one to John Walsingham and his wife, 1566. At Wixford one to Rise Griffin, 1597. In St. Mary's, Warwick, are brasses (1573) to Thomas Oken and his wife, which were 'rescued from the fire in 1694,' and which record the munificence of Oken to the town. At Chadshunt to William Askell, 1613. At Trinity Church, Coventry, to John Whitehead and his two wives, 1600. At Haseley a very fine brass to Clement Throckmorton, 1573. At Sutton Coldfield one to Jonas Bull, 1621. At Barcheston one to Flamochus Colburn, 1664, and several others of less interest as to subjects or dates which need not be recorded.

SEPULCHRAL MEMORIALS, originally memorial slabs or brasses, or recumbent effigies under canopies, gradually expanded into more sumptuous and more monumental structures in mortuary chapels, or 'chantries' as they were often called. The fourteenth century shows some of the earlier examples, as in the monument of Thomas Beauchamp, Earl of Warwick, who died in 1370, and whose effigy is in St. Mary's Church, Warwick—a tomb surrounded by recessed compartments or niches, in which figures of both sexes are placed. In Wolvey Church there is an effigy of two figures, Thomas de Wolvey and his wife, sculptured on one slab, and belonging to the early part of the fourteenth century. The fifteenth century was still more remarkable for large and imposing structures as sepulchral memorials of the dead, when special altars were erected in chantry chapels for prayers for the repose of the souls of benefactors, and these chantries or chapels soon developed into memorial or mortuary chapels in which one or more monuments were placed. These were often erected during the life of the donor, and endowed by him with the lands to secure the prayers for his soul, and to have his memory honoured.

One of the most famous in the kingdom, and certainly the greatest example of its class in the county, is the

Beauchamp Chapel in the Church of St. Mary, at Warwick. In the great fire in the seventeenth century this noble chapel and its tombs were practically unharmed. Although really the 'Chapel of Our Lady,' it is generally known by the name of its founder, Richard Beauchamp, Earl of Warwick, who devised its building during his lifetime, and who left minute and curiously detailed instructions in his will as to his own memorial tomb, the cost of which, with that of the chapel (which occupied twenty-one years in construction), was £2,481 4s. 7½d.—equivalent to about £40,000 now. The building was commenced in 1443 (21 Henry VI.), but, although completed in 1465, the chapel was not consecrated till 1475. The bold warrior had died at the Castle of Rouen, in Normandy, on the 30th of April, 1439, and on 'the iiiith day of October next following his cors was honorably conveied, as well by water as by londe, from Roon unto Warrewik, and there worshiply buried in the college of our Ladye Chirche, founded by his noble Auncestres, the bishop of lichfield being executor officii, and many lordes and ladyes and other worshipful people there beying present;' and when the chapel was completed, the body was reverently removed. An 'Inventory' of the furniture and dresses and gifts has been preserved, and gives full details of the costly and gorgeous services, but is too long for quotation, and would be useless if condensed. It is printed, however, in 'The Churches of Warwickshire' (by the Rev. W. Staunton and Mr. M. H. Bloxam, F.S.A.), to which reference has already been made, and from which many of the following details are quoted. The chapel is a magnificent building in the very finest style of the fifteenth century, but only some account of the monuments can be given here. On descending, under a magnificent door-canopy, the few steps to the lower level, the splendid proportions of the chapel are seen at a glance, and the graceful and gorgeous tombs in the 'dim religious light' There are four stately monuments:

that nearly in the centre being of Earl Richard, the founder, west of which, slightly southward, that of Ambrose Dudley, 'the good Earl of Warwick;' against the south wall, on the east, that of 'the noble Impe,' the youthful Lord Denbigh, the son and heir of Robert Dudley, the great Earl of Leicester (the favourite of Elizabeth), whose own fine monument and that of his Countess occupy the northern wall. All the monuments are not only historically interesting, but more especially so as well-preserved memorials of the changes in the style of sepulchral monuments from 1450 to 1590. In 1642 the 'rebels,' under Colonel Purefoy, 'did beat down and deface these monuments of antiquity,' according to the contemporary chronicles; but none of the tombs seem to have been damaged, and probably the altar of the chapel was the chief object of attack, and was broken up and removed, as its place is occupied by one erected in 1735.

The great tomb of Richard Beauchamp could only be adequately described by giving minute details, with drawings or photographs, of every part of the work. It is 'a high tomb of gray Purbeck marble, bearing a recumbent effigy. The sides are divided into five compartments. Each compartment contains a large canopied niche, called in the contract "a principall housing," and each of these divisions is flanked by sunk panel-work, with a smaller niche above; the "entail," or decorative part, is minutely and elaborately sculptured. Below each principal niche is a curved quatrefoil within a square. This contains a shield charged with armorial bearings enamelled on copper, and is thus described in the contract: "Under every principall housing a goodly quarter for a scutcheon of copper and gilt to be set in." The principal niches or "housings," fourteen in number, contain as many images, called weepers and mourners. These are cast in the metal called latten, and are gilt. Seven of these images are of males, and seven of females, and they represent persons of rank

p. 9

allied by blood or marriage to the deceased. The small images, eighteen in number, contain the like number of small images or angels, likewise cast in latten and gilt. These carry scrolls in their hands, on which is engraved (in black letter) the following legend : " Sit Deo Laus et Gloria, Defunctis Misericordia." The artist in metal of the effigy was William Austen, citizen and founder of London, who " covenanted " (and carried out his promise) " to cast and make an image of a man armed of fine latten garnished with certain ornaments — viz., with sword and dagger, with a garter, with a helme and crest under his head, and at his feet a bear musled, and a griffon perfectly made of the finest latten according to pattern and layde on the tombe ;" also " an hearse [open canopy] to stand on the tombe above and about the principall image, that shall lye in the tombe, according to a pattern."' This fully describes the artistic work, which is practically as perfect as when finished four hundred years ago. The 'hearse' referred to was an open metal canopy over which the 'pall' was thrown, and is one of very few now remaining. On the moulded verge of the tomb a long inscription runs in raised letters, with the 'bear and ragged staff' intermixed ; and all the details were in the contract that ' in the two long plates they shall write in Latine, in fine manner, all such declaration as the said executors shall devise that may be conteined and comprehended on the plates ; all the champes about the letter to be abated and hatched curiously to set out the letters.' But the inscription is in English (not 'Latine,' as first proposed), and, although somewhat long, is curious and historic enough to deserve quotation :

"Preieth devoutly for the sowel whom God assoille of one of the moost worshipful knightes in his dayes of monhode and conning Richard Beauchamp late Eorl of Warrewik Lord Despenser of Bergevenny and of many other grete lordships whos body resteth here under this tumbe in a fulfeire bont of stone set on the bare roock the which visited with longe siknes in the Castel of Roan therinne decessed ful cristenly the last day of April, the yer of our Lord God MCCCCXXXIX., he being at that tyme Lieutenant Gen'al and Governer of the Roialme of Fraunce and of the Duchie of Normandie by sufficient Autoritie of oure Sou'aigne lord the King Harry the VI. thewhich bodye with great deliberacon and ful worshipful conduit Bi see and by londe was broght to Warrewik the iiii. day of October the yer abovescide and was leide with ful solemn exequies in a feir chesle made of Stone in this Chirche afore the west dore of this Chapel according to his last wille and Testament therin to rest til this Chapel by him devised i' his lief were made at thewhiche Chapel founded on the Roock and all the membres therof his executors dede fully make and apparaille By the auctorite of his saide last Wille and Testament and therafter by the same Auctorite they dide translate fful worshiply the seide body in the vout abovescide. Honnerd be God therfor."

The effigy was re-gilt and the escutcheons were re-enamelled in 1681, but, with a few minor exceptions, the famous tomb and effigy are little altered by the chances and changes of nearly four hundred years, and still form a magnificent example of medieval metal-work of unrivalled excellence. The contrasts between the form and style of this and the other monuments of later date around are significant and instructive as lessons in the history of monumental art. The Church of St. Mary has some other monuments of considerable interest, and that in the Chapter House especially. As to style and fashion, it is later in date than those in the Beauchamp chapel, being a large and cumbrous and clumsy four-column canopy over a sarcophagus (cenotaph), but it was erected by Fulke Greville, the first Lord Brooke (who died in 1628), during his lifetime, and has a simple modest epitaph, quaint in its form and truthful in its facts :

'Fulke Grevill, Servant to Queene Elizabeth, Conceller to King James, and Frend to Sir Philip Sidney. Trophæum Peccati.'

Many of the old monuments perished in the fire of 1694, but some have been preserved by the engravings of Hollar and the descriptions of Dugdale, one seems to have been of the fourteenth century, others of the sixteenth century, and some 'brasses' of the Lucy, Maners, and other families. In the choir is still preserved a fine 'high tomb,' with effigy of Thomas Beauchamp and his countess (1369), and panels around the tomb with thirty-six figures of considerable interest, as the effigies are in fair condition and curiously valuable as records of costumes. Another, a mural monument with brass figures of Thomas Oken and his wife, great benefactors of Warwick, is remarkable as a post-Reformation monument (1573), with a Protestant inscription:

'Of your charitie give thanks for the soules of Thomas Oken and Jone his Wyffe, on whose soules Jesus hath mercy, Amen. Remember the Charyte for the pore for ever. Ao. dni. MCCCCCLXXIII.'

Another notable monument is a white marble slab with the incised effigies of the second Thomas Beauchamp, Earl of Warwick, who died in 1401, and of his wife, who died in 1406. Each of the effigies is gilt, probably re-gilt after the fire in 1694, and the details of the brasses and armorial bearings are in the best style of fifteenth-century art.

Altar-tombs, with sides, having arched or quatrefoil panels, and shields are also found in Warwickshire churches, one of the best examples being that in Meriden Church, and that of Geoffray Allesley (1401), in Newbold-on-Avon Church. Another variety, the mural altar-tomb, with a canopy, remains in a fine example of fifteenth-, or early sixteenth-century work in Wolston Church, near Combe Abbey. One of the few eccentric monuments in the county is a Memento Mori example—a skeleton beneath a figure of a man in armour—of the seventeenth century in Tarbick Church.

Sixteenth-century monuments show a marked decadence of taste, and prepare the visitor for the still more degraded examples of the next century and of the Georgian reigns. The use of alabaster instead of stone or marble had commenced. The figures had become kneeling, erect, truncated, or mere busts under canopies in regular succession of 'decline.' Examples of these classes are found among the numerous monuments in Coleshill Church, in

St. Michael's Church, Coventry, at Sutton Coldfield, and in many other places, but none of artistic and few of historic value.

Seventeenth-century monuments are also numerous, and some of these have been mentioned among the older and nobler remains at Warwick. The CHURCH of STRATFORD-ON-AVON also has some notable examples of various epochs of monumental art. The 'brasses' have long since disappeared, although an order of Elizabeth was issued to protect them. In the chancel of the church is a very fine altar-tomb of Thomas Balsall, who built the choir (*circa* 1480), but it is thoroughly mutilated, although its proportions, design, and decoration are charming, even in decay and ruin. Near it is the canopied bust of Shakespeare in striking contrast; and the still more striking contrast of the mural recumbent effigy of John à Combe, with two busts of members of his family above his tomb—a monument whose only merit is a pathetic inscription. Another and more remarkable example is seventeenth-century Clopton Chapel, where the same contrasts occur. A 'restored' memorial of a long lost altar-tomb to Sir Hugh Clopton (1496), is the oldest and best, and close by is a good altar-tomb of William Clopton, his wife and children (1592-1596); and another more imposing structure to George Carew, Earl of Totness and Baron of Clopton, Master of the Ordnance, *tempore* Elizabeth, who died in 1629. His monument is large and pretentious, with barrels of powder, piles of shot, and cannon, numerous armorial bearings, bright in colours and gold, and with long Latin inscription recording his services. It is an excellent example of its date and fashions, and the Clopton Chapel, as a whole, is a valuable relic of history and art, developing in later days into a 'squire's pew,' as the family is long ago extinct.

Another neighbouring example of a mortuary chapel is at Charlecote, near Stratford, where some monuments of the

Lucy family have been carefully preserved, but in so dark a chapel that their merits can scarcely be seen. The earliest is that erected by Sir Thomas Lucy to the memory of his wife (in 1595), and it is a very good example of sixteenth-century art. It has a special interest, too, in the pathetic epitaph in which the many merits and virtues of the Lady Joyce are described. Near it, in the same dark solemn chapel, is a monument to Sir Thomas himself, a lofty mural monument with conventional columns and a background of books, which may be assumed to indicate that he had some literary tastes. The later memorials have far less interest as to the deceased, and are little more than sad examples of the decline of art. The most famous and most interesting of all the Sepulchral Memorials in Warwickshire is the memorial of *Shakespeare* on the north wall of the chancel of *Stratford-on-Avon Church*. It was erected soon after Shakespeare's death in 1616, and before 1623, and doubtless by his widow and his son-in-law, Dr. John Hall, who had married their daughter Susannah. The social position of Shakespeare as part-owner of the Great Tithes, entitled him and his family to burial in the chancel, where his own body and those of his wife, his daughter Susannah Hall, Dr. John Hall, and of Thomas Nashe, who married their daughter Elizabeth, are buried beneath slabs across the chancel from north to south. All the inscriptions are of personal and historic value, and give nearly all the facts as to the family, and even as to their personal characters. The small brass plate over the grave of the poet's wife has a Latin inscription, probably by her son-in-law, Dr. Hall: 'Here Lyeth Interred the Body of Anne, wife of William Shakespeare, who departed this life the 6th day of August, 1623, being of the age of 67 years.' Alongside is the slab with the famous doggerel lines:

> ' GOOD FREND FOR JESUS SAKE FORBEARE,
> TO DIGG THE DOST ENCLOSED HEARE ;
> BLESTE BE YE MAN YT SPARES THES STONES,
> AND CVRST BE HE YT MOVES MY BONES."

The lines seem to be original, and no earlier example seems to have been found; but similar lines of later date have been discovered in Warwickshire, at Solihull and at Shustoke. Although it is not probable that the poet himself wrote like an 'unlettered muse,' there can be little or no doubt that he desired that his remains should never be removed to the charnel-house hard by, which contained the bones of so many of earlier generations. It is curious, too, that while many of the burials of his own family are recorded in the registers, no trace of the graves even of his father and mother, nor even of his own son Hamnet, has ever been found. The sacred rite of burial seems to have been required, and secured by this posthumous 'curse,' and the poet's remains have been left undisturbed.

The grave of Susannah Hall has a curious and characteristic inscription:

'Witty above her sex, but that's not all,
Wise to Salvation was good Mistress Hall,
Something of Shakespeare was in that, but this
Wholly of Him with whom she's now in bliss.'

And this, while recording her likeness to her father, indicates also the Puritanic character of herself and her husband, and leaves ample room for speculation as to what the religious belief of Shakespeare himself may have been. Another part of the inscription, in English also, is characteristic:

'Then, passenger, ha'st ne're a teare,
 To weep with her that wept with all?
That wept yet set herself to chere
 Them up with comforts cordiall.
Her love shall live, her mercy spread,
When thou ha'st ne'ere a teare to shed.'

The epitaph has further:

'Heere lyeth ye body of Susanna, Wife to John Hall, Gent., ye davghter of William Shakespeare, Gent., shee deceased ye 11th of July, Ao. 1640, aged 66.'

These graves of Shakespeare and some of his family

have an exceptional and impressive interest as memorials, and especially as so few facts are known as to his personal or family life. Some doubts have been expressed as to whether the slab which covers the poet's grave is the one originally placed by his family, or whether it has been replaced and the inscription copied; but there can be no reasonable doubt from the evidence which satisfied the late Mr. Halliwell Phillipps, and which was based on the traditions familiar to the late Mr. W. O. Hunt, and were handed down from his father and grandfather, and also from the evidence of the late Mr. R. B. Wheler, the historian of Stratford, which was personal knowledge down to 1800, that the slab was the original, and that only the letters had been deepened, and are now more carefully protected from injury than heretofore.

The mural monument of Shakespeare is too familiar from photographs and sketches to need any full description. Its exact date is uncertain, but it is referred to in the verses of Leonard Digges in 1623, and its characteristics are clearly of that period, except that the two cherubs may be of rather later date. Its principal interest is that it contains a life-size bust of the poet 'in his habit as he lived.' This is the more important as it is one of the only two 'true and original' contemporary portraits which have any real pedigree, or any claim to be considered genuine and authentic portraits of the 'poet of all time.' The Droeshout engraving prefixed to the first folio in 1623 and the Stratford bust are the only real claimants, and there is always a link or more missing in the pedigree of all the rest. The Stratford monument was the work of Gerard Johnson, 'tombe-maker,' of Southwark, who also executed the fine recumbent effigy of John Combe, in the same chancel, a proof, from the evident portraiture of Combe, that he was an artist of no mean skill. Portrait-sculpture was the fashion of the time, as is also proved by the characteristic individualized head and face of the Earl of Totness in the

Clopton Chapel in the same church, although of somewhat later date. Many sculptors, from Sir Francis Chantrey downwards, have had no doubt that the face was modelled from a *post-mortem* cast, also a common process of those days. There can, therefore, be no reasonable doubt that this bust shows Shakespeare as he was in his later years at Stratford, and that it was approved by his family and friends. A hundred years ago Edmond Malone was allowed to paint over all the colours of hair, face, and dress to a dirty drab, and in this state it remained till 1863—made famous by the severe but well-deserved lines:

> 'Stranger! to whom this monument is shown,
> Invoke the poet's curse upon Malone,
> Whose meddling zeal his barbarous taste displays,
> And daubed his tombstone as he marred his plays.'

In 1863 the paint was removed, and enough of colour was found to allow the whole to be really 'restored' to the state in which the bust had been left by Shakespeare's own friends. Now that the rawness of colour is 'toning down,' the monument has become a memorial of Shakespeare in the very 'fashion of his time.'

The Droeshout portrait resembles and yet differs from the bust sufficiently to confirm its accuracy, and was, indeed, very probably engraved from a sketch of the bust, with such variations as are inevitable in all copies. It is highly improbable that Droeshout ever saw Shakespeare, so that if he had another portrait (which has been lost) to copy from, the resemblances of the bust and engraving are further authenticated, and the Droeshout portrait has the poetical but clear and credible testimony of Ben Jonson (who knew Shakespeare well) in the famous lines:

> 'The figure that thou see'st here put
> It was for gentle Shakespeare cut;
> In which the 'graver had a strife
> With nature to out-do the life.

Oh! could he but have drawn his wit
As well in brass, as he hath hit
His face, this print would then surpass,
All that was ever writ in brass.
But since he cannot, Reader, look
Not on his picture but his book.'

The restored colouring shows the bust as originally painted—'a fine, full round face, the forehead towering, the eyes large and orbed, the lips expressive, the nose full, but not too prominent, the chin set, and the whole head well poised and massive, as originally painted after nature. The eyes are light hazel, the hair and beard auburn. The shoulders are free from stoop, the chest is broad and capacious, the right hand formerly held a pen. The dress is a scarlet doublet slashed on the breast, over which is a loose black gown without sleeves. The upper part of the cushion is crimson, the lower part green, the cord which binds it and the tassels are gilt. The inscriptions are:

'JUDICIO PYLIUM, GENIO SOCRATEM, ARTE MARONEM,
TERRA TEGIT, POPULUS MŒRET, OLYMPUS HABET.'

[In judgment a Nestor, in genius a Socrates, in art a Virgil. The earth covers, the people mourn, Olympus holds him.]

'STAY, PASSENGER: WHY GOEST THOU BY SO FAST?
READ IF THOU CANS'T, WHOM ENVIOVS DEATH HATH PLAST
WITHIN THIS MONVMENT, SHAKESPEARE WITH WHOME
QVICKE NATVRE DIDE: WHOSE NAME DOTH DECKE HIS TOMBE,
FAR MORE THAN COST; SITH ALL YT HE HATH WRITT
LEAVES LIVING ART BVT PAGE TO SERVE HIS WITT.'
OBIIT ANO. DOI., 1616.
ÆTATIS 53, DIE 23 AP.

As Dr. Hall, Shakespeare's son-in-law, was familiar with Latin, which his professional note-book shows, it is supposed that he may have written this epitaph; but the words 'within this monument' are puzzling, and could scarcely have been written by anyone who knew that the monument was mural, and the grave itself under the chancel-floor below. The classical references in the first two lines may probably have been from the pen of Ben Jonson, or some of Shakespeare's London friends, who had not seen the mural monument and the chancel grave.

The full effect of the bust can scarcely be appreciated on account of its height—eight or nine feet—above the chancel-floor, so that the features are foreshortened and somewhat distorted through being seen from below. When viewed as reproduced from careful casts of the face, the expression of the features is far more life-like and impressive, and 'appeals' (says Britton) 'to our eyes and understandings with the full force of truth;' and Fairholt, who had ample opportunities for minute and careful study, says: 'An intent study of this bust enforces the belief that all the manifold peculiarities of feature so characteristic of the poet, and which no chance could have originated and no theory account for, must have resulted from its having been a transcript of the man.'

Many old churches of pre-Reformation days contain mural remains which are sometimes mistaken for monuments from which the effigies have been removed. These, however, are readily explained and understood, and are really the remains of Easter sepulchres, and consisted of a low altar-tomb generally in the north wall of the chancel. They were sometimes, after the Reformation, converted into monumental or mural tombs. Originally they were typical of the Resurrection and the tomb hewn out of the rock, and at Easter certain ceremonies were performed before them. 'The Host and crucifix were carried in procession on Good Friday and deposited in the " sepulchre," which was generally a movable shrine. The door was then shut, and on that and the following night the " sepulchre was watched," in imitation of the narrative, and early on Easter morning the Host and crucifix were removed with great solemnity, the priest at the same time pronouncing the words, " Surrexit, non est hic." This is shown among the constitutions for the office of deacon in Trinity Church, Coventry, in 1462; one is "that he shall watch the sepulcur on Astur even till the resurrection be don."' The altar substructure and the arch above are generally the only vestiges now remaining, but the 'sepulchre' was sometimes constructed of stone of rich 'tabernacle work' with sculptured figures in relief. Few of these relics are found in Warwickshire, but there is one at Bilton Church, near Rugby, which Mr. Bloxam thus describes :

'The position which the Holy Sepulchre occupied is indicated by an elegant and enriched ogee-shaped arch in the north wall of the chancel ; near to it is a low door through which access was obtained to a small building adjoining the chancel, of which no other vestiges now remain, the building having been entirely demolished, probably early in the seventeenth century, when the church underwent considerable repairs.'

At Cubbington Church, near Warwick, the 'substructure of the sepulchre consisted of a low raised altar or tomb in the north wall, under a plain, pointed, elliptical-shaped arch, devoid of sculpture or ornament.' These seem to be the only Warwickshire examples, but Mr. Bloxam adds a remark which is curiously illustrative : ' The holy sepulchre was sometimes erected on a real and not an imaginary tomb. On the south side of the Clopton chapel or chantry, adjoining the north side of the chancel of Milford Church, Suffolk, and under an open arch formed through the entire thickness of the wall and open to the chancel, is the altar-tomb of Sir John Clopton, who died in 1497, and on this was placed the movable "sepulchre" at Easter. The custom of watching the "sepulchre" and other ceremonies, though generally discontinued at the Reformation, was revived during the reign of Mary ; but early in the reign of Elizabeth it was again discontinued.'

' Ancient churches now ruinated, desecrated or destroyed,' formed the subject of a sad but interesting paper by the late Matthew Holbeche Bloxam, F.S.A., not long before his lamented death at a great age, full of years and honours, devoted to Warwickshire, and given with unstinted care. His long life and methodical notes have preserved many records of forgotten places which have gone into oblivion in the resistless flood of the changes of time. The list is too long for anything like full record, but some well deserve a passing note. Although he did not give a complete list, he referred to more than forty without including any of those in the city of Coventry or in the county town of Warwick. Many of the places disappeared at the general Dissolution (*tempore* Henry VIII.), but some in earlier and some in later days. The proximity to the manor-house, the depopulation of villages and towns, the enclosures by lords of manors, and many less marked causes, helped to secure the loss of many ancient buildings, and also to obliterate all traces even of their sites, except from the vague accounts in ancient records. In the first year of the reign of Edward VI. an inquiry was made as to 'all the landes and rentes with stockes and cattel and money given to the maintenance of Obittes or Lights within the county of Warwick,' and as one of the first results, that of Thomas Fisher at Bishop's Itchington was destroyed, and no part of it remains; and under the same 'certificate' an 'olde decayed chapel' in Long Itchington, probably attached to Stonenthorpe, a mansion of the fifteenth century, was broken up, and only a part of it remained as a stable. At 'Stonely,' too, 'oone chapell covered with tyle and shyngle' disappeared, and another, dating from the time of Stephen, shared the same fate.

Among many other disappearances Sir W. Dugdale records (1656) at Bentley, in the parish of Shustoke, 'but the carcase of a chapel here.' At Bretford, near Wolston, on the Fosse Road, even the site of a chapel or hospital, with a list of incumbents from 1303, is now unknown. At Broadwell, near Leamington Hastings, Dr. Thomas records that a chapel was destroyed 'upon the report that it was like to be turned into a meeting-house.' At Caludon, Dugdale mentions a ruined chapel, but no trace of it remains. At Cestersover, on the Watling Road, one was not used in Dugdale's day, and has since disappeared. On Dunsmore Heath, at a place called the Stride, there was 'anciently a chapel which, with divers churches and other things, became appropriate to the Priory of Coventry in 1260 (44 Henry III.), and, as appears by the grant of Philip and Mary in the first and second year of their reign, was an enclosed grove, ' but the site is unknown.'

In Wedgnock Park there was 'Cuckow Church,' which as early as 1500 had been 'down to the ground a long time;' and the place where it stood, with the chapel road, had also been, and then was, 'employed to prophane uses: as also that there were no inhabitants who should rebuild it, the village whereunto this chapel did belong having been many years since depopulated.' At Dosthill, near Kingsbury, are the remains of a Norman chapel of the twelfth century, originally with a nave and chancel, the latter having been covered by the road to Tamworth, and the nave used as a schoolroom. At Lower Eatington the parish church has disappeared, except some ruins and a part used as a private chapel; and in 1795 an Act was passed to 'desecrate' the church at Upper Eatington. At Edston, near Henley-in-Arden, a chapel belonging to Wootton-Wawen, dating from Henry III., has been lost. At Fulbroke, near Stratford, a church of 1341 (Edward III.) was valued at nine marks, but was destroyed before 1535 (Henry VIII.); and in 6 Henry VI. (*circa* 1428) there were only four inhabitants, and only the manor remained. At Hurley, near Kingsbury, a chapel and chantry, founded by one of the Bracebriggs of Kingsbury in Edward II. (*circa* 1311), was used as late as 1667, and existed as late as 1712, but is now no more. At Luddington, in the parish of Stratford-on-Avon, there was 'anciently a chapel, the priest serving in which had in 26 Henry VIII. v*li*. vi*s*. and viii*d*. per annum for his stipend, and the like in 37 Henry VIII.' Tradition records that Shakespeare married Ann Hathaway in this chapel; but its site is uncertain, and its register was destroyed in the last century. At Newnham Regis the case was still more shameful, and, in Mr. Bloxam's own words, 'Of the old church here nothing remains but the towers and some portions of the external walls of the nave and chancel. This structure was perfect, and the walls internally covered with paintings in fresco or distemper of the Apostles, etc., till the close of the last century (*circa* 1795), when it was desecrated and the walls partially demolished by the steward, but without (it is believed) the knowledge of the then noble proprietor of the estate on which the church stood, near the manor-house.'

Many other examples might be quoted as instances of the vicissitudes even of consecrated places; but while in modern times these wholesale and shameless removals are less frequent, even more mischief is done under the pretence of 'restoration' than has been accomplished in the earlier four or five hundred years.

CHAPTER VII.

BIOGRAPHY.

Warwickshire Worthies.—County Family Names.—Antiquaries: Sir W. Dugdale, Sir Simon Archer, Henry Ferrers, William Staunton, William Hamper, R. B. Wheler, M. H. Bloxam. — Actors: Richard Burbage, Thomas Greene, William Shakespeare.—Artists: David Cox, Thomas Creswick, H. N. Humphreys, John Pye, J. T. Willmore, the Wyons.—Authors: Thomas Carte, H. F. Cary, 'George Eliot,' Philemon Holland, the three Holyoakes, William Hutton, W. S. Landor, Mark Noble, Dr. Parr, Dr. Priestley, John Rous.—Bishops: John Bird, Samuel Butler, Henry Compton, John Vesey (Harman), John Bird-Sumner.—Judges.—Martyrs.—Physicians.—Poets: Drayton, Shakespeare.—Industrial Worthies: Matthew Boulton, Edward Thomason. General: Dr. Arnold, Robert Catesby, Thomas Wright Hill, Mary Linwood.

THE 'English Worthies' of Thomas Fuller—nowadays far less read than its 'quaint and curious' pages deserve—gives a full and fair account of the 'Worthies' of Warwickshire, as well of the counties generally, as to 'Natural Commodities' (sheep, ash, cole [coal]), 'Buildings,' 'Wonders,' 'Medicinal Waters,' and 'Proverbs,' all described with that rough but pleasant humour and genuine wit which have made Fuller famous and readable even now. His 'worthies' are classed under various headings—'Princes,' 'Saints,' 'Martyrs,' 'Confessors,' 'Cardinals,' 'Prelates,' 'Statesmen,' 'Writers,' 'Romish Exile Writers,' 'Benefactors to the Public,' and 'Memorable Persons,' with a list of Warwickshire 'Lord

Mayors of London,' seven in number, from 1425 to 1619, of whom four were from Coventry, and one each from Stratford-on-Avon, Baddesley, and Rowington. He also gives a list of the sheriffs of the county in the reigns of Elizabeth, James I., and Charles I., and of the gentry of the county in 1433 (12 Henry VI.), principally from Dugdale's 'History of Warwickshire.' Although any classification of the 'Worthies' is arbitrary and indefinite, and somewhat formal, it is, on full consideration, the most convenient for reading and reference.

'The Worthies of Warwickshire who Lived Between 1500 and 1800,' by the Rev. Frederick Leigh Colvile, M.A., of Leek Wootton, was published in 1869 in a handsome volume of nearly nine hundred pages, compiled with great knowledge and care, giving the names in alphabetical order, with an alphabetical index, so that each of the memoirs can readily be found. The volume has the advantage of giving the titles of the works from which the facts are taken, and thus enabling the readers to test the correctness of the biographies and to guide them to any further researches. While most of these biographies are from well-known and authoritative sources, a large number are original contributions by 'experts,' and some of these will be used in this record of the 'Warwickshire worthies.' These 'three centuries' of 'worthies' include three hundred and twenty-one names, but do not include all the names of some who had some claim to notice; so that the present record must refer only to the more important names under the various headings, and only at such length as the character, history, or works deserve.

The county families are generally allowed precedence in all such records, but as they form a very special subject, which has been fully treated from time to time in many genealogical volumes, they will have little or no notice here, except as to individual members who have won some special honours. Among them, however, may be named the families of Conway, Craven, Compton, Digby, Dugdale, Dudley, Fielding, Ferrers, Greville, Holte, and Spencer, the last-named now more associated with Northamptonshire, although long known in Warwickshire at Wormleighton and Claverdon.

A very handy and valuable little volume, now out of print and very rarely seen, is 'Warwickshire Arms and Lineages: Compiled from the Heralds' Visitations and Ancient Manuscripts,' by the Rev. F. W. Kittermaster, of Meriden, in 1866. This work, in 120 pages, shows what families belonged to the old gentry before 1650—partly, of course, from Dugdale and other authorities, with numerous corrections from the visits of the heralds from 1563 to 1683; partly from the late Mr. Shirley's 'Noble and Gentle Men of England;' and partly from personal researches at Oxford, Cambridge, and among parish registers. An appendix includes the names and arms of some families 'now (1866) resident in the county;' but as the names 'do not appear in the Visitations, and have not been compared with heraldic records, they have been accepted only on the authority of the families who use them.' The one class of tested arms, etc., numbers 177, and the second class 27 names; but these later arms are those of 'old families,' although not strictly within the lines on which the larger part of the volume has been compiled. In all the cases the arms are fully described, and also the crests, and brief notes are occasionally given, and the references to the sources of 'authority' are always appended. The work is complete as it stands, but it might have been made more interesting and useful if some sort of distinction had been made as to the families still connected with the county, to those who are known elsewhere (and where), and also to those which may possibly be now extinct.

ANTIQUARIES form a goodly company among Warwickshire worthies, beginning with Sir Symon Archer (1581-1662), of Umberslade, the contemporary and friend of Sir

William Dugdale and of Henry Ferrers, of Baddesley Clinton, whose united labours preserved and described many of the rarest and most valuable records of the county. Archer was knighted by James I. at Warwick Castle, in the presence of George Villiers, Duke of Buckingham, and many others, and was Sheriff of the county and M.P. for Tamworth in 1640. In 1630 he became a friend of Dugdale, who in the dedication of his 'Antiquities of Warwickshire' wrote: 'But principally I must acknowledge the signall furtherance which this work hath received by my much-honoured friend, Sir Symon Archer, Knt.—a person, indeed, naturally qualified with a great affection to Antiquities, and with no small pains and charge, a diligent gatherer and preserver of many choice Manuscripts and other rarities whereof I have made a speciall use, as almost every page in this book will manifest.' In 1638 Archer persuaded Dugdale to accompany him to London, and introduced him to Sir Henry Spelman, who showed him much service. Fuller, who dedicates one of his books to the wife, 'the Lady Anne Archer,' writes: 'This worthy Knight is a lover of Antiquity and of the Lovers thereof. I should be much disheartened at his great age, which promises to us no great hope of his long continuance here, were I not comforted with the consideration of his worthy son, the heir as well of his *studiousness* as *estate*;' and further adds in a letter, 'It being questionable whether you be more skilful in knowing, careful in keeping, or courteous in communicating your curious collection in [of] that kind.' Archer was buried in Tamworth Church—' Symon Archer, miles, sepultus fuit 4° die Junii, 1662;' and Mr. Colvile adds: 'Some of his MSS. are in the library at Longbridge' (1866); but, alas! they are lost for ever. At Longbridge House, near Warwick, the late William Staunton had collected an unrivalled library of books and MSS. relating to Warwickshire, which included not only those of Archer, but everything which thirty years' industry and liberality could secure. The collection extended over more than three centuries as to dates, and had been continued down to our own days and carefully preserved by the late John Staunton, who generously sold it, on a friendly valuation, far below its mere market value, for presentation and preservation in the Reference Library, Birmingham, as 'The Staunton Warwickshire Collection'—a collection never surpassed by any county as to historic interest and future value from its *un*-copied treasures of MSS. and its many unique or rare books. The disastrous fire in January, 1879, during the extension of this library, destroyed nearly the whole collection, and not even the catalogue was saved.

Sir William Dugdale (1605-1686) was not only one of the most famous antiquaries of his own time, but one of the most illustrious in English history. He was born at Shustoke Rectory, in Warwickshire, not far from Blythe Hall, where he lived for many years, and from Shustoke Church, where his remains repose in peace. He was educated at Coventry, and among its famous sites and historic memories his antiquarian tastes were formed, and the course of his life marked out. In 1630 his friendship with Sir Symon Archer began, and their united life-work commenced. He had learned much law and history from his father, who was of a Lancashire family, but who had been attracted by the 'woodland part of Warwickshire' to reside there, and on the death of his father, in 1625, Dugdale sold the estate at Fillongley and bought Blythe Hall, near Coleshill, where he passed a large part of his long life. In 1638 he went with Archer to London, was introduced to Sir Christopher Hatton, and afterwards to Sir Henry Spelman, who introduced him to Lord Arundel, then Earl-Marshal of England, who first appointed him Blanche-Lyon, and afterwards, in 1640, as Rouge-Croix in Heralds' College, whence, as his official residence, he had ready access to the records in the Tower and elsewhere, so that all the materials of history were ready to his hand. In 1641, when the first clouds of the great Civil War were gathering, he was busy copying the inscriptions and monuments in Westminster Abbey and St. Paul's. In the following year he was, by virtue of his office, present when the King's standard was hoisted at Nottingham, and he was also present at the battle of Edge Hill. When at Oxford with the King he collected materials for his 'Monasticon,' and in 1644, when at Worcester with the King, he began collecting the materials for his 'History of Warwickshire,' one of the best known and most valuable of all his numerous works. About this date he met Antony à Wood, who in his 'Fasti' gave a memoir of Dugdale, evidently 'inspired' by Dugdale himself. In 1646 he removed to London, and was allowed to 'compound for his estate, which had been sequestered;' and then with Roger Dodsworth he began his 'History of St. Paul's Cathedral,' which was published in 1658, and continued his researches for the 'Monasticon.' During three months in Paris he began to study the history of the Alien Priories, the religious houses which had been 'cells' to the great abbeys of France. The cost of publishing the 'Monasticon' was necessarily very heavy, and Dugdale and Dodsworth had not only the enormous labour, but had to borrow money to complete the first volume.

In 1654 the death of Dodsworth left Dugdale with only one-tenth of the first volume ready, and the risks of lawsuits which the publication of so many old documents had brought forth, and also the active opposition of many Puritans, who became suspicious that the work was only a preliminary step to the revival of popery. The 'History of Warwickshire' was published in 1656, and Dugdale was nearly a year and a half in London to correct proofs and superintend the printing of the elaborate mass of facts and dates and references. The long-lost portion of his Diary of this period has recently (January, 1889) been discovered, and it gives many remarkable and curious details as to the cost of engravings, printing and paper, and shows how much microscopic care Dugdale gave to secure the correctness of every detail of his monumental work. A mere glance over any page suffices to show how elaborate and minute his researches were, not only among the official records, but among the masses of family papers entrusted to him. The numerous etchings by Hollar and others were generally supplied at the cost of the noblemen and gentlemen interested; but the transcripts of State papers, the copying of pedigrees, the sketches of monuments, the 'tricking' of arms, the long lists of rectors, vicars, patrons, etc., were wholly Dugdale's own work, and revised and corrected by his own hand.

The most careful critics have rarely found him wrong as to facts or dates, and the years of labour have had at least one reward, that the 'Warwickshire' is justly regarded as one of the greatest of its class. It is only to be regretted that Dugdale's tastes and the fashion of his time did not lead him to record many facts as to churches, houses and other buildings, which would have been of priceless value now that so many have been 'restored' or have entirely disappeared. His great work is too genealogical and heraldic for modern tastes. Much of what he passed over without notice would have been of infinite interest and value now. He gave himself very little trouble about remains which modern archæology regards as the very bones and marrow of history. He took too little notice of British, Saxon or Roman remains. Not only many of his crowded pages are of the 'dry-as-dust' order, but his style is curiously clumsy, and sometimes his sentences are far from clear. Still, he did collect 'facts' so far as they interested him, or were accordant with his plans of research and record; and he therefore deserves almost unstinted praise and honour as one of the most industrious, patient, careful and accurate of all who have explored the labyrinths of county history, with so little light in the dark recesses and so many pitfalls for unwary feet. Fuller, in his usual quaint way, well says :

'I cannot but congratulate the happiness of this county in having Master William Dugdale, now Norroy, my worthy friend, a native thereof, whose Illustrations are so great a Work, no young man could be so bold as to begin, or old man hope to finish it, while one of middle age fitted the performance. A well-chosen county for such a subject, because lying in the centre of the land, whose lustre diffuseth the light and darteth beames to the circumference of the kingdom. It were a wild wish that all the Shires in England were described by an equal degree of perfection as which will be accomplished when each star is as big and bright as the sun. However, one may desire them done *quoad specimen*, though not *quoad gradum*, in imitation of Warwickshire.'

At the Restoration Dugdale was made 'Norroy King of Arms ;' in 1667 'Garter Principal King of Arms' of Heralds' College—then a high heraldic dignity, but less honoured now. His 'History of Embanking and Draining of Divers Fens,' and his 'Origines Juridiciales' followed, and he was made a knight 'much against his will, as his estates were small,' on his rise to the dignity of 'Garter Principal King of Arms.' One of his daughters was married to Elias Ashmole, and the MS. collections for 'Warwickshire' are now in the Ashmolean Museum at Oxford, some at Heralds' College, London, and the author's rough copy of the 'Warwickshire' is reverently preserved at Merevale, near Atherstone, in Warwickshire. He died at Blythe Hall in 1686, and was buried in a vault at Shustoke Church with a Latin inscription, written by himself, in which he makes no mention of his invaluable contributions to English history, and records only the stages of his promotion to the highest honour which Heralds' College could bestow. His 'Life, Diary and Correspondence' were issued by the late William Hamper, F.S.A., of Birmingham, in an admirable volume, in which every known detail of his long, laborious and honourable life is fully given, and with such praise as the vast researches, the minute care, the untiring labour, the patient revision, and the unrivalled accuracy of so many important works so thoroughly deserve from all who value the life-work of one who was truly a 'Warwickshire worthy,' and a county historian of the highest rank.

Another of the antiquaries of Dugdale's time, and one of his literary helpers and personal friends, deserves some words of praise and honour. At Baddesley Clinton, near Knowle, in one of the most picturesque of the moated houses of Warwickshire, which remains almost unaltered, *Henry Ferrers* lived, and gave a large part of his quiet life to the discovery and preservation of the relics of the past. He was a careful student of heraldry, genealogy, and antiquities generally. He was a friend of Camden and Antony à Wood, and, excepting John Rous, he was the first collector of Warwickshire materials for history. He proposed to issue a 'Perambulation of Warwickshire,' like Lambarde's of Kent, but he never accomplished it, and was content to place his collections at the service of his friends. Eight of his manuscript volumes were in the Staunton Library at Longbridge, but all were lost in the great fire in the Birmingham Library already referred to. His neighbour, Sir Symon Archer, and himself combined to help Dugdale, who unfortunately used only portions of their materials, the originals of which have mostly perished. Happily, however, a few have been preserved by copies made by Archer and Ferrers, and some of these copies, as well as originals, have been saved by the fortunate habit of 'copying' old manuscripts, which the leisure and tastes of some of the ancient Warwickshire gentry allowed. So late as sixty years ago Captain Saunders, of Stratford-on-Avon, copied many of the manuscripts of the Ferrers and Archer collection (which had been borrowed and not returned), and these passed into the hands of R. B. Wheler, the historian of Stratford-on-Avon, and are now safely stored in Shakespeare's birthplace. These are the more valuable as they are now the only copies of documents which were not in accordance with Dugdale's plan of history, but which are of very curious value as parts of county history. Henry Ferrers died in 1633, aged eighty-four, but his tastes were not hereditary, and no engravings of Ferrers' monuments appear in Dugdale's 'Warwickshire,' 'because' (says that historian) 'so frugall a person is the present heir of the family, now (1656) residing here [Baddesley Clinton], as that he, refusing to contribute anything towards the charge thereof, they are omitted.'

Another of the antiquaries who greatly helped to preserve the materials of history was *William Hamper, F.S.A.*, of Birmingham (1776-1831), whose principal work was his 'Life of Dugdale,' but who devoted the small leisure of a busy life to antiquarian studies. He made very elaborate collections towards a new edition of Dugdale's 'Warwickshire,' as the edition of Dr. Thomas (two folio volumes, 1730) was very unsatisfactory, being little more than a reprint of Dugdale's of 1656, with later and fuller copies of monuments and inscriptions. The Hamper copy of Dugdale, interleaved, and with a mass of valuable notes and additions, is now safe in the British Museum, and is a monument *ære perennius* of his industry, vigilance, and knowledge of Warwickshire antiquities. He wrote, too, a singularly clear and correct 'hand,' and his copies of seals, facsimiles, rolls, charters, deeds, and pedigrees are as perfect and accurate as engravings. Like his predecessors, Archer and Ferrers, he was constantly contributing to the works of others, and greatly helped in Nichols's 'Leicestershire' and Ormerod's 'Cheshire,' and especially in Dr. Blair's 'Kenilworth Illustrated,' and he gave many of the details to Scott's famous semi-historical romance. He also annotated Hutton's 'History of Birmingham' with the purpose of a new edition, and collected a mass of facts previously unknown. His researches were extensive and profound, his records minute and careful, his notes and corrections of the highest value; and if his leisure had been greater and his life longer, he would have left a series of antiquarian works of the highest value. He was a frequent contributor to the *Gentleman's Magazine* under several initials and signatures, a friend of all the most learned men of his time, and, as an F.S.A., a frequent contributor to the 'Archæologia' of the Society of Antiquaries. He died in 1831 at Highgate, near Birmingham, and was buried in King's Norton Churchyard, admired and honoured by all who knew him and appreciated his life and work.

Another of the goodly company of Warwickshire antiquaries who have kept alight the lamp of history for so many generations was one whose name has already been mentioned—*William Staunton*, of Longbridge, near Warwick, where his family had lived for five hundred years. Although best known as the founder of the famous Warwickshire Collection, to which he devoted the larger part of his life, he was an author or editor of two priceless volumes on the 'Churches of Warwickshire' so far as the Deanery of Warwick was concerned. He was the author of the historical portion of the work, and the architectural parts were the work of the late Matthew Holbeche Bloxam, and the illustrations were by the late Allen E. Everitt, of Birmingham, and others. William Staunton was born at Kenilworth in 1765, was educated at Rugby and at St. John's, Oxford, was called to the Bar, but after a short service in the Life Guards he became, with the late Francis Douce, one of the chief numismatic collectors of the day. His friendship with Hamper of Birmingham, and Sharp of Coventry, led him to form a fine library, and to collect all manuscripts and prints relating to Warwickshire; and on the death of Hamper he acquired most of his MSS., deeds, rolls, and from Sharp his Coventry collections, which were extensive and valuable, and added from time to time all treasures from other sources as they occurred for sale, and thus formed an unrivalled collection, including records from the Archer Collection down to his own time. Among these were the original Register of the Gild of St. Anne at Knowle (1412); the Archer Records (1242 to 1485), the Cartulary of St. Mary's Priory at Coventry; the Gild-Book of St. Mary's, Coventry; the Inventory of the Earl of Leicester's household at Kenilworth (1584); the illuminated Order of St. Michael given to Leicester by Louis XI. in 1565; and many hundreds of original drawings of old churches and houses and of portraits of 'worthies,' and countless autograph letters of famous men, as well as volumes of antiquarian correspondence with all the chief people over a period of more than fifty years. All these treasures were included in the presentation by public subscription to the Reference Library at Birmingham, where they were unfortunately burned, and almost every scrap destroyed, by the fire in 1879. Even the original MS. catalogue perished, and only a small part of the proposed elaborate catalogue had been finished when the calamitous fire occurred. William Staunton died in 1848, aged eighty-three, and was buried in the family vault at St. Mary's, Warwick, where a mural tablet marks his memory as one of the worthiest of the Warwickshire worthies. His friend and neighbour, *Thomas Sharp*, of Coventry (1771-1841), well deserves much honour for his learned and laborious work. As early as 1792 he obtained access to the then long-neglected but priceless treasures which had accumulated in Coventry during many centuries of 'strange, eventful history.' He soon began to dust and clean and arrange and index the vast masses of neglected manuscripts, and his work, followed up a few years ago by the late John Fetherston, F.S.A., has now secured for Coventry a mass of well-cared-for manuscripts, records deeds, charters, merchant's marks, seals, autograph letters, etc., which no English city can surpass. Thomas Sharp, with George Howletts and George Nixon, all of Coventry, set to work to secure a record of all that remained of old-world lore. They engaged a drawing-master to make sketches of old churches, buildings, city gates, etc., to illustrate Dugdale's 'Warwickshire,' and one copy contained no less than 670 'illustrations'—108 engravings, 40 drawings of brasses, 223 of churches, and 300 of miscellaneous antiquities—most of which have long since been lost by vandalism or neglect. Sharp will long be remembered for his works on the 'Coventry Pageants,' his 'Ancient Mysteries and Moralities,' for his help in 'Kenilworth Illustrated,' and his generous assistance given to many other writers—as Dr. Harwood, of Lichfield, and others engaged in historical work. His many years of correspondence with Hamper, Staunton, and others had been carefully preserved as of great value, but the many volumes perished in the disastrous fire in 1879. He died in 1841, and was buried in St. Michael's Churchyard, in the heart of the city to whose history he had devoted his life.

Another Warwickshire antiquary is well known as the historian of Stratford-on-Avon, and although the range of his researches was limited, his work was well done, and has been universally known wherever the fame of Shakespeare has spread. He was not the first who had given some account of Stratford, for a former curate, the Rev. Joseph Greene (1711-1790), had carefully recorded some details of the history of the town, as well as of his own times. *Robert Bell Wheler* was born at Stratford in 1785 in the house in which he lived all his life, and in which he died in 1857. He was articled to the Town Clerk of Stratford, and, except one month in London, he rarely left his native town. His position in the Town Clerk's office necessarily brought under his notice the mass of old documents concerning Stratford which had been accumulating for several centuries, and his antiquarian tastes were acquired and developed in his very early life. He soon began to form the extraordinary collection of manuscripts,

books and relics which his sister, who survived him, gave
to Shakespeare's birthplace, where they are now carefully
preserved. His residence during so long a life continuously
in Stratford enabled him to secure every document which
formed part of the history of the town and neighbourhood.
His profession as a solicitor gave him access to many
private collections of papers, which he copied when he
could not acquire the originals. He wrote a singularly
neat, clear hand. He was an excellent draughtsman with
pen and ink, and also sepia, and his facsimiles of seals,
signatures and manuscripts, and his sepia drawings of
old houses and buildings which were ruined or destroyed
during his life, have the greatest interest and value as
authentic records of the ancient town. The Wheler Collection contains not only original records of unique
interest and importance, but volumes of scraps and cuttings
of all the principal incidents of the history of the town.
He had picked up and preserved many memorials of the
Garrick jubilee, and had saved from destruction many of
the small legal documents connected with Shakespeare's
properties and interests in the town. His own autograph
manuscripts, recording the facts in the history of Stratford
from the time of John of Stratford in the seventh century
down to the events of the first half of the nineteenth, are
probably as complete a series as any town possesses. His
first and most important work in literature—for his whole
life was spent in collecting materials for history—is the
'History and Antiquities of Stratford-on-Avon,' published
in 1806, and illustrated with some excellent plates. The
great merit of the text is its careful copies of manuscripts,
now lost, and of inscriptions long ago defaced or
destroyed. His own interleaved and annotated copy, with
many additional drawings, plans and notes, is, of course,
unique, and is more than ever valuable as a record of his
later researches, fifty years after his work was first produced. His 'Guide to Stratford' (1814), and his 'History

of Shakespeare's Birthplace' (1824), were also works of mark and merit, now rarely seen. His annotations in his own copies of these minor works—for he 'counted naught done while aught remained to do '—are excellent examples of all that such works should be—clear, concise, learned, accurate, even in the most trivial details. His books, and manuscripts, and sketches, given by his sister to Shakespeare's birthplace, number nearly three hundred volumes and relics, and his 'Collectanea de Stratford,' a quarto manuscript of more than five hundred pages, is 'so minutely (but clearly) written that an ordinary transcript would fill half a dozen volumes of the same size.' The rest of the collection has no surplusage; every portion grows more valuable as changes occur and landmarks are lost, and the Wheler Collection, although practically limited to Stratford and its immediate neighbourhood, is a noble monument to the memory and life-work of a Warwickshire author and collector who has enriched his county by the relics which he gathered and preserved. His good example was continued by his friend *William Oakes Hunt*, of an old Stratford family, and a resident there all his life, to whom the town owes an endless debt for his care of the Wheler Collection, his 'Index' to its contents, his long-continued care of the birthplace and museum, and his great services is assisting the late J. O. Halliwell-Phillipps to overhaul and calendar the long series of Stratford muniments which have been slowly increasing during seven hundred years.

One other name—*clarum et venerabile nomen*—completes the long and honourable list of those who have devoted their lives to the history of Warwickshire. Some were merely collectors—perhaps only 'hewers of wood and drawers of water,' ministering to the builders of the historic edifice— but others gave their genius, skill, and larger knowledge in the light of their times and the fashions of their day. Nearly all the earlier antiquaries were content to study the manuscript remains, and to record and illustrate the territorial, genealogical and heraldic history of the county. About a century ago new lights appeared, new sources of knowledge were sought and studied, new illustrations of early history were traced from neglected sources, and a new generation of antiquaries arose. The interest and value of ancient buildings, the relics which were recovered from old mounds and graves, were found to be as important records of history as the musty manuscripts and faded deeds and charters which Archer and Ferrers and Dugdale had delighted to explore. The fast-perishing memorials in earthworks, roads, old walls and ruins were found to be historic and illustrative, when carefully examined and described. Gothic architecture, which had never died out, but had only ceased to be understood and appreciated, slowly revived. No student or author of the time deserves higher praise for his share in this real 'revival' than *Matthew Holbeche Bloxam, F.S.A.*, who was one of the first to understand, to explain, and to popularize the genuine study of Gothic architecture, and to educate the taste of the early half of our century to the value, interest, and historical importance of the rich and rare remains of art which old churches and old houses have preserved. He was one of the first of the new school of antiquaries, who have developed into archæologists, and of the wider, systematic, and historic study of the buildings and monuments of the 'good old times.' He was one of the first to trace by personal observation, and to record with graphic pencil and pen, the remains of British, Celtic, Roman, and Saxon influences and relics, and especially to note and compare the growth and perfection of the architectural remains of the early centuries of English history, from the Norman Conquest to the sixteenth century, as priceless architectural and monumental remains. He filled up, in fact, the register of our national story by the study of long-neglected or misunderstood 'survivals,' and traced the links of evolution with a masterly hand during a long and honourable, a modest and blameless life.

Matthew Holbeche Bloxam was born at Rugby in 1809, and was educated at the school where his father was one of the masters. He was articled to a lawyer there, and his early duties — to search the registers of country churches — took him to many of the old villages of Warwickshire and the neighbouring counties, and formed the 'environment' by which his early tastes were moulded and the work of his life slowly matured. He began to make sketches of monuments and porches, fonts, windows, and crosses, and then to study and compare his observations. His interest was soon aroused by the remains of British camps and Roman roads, and he devoted all his leisure to the study of all ancient remains, long before their value and interest were generally understood. In 1829 he published a small volume, 'The Principles of Gothic Architecture,' and, according to the Pinnock-fashion of the time, it was 'elucidated by question and answer.' This volume, printed at Leicester, soon became popular, and aroused a new interest and admiration of the too long neglected remains, and it soon became a handbook and guide, especially to the numerous ecclesiastical buildings. The work became so popular that in 1845 it had reached a fifth edition, and soon afterwards was translated into German, with more than two hundred of the excellent woodcuts which so largely increased its usefulness and spread its fame. Its accuracy was so notable that it was accepted as evidence in a Chancery suit as to an ancient chantry chapel at Icklesham, in Sussex. In 1882 the final edition was published in three volumes, and the work holds its place as one of the most handy, accurate, and complete handbooks of Gothic ecclesiastical art. A special work on 'Monumental Architecture and Sculpture' was issued in 1834, and soon became scarce; but its substance and illustrations were included in the edition of

1882. Another work, 'Fragmenta Sepulchralia'—now still more rare—was only a fragment, but it related to the sepulchral remains of the Celtic and Belgic Britons, the Romans, the Romanized Britons, the Early Saxons, and the forms of burial from the seventh to the seventeenth century. The principal parts of this volume are, however, also included in the edition of 1882. The two volumes on the 'Churches of Warwickshire,' already referred to, owe all the descriptions of architecture and monuments to Bloxam, and greatly increase the authority, accuracy, and value of the work. He also had a large share in the 'Memorials of Rugby,' which were illustrated by C. W. Radclyffe; and in the ' Brasses of Northamptonshire,' by the late Franklin Hudson, ninety brasses were described by Bloxam from his rubbings and notes. His long life and comparative leisure enabled him to visit many parts of England where Gothic remains were found, and to prepare more than two hundred papers on various subjects to various archæological societies. He modestly regarded them as 'ephemera,' but all have curious interest and authority as the records by a competent author of a long series of observations.

He was not elected a Fellow of the Society of Antiquaries till 1863; but no candidate was ever worthier of that honour, and he was soon afterwards chosen as one of the local secretaries for Warwickshire, with the late Evelyn Philip Shirley. He frequently attended the meetings of the society, and contributed several papers to the *Archæologia*. Nearly all his life was passed at Rugby, and he naturally felt a great interest in the famous School, and delighted to take some of the boys—his 'young archæologists'—to look over his crowded rooms and to understand some of the treasures and relics of old times. One of his latest works was a modest 'Fardel of Antiquarian Papers,' a list of the pamphlets and papers he had written during fifty years, with valuable notes and comments of an autobiographical sort. Almost to the last he kept at his congenial work, sketching, noting, illustrating, and until the year of his death he took every opportunity of going out with the Warwickshire Field Club on its archæological excursions, and revisiting the places, some of which he had not seen for sixty years! Although a reverent preserver of all relics of the past, and a hater of modern 'restorations,' he was a stern critic and a thorough iconoclast as to some of the traditions about Guy, Earl of Warwick and Godiva of Coventry, Wycliffe's chair at Lutterworth, and other similar legacies of the 'ages of faith.' His love of Warwickshire, and especially of Rugby, formed a pleasant part of his character. He sometimes read papers on his recollections of Rugby School, and of life at Rugby sixty years before. He wrote many special descriptions of the more interesting remains in Warwickshire, in which historic research and personal observation were pleasantly combined. As early as 1836 he read a paper on the 'British Antiquities of Warwickshire,' and he continued his papers about Rugby School till a few weeks before his death. He died on April 24, 1888, in his eighty-third year, and was buried at his own desire in a spot he had chosen, at Brownsover, not far from Rugby, 'near the site of an ancient British fortress.' His personal life was uneventful. His health was almost unbroken all through his life. He was cheerful and active almost to the last, and paralysis left his mind unclouded and his memory clear. All he knew or all he could learn was ever at the service of his friends. He was a gentleman of the old school in mind and manners, kindness and courtesy. His additions to Warwickshire history are perhaps not yet fully appreciated as to completeness and extent. Among all who knew him personally, only pleasant memories remain, and he has left to literature at least one monumental work which has been the teacher and the text-book of two generations as to the glories of Gothic art.

ACTORS have not been numerous in connection with Warwickshire, but three at least were among the foremost of the players of the Elizabethan stage. Curiously, too, and almost inexplicably, all the three belonged to Stratford-on-Avon. *Richard Burbage* (or Burbadge), the 'Roscius of the Elizabethan age,' is recorded with Thomas Greene as amongst the townsmen of Stratford; and they were certainly natives of Warwickshire, and probably of Stratford. In 1574 Elizabeth granted a license to Burbage and others for plays of every sort, they 'being before seen and allowed by the Master of the Revels.' In 1583 Burbage's company was incorporated as the 'Queen's Players,' and Shakespeare himself was probably, or at least possibly, in his townsman's 'company' as early as 1587, when they visited Stratford, and were more highly rewarded than any previous players had been. Even if Shakespeare was not a member of the company, there can be no reasonable doubt that his connection with the stage was due, sooner or later, to the example and influence of his successful townsman. The details may never be fully known, but the happy accident of one Stratford man being a successful player when Shakespeare had gone to London may fairly be claimed as the immediate cause of Shakespeare becoming a player and a dramatic author, who might under less favourable circumstances have lived and died unhonoured and unknown. In 1603 Shakespeare's name appears in a royal warrant of May 17, with those of Laurence Fletcher, Richard Burbage, Augustine Phillips, William Sly, Robert Armyn, Richard Cowlye, John Hemmings, and Henrie Condell, and the rest of their associates; the two last-named being those of the two friends who collected the plays of Shakespeare in the famous first folio of 1623, seven years after the poet's death. This 'company of players' had the 'warrant to use and exercise the arte and faculty of playing comedies, tragedies, enterludes, histories, moralls, pastorals, stage-plaies, and such-like, as they have alreadie studied, or hereafter shall use or studie, as well for the recreation of our lovinge subjects as for our solace and pleasure . . . as well within their now usuall howse called the Globe, within our County of Surreye, as also within anie town halls or mote halls, or other convenient places within the liberties and freedome of anie other citie, university, towne, or borough whatsoever within our said realms and dominions,' etc. Burbage was one of the first and principal players of Shakespeare's greatest tragic characters, and the fact that he is mentioned in Shakespeare's will is another proof of their close and life-long personal relations. One of Burbage's favourite plays was 'Romeo and Juliet,' and his first daughter was named Juliet; and after her death, in 1608, another daughter, born in 1614, received the same memorable name. Burbage was a painter as well as a player, and a portrait said to be of Shakespeare, and evidently of early date, was held by the late Abraham Wivell to be a genuine portrait of Shakespeare by Burbage, but the genuineness has never been fully proved. Burbage died about three years after Shakespeare (*circa* 1620), and the characteristic epitaph on his grave was '*Exit* Burbage.'

Thomas Greene was less famous, but a comedy-actor of considerable power and fame. He, also, is traditionally said to have introduced Shakespeare to the stage, *circa* 1586. Heywood says of him: 'There was not an actor of his nature, in his time, of better ability in the performance of what he undertook, more applauded by the audience, of greater grace at the Court, or of more general love in the City.' Little more is known of him, except as to his name as one of the *dramatis personæ* in many of the contemporary plays; and one of his most popular parts was that of Bubble, in 'The City Gallant,' a character who, in answer to every compliment, shouted out 'Tu quoque;' and a portrait of Greene, with a label issuing from his mouth and bearing these two words, was added as a frontispiece to the two contemporary editions of the play. He was doubtless connected with the Thomas Greene, Town Clerk of Stratford, who held a good position there.

William Shakespeare himself must be included among these Stratford actors, although his fame as a player has been lost in the splendour of his genius as a dramatic author. His name appears as an actor, but he is not known to have taken any very great position on the stage. Tradition records that he played the Ghost in 'Hamlet,' and also old Adam in 'As You Like It;' and in his early life in London, and his first connection with the stage, doubtless he played minor characters, at least, from time to time. Whatever his personal experience as a player may have been, there can be no sort of doubt that it was invaluable to him in the works which his genius produced in later years. Not only his stage knowledge, but his unrivalled skill in working out plots and creating characters, was vastly influenced by his personal observations and experiences on the stage. No dramatic author has ever approached him in the extraordinary life-likeness of characters, and brilliant dialogues and arrangements of parts. Not only as a dramatist, but as a critic, he stands in the first rank and the first place, and his 'Advice to the Players,' which Hamlet gives, is wholly unsurpassed as genuine criticism, and as laying down the conditions, laws, and expressions upon which all really great acting must ever be based.

ARTISTS.—A school of artists—painters and engravers—flourished in Warwickshire in the latter half of the last and the first half of this century, and secured far more than merely local fame. While their works are well known and highly valued, comparatively little has been preserved of their lives and progress. All that could be traced was recorded in a valuable paper by Mr. J. Thackray Bunce in a series of 'Biographical Notes' as a preface to the catalogue of an exhibition of engravings by

Birmingham artists formed at Birmingham in the spring of 1877, and from which many of the following details are condensed.

Allen, J. B. (1802-1876), was born in Birmingham, and was a pupil of J. V. Barber and S. Lines. He left his native town in early life, and was engaged as an engraver for the Bank of England for many years. His early landscape works were for the then popular 'Annuals,' and afterwards for Finden's ' Gallery of Art,' and the *Art Journal.* He was an intimate friend and associate of John Pye and Joseph Goodyear all through his London life. His ' Bull-Fight at Seville,' for Jennings' 'Landscape Annual,' was undertaken for eighty, but the publisher gave him one hundred, guineas on seeing the first proof.

Barber, J. V. (1787-1838), was the son of Joseph Barber, an eminent drawing-master in Birmingham, and he continued his father's school till 1836, when he retired on a competency, and devoted the rest of his life to landscape art. In 1837 and 1838 he visited Italy, where he was attacked by marsh-fever, and he died in Rome in 1838. Some of his best work was given to local drawings for the 'Graphic Illustrations of Warwickshire,' and to some fine oil-pictures presented by his widow to the Birmingham Art Gallery. He was honorary secretary to the first Society of Artists in that town, and he was the teacher of many of the local engravers and painters who won distinction, such as Baker of Leamington, J. T. Willmore, A.R.A., and F. H. Henshaw, who still survives his early friends in a genial old age.

Brandard, R. (1805-1862), was also born in Birmingham, where he received his early art-training, and then went to the studio of Edward Goodall, where he engraved many of Turner's works. He sometimes exhibited oil-pictures at the Royal Academy and the British Institution. He contributed many fine engravings of the Vernon Collection to the *Art Journal,* and won great fame and honour as a draughtsman, an engraver, and an etcher of a very high class.

Cox, David (1783-1859), has so long been famous that only a few details of his local life and associations need be given. He was born in Birmingham, near which he spent the last years of his life, and was buried at Harborne, near Birmingham. As an etcher, by the soft-ground process, he won great fame by his fine folio of drawing-lessons in all stages, under the title of 'A Treatise on Landscape Painting and Effect in Water-Colour,' in 1814, and later by a fine quarto volume, 'The Young Artist's Companion and Drawing-Book,' in 1825. Both works are now rarely met with, and they secure very high prices whenever a copy occurs for sale. The first-named work had forty pages of etchings, twenty-four of aquatints, and some in colour, with remarkable details of Cox's own method and practice, as given to his pupils and employed in his own work. The fame of David Cox as one of the greatest water-colour artists of his day is world-wide, and the Art Gallery of Birmingham contains a large number of his less known but highly valued landscapes in oil.

Creswick, Thomas (1811-1869), was born at Sheffield, but was educated at the famous Hazelwood School, Birmingham, which, under Thomas Wright Hill and his son (Sir) Rowland Hill, formed the characters of so many men of eminence. Creswick showed so much talent and skill that he was a pupil of J. V. Barber for some time, and in 1828 he went to London, where, although only in his seventeenth year, two of his pictures were hung at the Royal Academy, to which he was a frequent contributor for more than thirty years. He excelled in etching, and was constantly engaged in book illustrations, for which he became famous. In many of his pictures he was modest and wise enough to accept the aid of his friends, as Ansdell, Elmore, Frith, and Goodall, for figures and cattle; but as a patient student of nature, and a brilliant painter of trees and landscape, he won the highest praise. He died in 1869, and was buried at Kensal Green.

Eginton, Francis (1737-1805), was one of the illustrious artists whom Matthew Boulton gathered around him at Soho in the latter half of the last century. He was born at Eckington, Worcestershire, but passed nearly all his life at Handsworth-juxta-Birmingham and close to Soho. He began life as an enameller at Bilston, near Wolverhampton, now only known as a smoky town in the 'Black Country,' but which was famous a century ago for 'patch-boxes' and other works in enamelled copper, which competed with those of Battersea as works of art. In 1764, just before Boulton began at Soho, Eginton was working as a decorator of japan-ware; but he also worked at modelling, and soon afterwards was working for Boulton, with Flaxman, Küchler, Pidgeon, and others, in many departments of art. Eginton was the inventor of a process of copying oil-pictures in colour which excited much interest and discussion some years ago, as most of the original facts had been forgotten. It was, in fact, a method of colour-printing by aquatint transfers for each colour, afterwards revived and improved in the Baxter oil-pictures, and still later on lithographic stones in the modern oleographs. Large numbers of these were sold, and some were of very large size, and so excellent that they were sold as genuine original oil-paintings, when discovered a few years ago. The process was probably suggested by the transfer-printing used on pottery; but it did not pay, and Boulton, who was eminently practical, ceased to produce such pictures in 1780. Local tradition asserted, on the ground of some words of Sir William Beachy, that the process was suppressed in the interests of art; but the commercial failure was the real cause. Eginton's name was also associated with some alleged early photographs long before Daguerre and Niepce. Wedgwood had certainly observed the effects of light on plates of nitrate of silver, but the means of fixing the impression were really not known in Eginton's century, and the supposed photographs of buildings were proved to be the work of half a century later. After the partnership of Boulton and Eginton was ended, the ingenious inventor turned his attention to producing windows of coloured glass, but perhaps more exactly to the production of pictures on glass, which were formed into windows. In 1784 he had a house and workshops near Soho, where during the next twenty years he produced a large number of windows in 'stained glass.' His work was really painted on glass in sections of the whole work, and then generally fitted in rectangular frames, and not with the various lines of 'leading' used in mediæval glass. The novelty and effects of his process—which was practically 'transparencies on glass,' to be looked through rather than looked at, and largely opaque—and the fashion of the day brought him large commissions, his first work being the Arms of Knights in St. George's Chapel, Windsor, followed by others in numerous cathedrals and mansions; and at Beckford's famous 'Fonthill Abbey' his numerous works cost £12,000. He was buried at Handsworth in 1805, and the only worthy memorial of his life and work is in a privately printed memoir by William Costen Aitken (1817-1875), who devoted his life and labours and genius to the heroes of Soho, and whose mortal remains rest, as he desired, by Francis Eginton's grave.

Eginton, Francis, jun. (1775-1823), was a nephew of the artist described above, and was born in Birmingham. He was an engraver in 'stipple,' and was well known and admired for his great care and taste. He executed many very fine engravings for Shaw's 'Staffordshire,' Wheler's 'Stratford-on-Avon,' Bissett's 'Directory,' Pratt's 'Leamington Guide,' Price's 'Hereford and Leominster,' and many local topographical and historical works of his time. His name and works are frequently assigned to his relative; but the dates give a safe clue generally, and the older

Eginton is not known as an illustrator of books, but conducted his works as a glass-stainer till his death in 1805, and they were continued by his son, William Raphael Eginton, for many years.

Garner, Thos. (1789-1868) was the son of a Birmingham engraver, and was also born in that town. He was a pupil of S. Lines, and afterwards of the schools of the Royal Academy, and then went to the studio of the Heaths for some time, and returned to his own town, where he passed most of his life. He engraved for the *Art Journal* and the earlier annuals, and was especially successful as a pure 'line-engraver' and in portrait-work. He was a thorough artist in all he undertook, and he gave great service to all local art by his kindly modesty and generous encouragement of all young folk who showed a taste for art.

Goodyear, Jos. (1797-1839), was a pupil of J. V. Barber and S. Lines, and was engaged by Charles Heath as an historical engraver. He was also a frequent and excellent contributor to the annuals, and produced a large number of fine engravings which were popular in his own day, and are still highly prized. His largest, latest, and most important plate was that of Eastlake's 'Greek Fugitives.'

Green, Valentine (1737-1812), was born at Salford Priors, near Alcester, Warwickshire, and was one of the most famous engravers and antiquaries of his time. He was meant to be a lawyer, but in 1760 he left home and articled himself to Robert Hancock, a well-known 'line-engraver,' of Worcester. As he was not quite at home in his choice, he compiled a 'History of the City of Worcester,' with sixteen copper-plates from his own drawings, which he published in 1764. In the next year he went to London and started as a mezzotinto engraver, an art which he had taught himself, and in which he won laurels for forty-four years. One of his best works was the 'Dusseldorf Gallery,' the Duke of Bavaria having given him the 'concession' to engrave and publish the collection of twenty-four plates, which he completed in 1795; but the French siege, and the removal and dispersion of the pictures, caused him heavy losses. In 1776 he was elected one of the six Associate Engravers of the Royal Academy, and soon after a Fellow of the Society of Antiquaries. His 'History of Worcester' has long been accepted as authoritative up to date, and is interesting even now, when a different standard is fixed for all such works. His other works were: 'A Review of the Polite Arts in France' (1782), 'The Discovery of the Body of King John in Worcester Cathedral' (1797), and the 'Acta Historica Reginarum Angliæ,' with a series of rare and fine portraits of the 'ancestors of the first families in Great Britain.' In 1804 he was Keeper of the British Institution of the Fine Arts, and he died in London in 1812.

Haughton, Matthew (1734-1804), was a brother of Moses Haughton, a painter who secured a high local reputation, and who as an engraver showed great powers and skill. Matthew Haughton was a wood-engraver, but only few of his works, and fewer details of his life, are now known.

Moses Haughton was a prolific worker, and originally a painter of tea-trays and similar articles, such as were made by Baskerville, before he devoted his taste to type-founding and printing, and by Henry Clay, who raised such productions to the rank of art. The fashion of the time led to the production of finished hand-paintings on 'trays' and 'waiters;' and many of these, after the artists had become famous, have been treasured as valuable pictures. Haughton not only designed, but engraved, pictures of Scriptural subjects as plates to editions of the Bible, which were issued in Birmingham by Pearson and Rollason, and by Boden and Adams in the later years of the last century. He was buried, and has a monument to his memory, in St. Philip's Church, Birmingham.

Humphreys, Henry Noel (1809-1879), was born in Birmingham, and was educated in King Edward's Grammar

School, where he won distinctions; but the future work of his life was given to archæology and art. His name has long been well known in connection with illustrated books on history, natural history, archæology, and art, and many of them have become the text-books on their various subjects. He was one of the first to see the usefulness and to develop the advantages which chromo-lithography affords in reproducing in a comparatively cheap form the choicest examples of the mediæval illuminated manuscripts, which had been almost inaccessible for the use of students as examples of design and colour. Among his works only the most important need be named to show the extent and variety of his labours, and they are too well known and appreciated to need special praise. There were 'The Art of Illumination and Missal Painting' (1848), 'The Coins of England' (1847), 'The Origin of Coins and the Art of Coining' (1849), 'The Illuminated Books of the Middle Ages' (1847-1850), 'The History of Ancient Coins and Medals' (1850), 'The Origin and Progress of the Art of Writing' (1852), 'The Coin-Collector's Manual' (1853), 'The Ocean and River Gardens' (1857), 'The Butterfly Vivarium' (1858), 'The Genera of British Butterflies' (1859), and of 'Moths' (1860), 'The Coinage of the British Empire' (1860), and the great work, in conjunction with Westwood, on 'Butterflies,' the same year. 'The Illustration of Froissart's Chronicles' (1862) was also a fine and valuable work.

Lines, Sam (1778-1863), was born at Allesley, near Coventry, but removed to Birmingham in 1794, and passed his long life in that town. He was apprenticed to a clock-dial enameller, but his love of art and his graphic skill induced him to open an 'Academy' in 1807; and he continued his teaching to the last years of his long life. He had the merit of being the art-father of nearly all the local men who became famous in later years. In 1814 he joined Barber, Radclyffe, and others in the collection of the first Art Exhibition in Birmingham, and took an active part in all the later exhibitions till his eightieth year. As an artist he did some good work, and was in his early life an etcher of figures and inscriptions on swords, a designer of war-medals, and also for the papier-maché ware first made by Henry Clay.

Pye, John (1782-1874), was also a native of Birmingham and one of the foremost of the 'School.' He entered the studio of Charles Heath in 1801, and in 1820 he engraved Turner's 'Pope's Villa at Twickenham,' which soon brought him fame. Turner was so well pleased that he said to him; 'This will do; you can see the lights. If I had known there was a man living who could do that I would have had it done before.' He afterwards spent ten years over Turner's 'Ehrenbreitstein,' and contributed other plates to the 'Liber Studiorum.' This 'high art' was not profitable, and many of his best engravings are buried in Peacock's 'Pocket-Books' and similar works. His pen as well as his pencil was well used, for in 1845 he issued 'The Patronage of British Art,' and was ever ready to help his brother artists who were struggling to succeed.

Radclyffe, William (1796-1855), was born in Birmingham and apprenticed to the art of letter-cutting, but with his friends J. V. and Charles Barber and John Pye he developed a taste for higher art, and commenced engraving in the 'line manner,' which applied to portraits, landscape, and all varieties of art. He engraved several of Turner's pictures and others by Reinagle, Copley Fielding, and other artists. He illustrated many books, but his best and best-known work was in the 'Graphic Illustrations of Warwickshire.' All the fine engravings were his own work, and he had the good taste to insist that the editor, Dr. Blair, should engage artists of eminence to make the drawings. This resulted in the choice of David Cox, Dewint, J. D. Harding, W. Westall, and J. V. Barber, all the original drawings being found, among a mass of papers, some years ago, and purchased and presented to the Birmingham and Midland Institute, where they are carefully preserved. These drawings are of exceptional excellence and singular interest, and the engravings are of the very highest order of art and taste. Another series of examples of his best work is Roscoe's 'Wanderings in North and South Wales,' which are always highly praised and valued as among the best examples of landscape art in the engravers' hands. He was active in all art work, and in helping to found and assist societies; and he was, in fact, the father of the Birmingham and, to a large extent, of the later English School. Three of his sons followed his example, two as engravers, and one is still known as a landscape-painter of extensive fame.

Willmore, J. T. (1801-1863), was born at Handsworth-juxta-Birmingham, and was a pupil of Radclyffe. He is recognised as 'one of the most eminent landscape engravers of the English School, an excellent draughtsman, a true artist in feeling, and possessing the rarest executive skill.' His chief successes were his illustrations of Turner's works, such as 'The Fighting *Téméraire*,' 'The Golden Bough,' 'Ancient Italy,' and others in Turner's 'Rivers of France.' His 'Byron's Dream,' after Eastlake; 'Tilbury Fort,' after Calcott; 'Wind against Tide,' after Stanfield, are well-known examples of his genius and skill. In 1843 he was elected an Associate of the Royal Academy, a distinction which his long series of brilliant works well deserved.

Wyon, Thomas, jun. (1792-1817), was the son of Thomas Wyon, the chief engraver of 'his Majesty's seals,' and was born in Birmingham. His father's fame and the European reputation of the art of medalling, which was so brilliantly accomplished by Matthew Boulton and his artistic workers at Soho, helped to guide young Wyon to the pursuits which were to secure him so high a place. When he was fourteen he was apprenticed to his father, and he began to engrave on steel. He won prizes at the Royal Academy School, and in 1809 his first medal was finished and his fame was secured. In 1801 he received an appointment at the Royal Mint, and was engaged on coins and tokens, but he found time for larger and more important works. In 1816 he brought out the new silver coinage, but he was not responsible for the portrait, as he had to follow a copy, but the 'reverse' was left to his own taste and skill. In 1817 he struck the Maunday silver coins, the penny, twopenny, threepenny, and fourpenny pieces. In the same year he executed the Waterloo medal, which he had to engrave twice, as the first was considered to be too large. His last work was the medal on the opening of Waterloo Bridge, which was considered to be one of his best works. As he died when he was only twenty-five, the number and excellence of his works—really within nine years—show how thoroughly he had mastered the details of his art and how industriously he had laboured over his numerous productions. Symptoms of consumption had appeared, and although he sought rest and relaxation, he died in September, 1817, at Hastings, and was buried in the graveyard of Christ Church, Southwark.

AUTHORS.—Among the pleasant recollections of authors connected with Warwickshire *Joseph Addison* perhaps deserves first mention. He was not born in the county, and only part of his life was spent within its boundaries, but it was for some years his home. Soon after his marriage, in 1716, with the widow of Edward Rich, sixth Earl of Warwick, he bought the manor of Bilton, near Rugby, and at Bilton Hall he passed a few peaceful years. The gardens were very beautiful, and a long walk of fine Spanish chestnuts was planted by Addison himself, and they grew and flourished till after the death of his daughter in 1797. Since that date the house and grounds have known many changes, but Addison's Walk still preserves the memory of 'Mr. Spectator,' and his retirement from busy London to the scenes of rural life.

Thomas Carte, the historian (1686-1754), was born at Clifton-on-Dunsmore, near Rugby, and was educated at the school, since so famous. On the accession of George I. he refused to take the Coronation Oath, in 1715 he joined in the Rebellion, in 1722 he was again in danger, and fled to France. He returned to England (1728-1730), and soon after commenced his 'History of England,' in three folio volumes, and the fourth appeared after his death. His contemporaries called him the 'historian of facts,' and he certainly spared no pains in his researches.

Edward Cave (1691-1754) has long been a familiar name as the early friend of Samuel Johnson and the founder of the *Gentleman's Magazine*. He was born at Cave's Inn, near Churchover, and when nine years old was sent to Rugby School. A petty dispute and a harsh master caused him to leave the school, and on reaching manhood he became a clerk of Excise, but soon after went to London, where he bound himself as apprentice to a printer. At the end of his term he became a clerk in the post-office, and held a responsible place as clerk of the franks, in which office he discovered some abuses, and he was cited before the House of Commons, where he refused to break his oath of secrecy, and was discharged. His office enabled him to procure many country newspapers, and he supplied a London paper with news for a guinea a week. He earned some money as a 'printer's reader,' and in 1731 he started under the name of 'Sylvanus Urban' the *Gentleman's Magazine*, from St. John's Gate. Six years later Samuel Johnson began to contribute, and the fame of the magazine grew rapidly, and continued for nearly one hundred and thirty-six years. His association with Johnson was honourable to both, and Johnson's sketch of the life and work of his friend is a fine example of excellent biography—clear, vigorous, candid, and sincere.

Henry Francis Cary (1772-1844) has won a more permanent place in English literature than his studies and pursuits were likely to secure. He was born at Gibraltar, and in 1783 he was sent to Rugby, went two years after to the Grammar School of Sutton, and afterwards to that of Birmingham. He was a diligent and careful student, and made rapid progress. In 1788 he published a volume of 'Sonnets,' and before he was out of his 'teens' he had carefully studied French and Italian, as well as the classical tongues. He took his M.A. degree at Christ Church in 1796, and was forthwith ordained, and soon after became Vicar of Abbot's Bromley, Staffordshire, where he began his brilliant and famous translation of 'Dante,' which he finished at Kingsbury, Warwickshire, in 1812. His translation and annotations are even now, when so many have been made by more eminent authors, among the best in the language, and certainly have been most generally popular and most widely read. As Vicar of Kingsbury his stipend was but small, but he had ample leisure for his favourite studies, and he did much excellent work. In 1810 he removed to London, and from 1825 to 1836 he found welcome work and congenial pursuits as Assistant-Keeper of Printed Books at the British Museum. He was a friend of Charles Lamb, Hazlitt, De Quincey, and Carlyle, and he had the final honour of burial in Westminster Abbey by the side of Samuel Johnson.

'*Eliot, George*' (*née* Mary Ann Evans), was born at Arbury Farm, near Nuneaton, on November 22, 1819. In 1820 her father removed to Griff, where he was agent to the Newdegate estates of Arbury, near which her early life was passed. He was famous for his physical strength, energy, and skill, and his character is sketched in Adam Bede and Caleb Garth of his daughter's novels. His second wife was the original of Mrs. Poyser in 'Adam

Bede.' Mary Ann was at school at Attleburgh, and afterwards at Nuneaton and Coventry, but was not remarkable for studious tastes till she devoted herself to reading Bunyan, Dr. Johnson, Charles Lamb, and Sir Walter Scott. In 1832 she showed a great love of music, which was the solace of her quiet life. After her mother's death she managed her father's house, held very 'Evangelical views' of the stricter sort, learned Italian and German, and read Greek and Latin with the master of the Coventry school. She even doubted if it was lawful to use music except in strict worship, but showed much practical piety in forming clothing clubs, and in other charitable works. Her aunt Elizabeth was a Methodist preacher, and from her came a story which developed into 'Adam Bede,' and her aunt was the original of Dinah Morris. She wrote some religious poems, and firmly held the orthodox faith till her father's removal to Foleshill, near Coventry, where she became a constant visitor and life-long friend of the late Charles Bray, of Coventry, who married the sister of Charles Hennell, whose 'Inquiry into the Origin of Christianity' was read by Mary Ann Evans, and which slowly altered her religious convictions and led her to form far wider views of the history of theological growth. On one of her many visits to the Brays she met Miss Brabant, who had undertaken the translation of Strauss's 'Leben Jesu' at the suggestion of Joseph Parkes, of Birmingham, and Charles Hennell, who had married Miss Brabant. The translation was left to Mary Ann Evans, and was her first work. Her health was feeble, but she persevered, and the book was issued in 1846. After some time at Geneva in the house of M. d'Albert she lived for some months with the Brays, and in 1850 she began as a contributor to the *Westminster Review*, afterwards assistant editor, and lived with John Chapman and his family in London. Her first work with her name was Feuerbach's 'Essence of Christianity,' in 1854. Her interest in Auguste Comte led her to friendships with Herbert Spencer, J. S. Mill, Harriet Martineau, and G. H. Lewes, with whom in 1854 she lived (in Mr. Leslie Stephen's words) in the 'connection which she always regarded as a marriage, though without the legal sanction.' In 1854 they went to Weimar and Berlin, and met many German celebrities, and they returned to England in 1855, where she continued her work for reviews and magazines. At Berlin she had read to Lewes 'a fragment of a description of a Staffordshire farmhouse,' in which Lewes saw so much dramatic power that he urged her to try a novel, and the first part of 'Amos Barton' appeared in *Blackwood's Magazine* in January, 1857, followed by 'Mr. Gilfil's Love-Story,' 'Janet's Repentance,' 'Adam Bede,' and 'Scenes from Clerical Life.' Warwickshire readers who knew the neighbourhood of Nuneaton had no doubt about the real 'George Eliot' from the numerous local descriptions of persons and places. Arbury Hall was the 'Cheverel Manor,' and Mrs. Poyser's 'farmhouse' near Corley remains unchanged, with its two griffins on the gate-posts, its clipped yews on the lawn, and its double row of walnut-trees behind. Astley Church and the moated castle were identified as 'Knebley Church,' 'Milby' with Nuneaton, and Chilvers Coton with 'Shepperton.' 'Milby' was the corn-mill at Nuneaton, the 'Red Lion' in the same town is the Bull Hotel, and 'Orchard Street' is Church Street. 'Paddiford Common' is Stockingford; and 'Silas Marner,' 'Felix Holt,' and 'Middlemarch' all owe most of their local colour as to persons and places from the neighbourhood of Nuneaton, which is especially 'George Eliot's Country,' with the impressions, indelible and graphic, of her early life. It is curious that Coventry contributed so little, but she saw it later in life; and her tastes and feelings were more with people and incidents rather than old city life and scenes. 'Rufus Lyon,' however, in 'Felix Holt' is well remembered as a local worthy, and 'Esther Lyon' is largely an autobiographic portrait. The election riot was a scene in Coventry in 1832, which Mary Ann Evans saw when a girl of thirteen, and which evidently made a permanent impression, for she reproduced nearly every detail. The larger number of her characters and her first three stories were of Warwickshire origin, and only those who knew the people or are familiar with the scenes can realize the graphic skill and dramatic power of her artistic realism. Her later life was romantic in one incident, for in 1867 Herbert Spencer had introduced 'George Eliot' to Mrs. Cross and her son; and in 1869 they met in Rome; also after the death of Lewes in 1878; and in 1880 she was married to Mr. J. W. Cross in May. After a Continental tour they returned to London, and on December 18 of the same year 'George Eliot' died at Cheyne Walk, Chelsea. Mr. Leslie Stephen ('Dict. Nat. Biog.,' s.v.) 'Cross,' thus briefly sums up her character and work :

'Where the philosophic reflectiveness widens her horizon and strengthens her insight, without prompting to excessive didacticism, her novels stand in the very first rank. In her own peculiar province no contemporary equalled or approached her power and charm; while even the comparative failures reveal a mind of extraordinary grasp and perceptive faculty.'

William Field (*Rev.*), of Warwick (1768-1851), was an author of marked ability, and especially as an historian. His mother was one of the last two lineal descendants of Cromwell who bore the name. He was a Dissenter as to training and convictions, and in 1789 he became pastor of the Unitarian Church at Warwick, and occupied the pulpit for fifty-four years. He was a friend of Dr. Priestley (during his residence in Birmingham, 1780-1791), till his departure from England, and Priestley had conducted the ordination services of the young minister (Dr. Parr, of Hatton, being present as a spectator of the ceremonial), and ever afterwards was on most friendly terms with his young neighbour, whom he described as 'a dwarf in stature, but a giant in literature.' In his later years Field was one of the founders of the Public Library at Warwick, and although an earnest and eloquent controversialist, he lived in peace with the clergy of the neighbourhood. His principal literary works were 'The History of the Town and Castle of Warwick' (1815) and 'Memoirs of the Life of Dr. Parr' (1826), in both of which elaborate research, patient care, and untiring industry were shown. 'The History of Warwick Town and Castle' has not been superseded, and is accurate and authoritative, and 'The Life of Dr. Parr' is a worthy and faithful summary of the general learning, and classical knowledge, and social life of the famous Greek scholar and Vicar of Hatton.

Mary Anne Galton, afterwards Mrs. Schimmelpenninck (1778-1856), was the daughter of Samuel Galton, F.R.S., and was born in Birmingham, where the family had come from Dorsetshire and Somersetshire about 1730. They were members of the Society of Friends, and Miss Galton belonged to the same society till some years before her death. The social position of her family and their scientific and literary tastes attracted the principal scientific and literary celebrities of the time, and these influences soon developed and matured a more than ordinary mind. In 1806 she married Mr. Schimmelpenninck, a Dutch merchant, of Bristol, who died in 1840. Her early life and surroundings led to very liberal and tolerant opinions as to the search for truth in theology and politics, and she was for some time a Methodist and afterwards a Moravian. Her several works show how varied were her tastes, and all of them are marked by originality and independence, and no little taste and skill. They were,' Memoirs of Port Royal,' 3 vols. (1826), 'Theory of the Classification of Beauty and Deformity' (1815), and essays on 'The Temperaments,' and on 'Gothic and Grecian Architecture,' etc. (1820). The details of her life and of the literary, scientific, and famous public men she knew are singularly interesting, and Hankin's 'Life' of her is a curiously vigorous and valuable record of facts not obtainable elsewhere.

Philemon Holland (1551-1636) is one of the worthies of Warwickshire whose name and fame have long been known. He was facetiously called by Fuller the 'Translator Generall,' from his numerous works of that class. Although born at Chelmsford in 1551, he became a citizen of Coventry in 1612, and was a 'sworn freeman'; and on the visit of James I. in 1617 he was chosen by the recorder to address the king, which he did in a long and elaborate speech, and in 'a suit of black satin, the cost of which was £11 1s. 11d.' In 1628, at the age of 77, he was appointed headmaster of the Free School at Coventry, where he had been usher for twenty years. Like many of the clergy of his time, he studied medicine, and graduated M.D. at Cambridge. He held his appointment less than a year, when age and infirmity obliged him to resign. His last years were passed in poverty and distress; but he was highly esteemed, and the Common Council Book of 1632, October 23, records:

'Forasmuch as Dr. Holland, by reason of his age, is now growne weake and decaied in his estate, and being a man of good deserts in respect of the abilities wherewith God hath endowed him: this house, taking him into consideracon, are pleased and agreed that there shall be three pounds six shillings and eight pence given him from henceforth on the 24th October for three yeres, if he shall so long live.'

And as he had also 'some benevolence' from his old University, he probably was not allowed to starve. He died in 1636, and was buried in Holy Trinity Church, where a monumental slab with a quaint and quibbling Latin inscription, composed by himself, records his memory. Among his many works were a translation of Camden's 'Britannia,' with additions 'not found in the original'; Plutarch's 'Morals'; Xenophon's 'Cyropædia'; Pliny's 'Natural History'; Suetonius, and Livy, in which last-named he took great pride, as the whole was written with one pen, concerning which he wrote the lines:

The Holyoke Family.

'With one sole pen I wrote this book,
Made of a grey goose-quill ;
A pen it was when it I took,
A pen I leave it still.'

'This monumental pen,' says Fuller, 'he solemnly kept, and showed to my reverend tutor, Dr. Samuel Ward. It seems he leaned very lightly on the nib thereof, though weightily enough in another sense, performing not slightly, but solidly, what he undertook.' His only surviving son (of seven), *Henry Holland,* became a bookseller in London, and was the editor of that rare and valuable collection of lives and portraits, ' Hero-ologia Anglicana '—from 1509 to 1620—a series of sixty-five fine portraits, many of which have never been re-engraved nor even copied since.

The Holyoke family—three generations—are far less honoured than their works deserve. *Francis Holyoke,* who Latinized himself into ' De Sacra Quercu,' was born at Nether Whitacre, near Coleshill, in 1567. He studied at Queen's College, Oxford, and seems not to have taken a degree, but to have taught a school—first at Oxford, and afterwards in his native county, where he became Rector of Southam in 1604. In the first year of Charles I. he was elected a member of the Convocation of the Clergy, and he suffered severely in the Civil War for his devotion to the royal cause. He died in 1653, and was buried in St. Mary's Church at Warwick. His chief claim to remembrance is the Latin-English Dictionary which he compiled and published in 1606—a revised and enlarged edition of Rider's Dictionary, of which Fuller humorously says :

' This Rider did borrow (to say no worse) both his saddle and bridle from Thomas Thomatius, who, being bred Fellow of King's College in Cambridge, set forth that Dictionary known by his name ; than which Men have not a better and truer, Children no plainer and briefer. But Rider, after Thomas's death, set forth his Dictionary, the same in effect, under his own Name, the property thereof being little disguised by any Additions.'

The Holyoke Dictionary is a wonderful work for a quiet

country rector in a small place to have compiled two centuries ago, and it is curious and even useful now, although practically superseded by the countless Latin-English dictionaries of later days. It was so useful and so popular that a fourth edition was issued in 1633. Holyoke's son, *Thomas*, made many and valuable additions to his father's work, but died before its publication, and it was edited by *his* son *Charles,* and published as a folio in 1677, and dedicated to Fulke, Lord Brooke. This *Thomas Holyoke* was born at Stoneythorpe, near Southam, in 1616, and educated at Coventry and at Queen's College, Oxford, where he graduated M.A., and became chaplain of the college. When Oxford was garrisoned for the king he was captain of a foot company, chiefly of undergraduates, for which service he received the degree of D.D. at the king's express desire. For some time he practised medicine successfully in Warwickshire and until the Restoration, when he was preferred to the Rectory of Whitnash, near Leamington, and afterwards to a living in Hampshire, but he died soon after in 1675. His son, *Henry Holyoke,* was born in 1657, and probably in Warwickshire. He began life as a chorister of Magdalen College, Oxford; then became a scholar, and in 1678 took the B.A. degree, and became clerk and sub-librarian in 1676, and chaplain in 1681. In 1687 he was made headmaster of Rugby School, and held the office till his death in 1730. 'It seems to be universally maintained that he treated the boy Edward Cave with unnecessary harshness (which led to Cave's removal from the school) by habitually oppressing him with unreasonable tasks;' but, generally, he seems to have managed the school successfully, and to have increased its reputation. He died at Rugby, and was buried in St. Mary's, Warwick, where a Latin epitaph, from his own pen, commemorates his father and grandfather, as well as himself. His forty-four years of rule at Rugby were eventful, for he had only £63 6s. 8d. income for the school, and yet was the first to appoint an assistant-master, and in other ways to advance the interests of the school. He seems to have been a bachelor, for his sister Judith 'kept house,' and his will left her a legacy on the express ground that she had been 'very serviceable and seemingly kind' to the boys. An odd glimpse into the domestic arrangements of Rugby School at that time is that this master, in his will, left the 'large sum of £30 to the daughter of Widow Harris,' his 'tripe-woman,' who seems to have been a popular caterer in the days when Rugby had no playground, and probably the boys of that period (says the author of 'Public Schools') 'had only the tombstones of the churchyard for their leap-frog and hide-and-seek.'

William Hutton (1723-1814), although born in Derbyshire, was practically a Warwickshire man so far as authorship is concerned, for nearly all his long life was passed in Birmingham. His life, from his own narrative and the additions of his daughter, is too familiar to readers generally to require any details here. 'The Hutton Family,' edited by the late Llewellyn Jewitt, is a thoroughly delightful summary of facts about the men and manners of the middle of the last century, and is well worth reading from its frank and charming *naïveté* as to the incidents of Hutton's own life. The first and most important work of Hutton's pen was his 'History of Birmingham,' which he issued in 1781. If measured by the modern standard, it is scarcely to be called 'history'; but it is a most readable and amusing work. He had not the knowledge nor the leisure to look out the facts of history, and was far too ready to speculate in all sorts of etymologies of names of places. He considered himself an 'antiquary,' and yet he not only took no trouble to collect and preserve, but he confesses that he used up large quantities of the remains of the Priory at Birmingham in a cellar, although they were mostly of 'the Gothic manner.' He has even neglected to record many of the facts of his own times which would have been of the utmost interest and value now. His work is, however, full of interest, most readable, and often highly amusing from the quaintness of his style. He also wrote a 'History of Blackpool' (1788), a 'History of Derby' (1791), the 'Battle of Bosworth Field' (1788), the 'History of the Roman Wall' (1801), all being more or less historical in form, and trustworthy as far as his own knowledge would allow. Many of his miscellaneous works are also well worth reading even now, as they are full of keen observations, vigorous descriptions, quaint, but sometimes rough, humour, and out-of-the-way facts as to his travels and adventures. One of his works, the 'Court of Requests,' is original and dramatic all through. He was one of the Commissioners in the Court of Requests at Birmingham— the forerunner of our County Courts—and the court [himself] not only 'hears the causes and adjudicates,' but records its own proceedings, with descriptions of the litigants, in a most amusing style. His 'Autobiography,' with its recollections of the cruel treatment in his early days, its pictures of old customs and manners, its graphic sketches of his own failures and successes, has sometimes a pathetic, and always a most attractive, interest. He enjoyed almost unbroken health nearly to his death, at the age of ninety-two, and his industry, and intelligence, and energy will keep his memory green for many a year.

Catherine Hutton, his daughter (1756-1846), was also an author, and between 1815 and 1819 she published several novels in the regulation three-volume form—'The Miser Married,' 'Oakwood Hall,' and 'The Welsh Mountaineers' —and also contributed some sixty articles to various periodicals. One original and curious paper was her sketch of the life of her father's old friend Robert Bage (himself an author of several novels of much note in their day) to the Edinburgh edition of the 'Lives of the Novelists.' She also edited an edition (fourth, in 1819) of her father's

'History of Birmingham,' with some valuable additions, and in 1821 she compiled from general sources 'A Tour in Africa,' in three volumes—a complete and useful summary of all that was then known. Her greatest pride was, however, her large collection of autograph letters, fashion plates, costumes, etc., which she continued persistently to gather for nearly seventy years. As a history of dress —for she had not merely collected, but had annotated with names, dates, and descriptions—her collection was unique. Her holograph letters numbered more than three thousand, many of the greatest historical interest. Like her father, she retained her faculties and lively manners to the very last, and died, aged ninety, eight months after the death of her only brother, Thomas Hutton, who had collected a vast number of fine engravings, and valuable, rare and costly books.

Walter Savage Landor (1775-1864) was for many years regarded as one of the great English classics, representing the form and style of the old 'classic' authors. His works are less talked of and less read and appreciated than they were a few years since; but they are still ranked among the most scholarly productions of his day. He was born at a large house adjoining the East Gate, Warwick, where his father was an eminent physician; and in 1785 he was at Rugby School, but removed for some insubordination or other offence to the headmaster, for which he expressed his regret in his later life. At Trinity College, Cambridge, his animal spirits and recklessness again brought him into trouble, and he was rusticated for firing a gun in the quadrangle of the college, and never returned to take a degree. His erratic temperament unfitted him for the legal profession, and he went to live at Swansea and Tenby on an allowance from his father. As he had too much of the 'noble savage' in his nature to be content with civilized life, he went in 1808 to Galicia and raised a few troops at his own cost, but soon quarrelled with his superiors, and declared that, 'although willing to aid the Spanish people in the assertion of their liberties against the antagonists of Europe, he would have nothing to do with a perjurer and traitor.' After the death of his father he retained Ipsley Court, Warwickshire, and purchased Llanthony Abbey (which he once proposed to restore), and lived chiefly at Bath and Clifton. His restlessness and waywardness soon broke out again. He quarrelled with his neighbours and tenants, and in 1814 he went to live on the Continent, and commenced the work by which he is best known to the literary world, the 'Imaginary Conversations of Literary Men and Statesmen,' which was published in 1824. This work, from its dramatic vigour, fine personifications, and brilliant language (of the 'classic' style), was received with great honours, and still holds a high place in English literature; but the fashions have changed, and it has now scarcely full justice from the reading public. He returned to Bath about 1835, but in 1858 he settled in Florence, devoted his life to literature and art, became famous in the English circle, and he died there in 1864. Dr. Parr considered him one of the best Latin scholars of his time, and his poems 'Gebir' and 'Count Julian' showed brilliant powers. His irascible temper and his courteous manners, his generous instincts and his impetuous words, formed a strange mixture; and although he had the greatest contempt for social observances, he secured a large circle of life-long and admiring friends.

Mark Noble (1754-1827) has secured far more than local fame as an antiquary and historiographer. He was born in Birmingham in 1754, and was the son of a merchant, who was taught the art of writing by John Baskerville, the famous typefounder and printer, who began his life in Birmingham as a 'writing-master,' and whose slate window-slab or sign still exists, with the inscription 'Grave-Stones Cut in any of the Hands by John Baskervill, Writing-

Master,' all the letters and floriations being forecasts of the type which was 'to astonish the librarians of Europe' some years later. On the death of his father, who had left him a small fortune, Mark Noble was anxious to take holy orders, but was at last persuaded to be articled to a solicitor; and he commenced business on his own account, but thought more of literature than law, and began his 'Memoirs of the House of Cromwell,' and spent much time and travel and money in collecting materials. In 1781 he was ordained and appointed to the curacies of Baddesley Clinton and Packwood, and on the death of the incumbent he was presented to the two livings—or 'starvations,' as he called them. Having married, he took a house at Knowle, dividing his interest between his flock, his books, and a farm. During his residence at Knowle his work, the 'Cromwell Memoirs,' introduced him to the Earl of Sandwich, who invited him to visit him with a view to a new edition; and he passed much time at Hinchinbroke. His next work, the 'History of the College of Arms,' was dedicated to Lord Leicester, afterwards Marquis of Townsend, and the two noblemen induced Lord Thurlow to give Noble the rectorship of Barming in Kent, in 1786. There he lived for forty-two years, and there his later works were written. Among them were: 'Two Dissertations on the Mint and Coins of the Episcopal Palatine of Durham' (1780), 'Genealogical History of the Royal Families of Europe' (1781, and another edition in 1787), 'Historical Genealogy of the House of Steward' (1795), 'Memoirs of the House of Medici,' 'Lives of English Regicides' (1798), 'History of the College of Arms' (1805), and many other papers in *Archæologia*, etc. He had formed a fine library, and had collected a large number of MSS., many of which were sold by auction after his death at Barming in 1827, in the seventy-third year of his age; but some of the collections and manuscripts were retained by his descendants, and are probably still in private hands.

Samuel Parr, LL.D. (1747-1825), is too well known as the great Greek scholar of his time to need many descriptive details. He was born at Harrow, and was the son of an apothecary who had spent his fortune on the Young Pretender. When six years old he was at Harrow School, and was removed at fourteen to help his father in his business; but he so persistently followed his classical studies that he was entered as a student at Emmanuel College, Cambridge. He left without taking a degree, and was soon after appointed assistant-master at Harrow School. He failed to secure the headmastership at Harrow, and opened a private academy at Stanmore, but left it in 1776, and afterwards became the master of the Grammar School at Colchester, and curate of Holy Trinity Church. In 1783 he was instituted to the perpetual curacy of Hatton, near Warwick, which he held till his death in 1825. His admiration of Charles James Fox led him to many controversial pamphlets; but his works were generally classical and critical, and they were collected and published by his literary executor, Dr. Johnstone, in eight large volumes, which are quite out of fashion now. The sale of his great library excited much interest, and the catalogue is still interesting; but his voluminous works are now rarely referred to, and still more rarely read. 'Dr. Parr at Hatton' was, however, a great celebrity, famous personally and socially for very many years.

Joseph Priestley, LL.D., has been so long and so widely known as associated with Birmingham that his name may be expected in any record of Warwickshire authors. His residence in the county was, however, only brief—from 1780 to 1791; and even during that period he made none of his wonderful discoveries, nor wrote any of his important works, the principal book published during his residence in Birmingham being his 'History of the Corruptions of Christianity' (1782). He was frequently engaged in controversies of some sort even with his immediate neighbours, but he managed to live in peace and goodwill with all. Among his local friends and frequent associates were Dr. Parr (the Churchman), Rev. J. Berington (the Roman Catholic), Rev. J. Proud (the Swedenborgian), Galton (the Quaker), Watt (the Presbyterian), and 'all sorts and conditions of men.' It was only on a sort of side-issue, in which he took no part, that the digraceful riots of 1791—the cry of 'Church and King'—were supported, if not instigated, by fanatics; and the town and the age were disgraced by the destruction of Priestley's house, laboratory, books, apparatus, and records (the results of many years' researches), his life was threatened, and his neighbours' houses destroyed. Some sort of reparation has been made to his memory by the erection of a statue (celebrating the centenary of his discovery of oxygen) in the heart of the town where he lived for eleven years, and whence he was driven by political intolerance and wild mob-law.

Rous, John (died 1491), was one of the early and notable authors connected with Warwickshire, not only by birth, but by residence and work. According to Dugdale, he was descended from the Rous family of Brinklow; but Leland assigns him to the Rous family of Ragley, near Alcester. He was born at Warwick in the reign of Edward IV. (1460-1483), and received his early education there; but afterwards went to Oxford, where he greatly distinguished himself by his extensive learning. On leaving the University he became one of the chantry-priests at the still picturesque and romantic Guy's Cliff, where he wrote several of his works, one of which, the 'Chronicon de Regibus Angliæ,' has long been accepted as authoritative, and others on the history and antiquities of Warwickshire. He erected a library over the south porch of St. Mary's, Warwick, to which he bequeathed his writings; but even in Dugdale's time these had disappeared, and only a fine heraldic roll of the Earls of Warwick, in his own handwriting, with portraits and 'arms,' has been preserved, and printed, forming a very valuable record, historical, genealogical, and heraldic. Rous died at Guy's Cliff in 1491, and was buried in St. Mary's Church, Warwick. His monument, and even its site, cannot now be traced; but a brass plate records the memory of one of his relatives, 'Thomas Rous, of Rous Lench, in the county of Worcester, who died on the 9th of September, 1645.'

BISHOPS.—Warwickshire has had a larger number of prelates than is generally known, who either by birth or residence or works have been associated with the county during the past three hundred years.

John Bird, D.D. (―― 1558), was born at Coventry, and was educated as a Carmelite at Oxford, and of that order he was the Provincial, and managed its affairs from 1516 to 1519. He was appreciated as a preacher by Henry VIII., as he earnestly impugned the primacy of the Pope, and was despatched by the King to Catherine of Arragon in 1535, to persuade her to abjure the title of queen. In 1539 he was sent on an embassy to Germany with Dr. Wotton, to interview Ann of Cleves, but he afterwards signed the decree for her divorce. In 1541 he became Bishop of Chester; in 1544 he ordained Edmund Grindal, afterwards Archbishop of Canterbury; and in the reign of Mary he returned to the Roman Church, but lost his bishopric through his marriage. In 1554 Bonner appointed him his Suffragan, and gave him the Vicarage of Dunmow, Essex, where he died in obscurity in 1558. He was a thorough temporizer, and constantly engaged in State intrigues. He said in repudiating his wife, that 'he had married her against his will,' and 'for bearing with the time;' but he afterwards showed so much penitence for his sin that he seems to have softened even the heart of Bonner. He wrote several works, but none were printed.

Samuel Butler, D.D. (1774-1839), was born at Kenilworth,

was sent to Rugby, and afterwards to Cambridge, to St. John's College, where he showed great tastes for classical studies, and won honours and prizes. In 1798 he was appointed, soon after his ordination and marriage, to the headmastership of Shrewsbury School, which had long been neglected. On his arrival he found one boy, the buildings almost in ruins, and the school funds in Chancery; but his ability and energy soon raised the school to great eminence, and he remained master for thirty-eight years. In 1802 he became Vicar of Kenilworth, and in 1836 he was appointed Bishop of Lichfield and Coventry. While Archdeacon of Derby he accomplished a work which he originated, and which few have followed, for he left his successors elaborate details and careful drawings of all the churches in his archdeaconry. *O! si sic omnia!* His school life allowed him scanty leisure, but he prepared his long well-known Geography and his ancient and modern Atlases, which stood alone for many years as excellent works, and have only recently been superseded by the advance of geographical science and the improvements in the cartographic art. He governed the school with a firm but gentle hand, acquired, as he deserved, a great moral and social influence over the boys, and well deserved the esteem and honour which marked his later years.

Henry Compton, D.D. (1632-1713), was one of the Warwickshire family of Compton Wynyates—the most romantic and picturesque house in Warwickshire—where he was born in 1632. From Queen's College, Oxford, he travelled abroad, and on his return he joined the Horse Guards, but afterwards took his M.A. degree at Cambridge. In 1667 he was Master of the Hospital of St. Cross at Winchester, and after his D.D. degree became a Canon of Christ Church, and in 1674 Bishop of Oxford. Charles II. entrusted his two nieces, the Princesses Mary and Anne, to his care, and both were married by him—professionally, of course. He tried to effect a union of Protestants, and he consulted many foreign divines, but without success, and his earnest Protestant opinions caused his dismissal from the deanery of the Chapel Royal when James II. became King. He was even suspended from his bishopric by a royal mandate, and the Princess of Orange interceded in vain, till the Prince of Orange was expected in England, when the King removed the suspension, and the Bishop sided with the Prince. His first act in the Revolution was to safeguard the Princess Anne of Denmark on her way from London to Nottingham, when his old military ardour was aroused, and he laid down mitre and staff, and preceded the carriage of the Princess in 'a buff coat and jack-boots, with pistols in his holsters and a sword by his side.' The body-guard of gentlemen, who were volunteers in this escort, 'invited the Bishop to act as their colonel, and he consented with an alacrity which gave great scandal to rigid Churchmen, and did not much raise his character even in the opinion of Whigs.' After this personal service it was reasonable that the Bishop should crown William and Mary, and be 'the only prelate who accompanied William to the Hague in 1691.' He was one of the Royal Commissioners for the Revision of the Liturgy, and he laboured to reconcile Dissenters to the Church. He died in 1713, and was buried in the churchyard of Fulham, in strict accordance with his own instructions and opinion that 'the Church was for the living and the churchyard for the dead.' His literary works are not numerous, nor very important, but he translated 'The Life of Donna Olympia Maldacchini' from the Italian, also Lortie's 'Traité de la Sainte Cêne' from the French, and his 'Episcopalia' to his clergy have had life enough to be reprinted as late as 1842. He was a friend to men of letters generally; he even believed in and helped that arch-impostor, George Psalmanazar, the hero of Formosa. He kept his grounds at Fulham in excellent and tasteful order, and devoted much time to botany—especially to exotics—and Ray in his 'History of Plants' makes special reference to fifteen rare plants in Compton's garden, and Petiver engraved many specimens from the Bishop's garden.

Richard Smalbroke, D.D. (1672-1749), was born at Birmingham, where his ancestors had lived for several generations, holding much landed property, and one street still bears the family name. He was probably educated at King Edward's School, but went to Magdalen College, Oxford, and took his B.A. degree in 1682, his D.D. in 1708, and became a Fellow of the college. He was appointed Chaplain to Archbishop Tenison, and rose through Treasurer of Llandaff, and Canon Residentiary of Hereford, where he held what was called 'the golden prebend,' to be Bishop of Lichfield and Coventry in 1731. He is described as a 'prelate of the ordinary Hanoverian type, a fair scholar, and a learned, though not profound, controversialist.' He wished infidels prosecuted by law, lest, among other presumably minor evils, they should bring in popery; and in his 'Vindication of Christ's Miracles,' in answer to Woolston, he won much ridicule, by an unlucky calculation that six thousand evil spirits (a legion) to one man was mercifully exchanged for three apiece 'to each hog'; but on the whole he replied to Woolston, who had provoked the controversy, 'with very sufficient sense and considerable learning.' He wrote various sermons, some pamphlets, and episcopal charges (one of which was criticised by Warburton in 1741), died in 1749, and was buried in Lichfield Cathedral, where a monument, 'suitable apparently to the taste of the time,' was erected to his memory.

John Bird Sumner, D.D. (1780-1862), born at Kenilworth, where his father was Vicar, was not only a Bishop of eminence, but rose to Archiepiscopal rank. After some time at Eton he went to King's College, Cambridge, in 1798, and after taking his B.A. degree in 1802, he was appointed assistant master at Eton in the following year.

In 1807 he was installed as one of the 'golden' Prebends of Durham, and in 1828 the Duke of Wellington nominated him to the Bishopric of Chester, 'with the view of conciliating the Protestant party,' when the Roman Catholic emancipation contest was the subject of much strife. The first vote of the new Bishop in the House of Lords was in favour of the repeal of the Test and Corporation Acts, and of Roman Catholic emancipation, and afterwards in favour of the Reform Bill, for which he gave a silent vote. On the death of Archbishop Howley, Dr. Sumner, who had worked hard at Chester, was chosen as Archbishop of Canterbury. He was an earnest and active Archbishop and generally popular. He died at Addington, and was buried in the churchyard there in 1862.

John Vesey, alias *Harman*, D.C.L. (1452-1555), was more emphatically, both by birth and residence, a Warwickshire worthy, for he was born and died in the county, and lavished gifts upon his native town, Sutton Coldfield, during the whole of his long life. His father was William Harman, but the Bishop adopted the name of Veize or Vesey, which he seems to have held to be the orignal name of the family, although 'Harman' had been used for several generations. Thomas Fuller is more than usually facetious in his description of this famous prelate. He says:

'He was born at Sutton Colefield, educated at Oxford: a most vivacious person if the date of these remarks be seriously considered: (1) In the twentieth year of King Henry VI. he was appointed to celebrate the Divine Service in the Free Chappell of St. Blase, of Sutton aforesaid. (2) In the twenty-third year of Henry VII. he was made Vicar of Saint Michael's Church in Coventry. (3) Under King Henry VIII. he was made Dean of the Chappell, tutor to the Lady Mary, and President of Wales. (4) In the eleventh of King Henry VIII., 1519, he was advanced to be Bishop of Exeter. Which Bishoprick he destroyed, not onely shaving the hairs (with long leases), but cutting away the limbs with sales outright, in so much that Bishop Hall, his successor in that See, complaineth in print, that the following Bishops were Barons, but Bare-ones indeed. Some have confidently affirmed in my hearing that the word to *veize* (that is, in the west, to drive away with a witness) had its originall from his profligating of the lands of his Bishoprick; but I yet demurre to the truth hereof. He robbed his own Cathedrall to pay a Parish Church, Sutton, in this county [Warwick], where he was born, whereon he bestowed many benefactions, and built fifty-one houses. To inrich this his native town he brought out of Devonshire many clothiers, with desire and hope to fix the manufacture of cloathing there. All in vaine; for as Bishop Godwin observeth, "*Non omnis fert omnia tellus.*" Which, though true conjunctively, that all countrys put together bring forth all things to be mutually bartered by a reciprocation of trade, is false disjunctively, no one place affording all commodities, so that the cloathworkers here had their pains for their labour, and sold for their lost. It seems, though, he brought out of Devon-shire the fiddle and fiddle-stick; he brought not the rosen therewith to make good musick; and every country is innated with a peculiar genius, and is left-handed to those trades which are against their inclinations. He quitted his Bishoprick (not worth keeping) in the reign of Edward VI.; and no wonder that he resumed it not in the reign of Queen Mary, the bone not being worth the taking, the marrow being knocked out before. He died (being 103 years old) in the reign of Queen Mary, and was buried in his native town, with his statue mitred and vested.'

'John Harman' was elected a Fellow of Magdalen College, Oxford, in 1487, and with the same name was Vicar of St. Michael's, Coventry, in 1507. In 1509 he became Dean of Exeter and also of Windsor and Wolverhampton, in accordance with the pluralist practices of those times. He was admitted as a Brother of the Corpus Christi Gild of Coventry, and his name remained on the books till 1518, but about two years later he resigned his Coventry holdings, and was appointed Bishop of Exeter by Henry VIII., who had formed a high opinion of his business habits and general good manners. In the early years of his episcopate he passed most of his time in his diocese, but he afterwards left the care of it to 'grand vicars and coadjutor Bishops,' and incurred the censure of Latimer. In 1533 he officiated at the consecration of Cranmer, and was on the King's side in 'the Divorce of Catherine, in the supremacy, and in the Dissolution of the Monasteries.' In fact, in Mr. Colvile's words, 'the obsequious prelate went all lengths,' and 'was, in truth, a perfect courtier,' rather than a Christian Bishop. It is claimed for him that, although he certainly alienated many of the possessions of the See, he had always the 'express command and requisition of the Sovereign under the Privy Seal,' and as Mr. Colvile adds: 'Probably if he and his Chapter had been restive, and had refused to sacrifice a portion to the royal demands, the whole would have been snatched from them.' On the accession of Edward VI., Bishop Vesey was suspected of aiding or fomenting a rebellion in Devonshire against the Protestant cause, and was peremptorily ordered by the Privy Council to surrender his See to the King, which he duly did, and was allowed a pension of £495 9s. 3d. He retired to his own town and continued his benefactions. He obtained the incorporation, and Sutton became a royal town. He gave the Chase, Park and Manor in trust to the inhabitants for the use of the poor, and the sports of the field. He built two aisles to the Parish Church, gave an organ, and built the Town Hall and Market Place. He built fifty-two houses, most of which were to be rent-free to workers in woollen kersey, as made in Devonshire. He founded and endowed a Grammar School, gave a meadow for the support of poor widows, and paved the whole town; and he built two fine bridges (one of which still remains, with fragments of old buildings used up in its walls) at Water Orton and Curdworth, over the river Tame. Among other benefactions he provided, to encourage marriages, that four poor women, of good character, born or resident in Sutton, should have five pounds each on their marriage, and that sum has now risen to twenty-five pounds, and is dispensed by the Warden and Corporation every year. All the gifts did little to increase the population or the interests of the town, but greater progress has recently been made by residents from Birmingham, in the neighbourhood of the fine Sutton Park (3,500 acres), near which numerous villas have been built; and the town has recently received a Charter of Incorporation, and has now a Mayor and Corporation. The aged Bishop was restored to his See by Queen Mary, and passed two months at Exeter, but early in 1554 he returned to Moor Hall, near Sutton, where he died suddenly in 1555, at an advanced age—whether 93 or 103 is not certainly known; but the inscription on his monument states 103. He was a princely prelate, and lived and travelled in great state, his retinue being one hundred and forty men, in scarlet caps and gowns. His effigy represents him in the episcopal vestments worn before the Reformation, with the mitre and pastoral crook.

Edward Willes, D.D. (1693-1773), was another of the Warwickshire-born Bishops, and he was born at Bishop's Itchington, where his father was Rector. He entered Oriel College, Oxford; graduated B.A. in 1712, M.A. in 1715, and B. and D.D. in 1726; became Rector of Barton, Staffordshire, Prebendary of Wells, Dean of Lincoln; and in 1742 Bishop of St. David's, whence he was translated in the same year to the See of Bath and Wells, which he held for thirty years. The influence of his brother, Chief Justice Willes, doubtless helped in these promotions, but, according to Mr. Colvile, his episcopal appointment 'was mainly attributable to his tenure of the office of "Decypherer" to the King, the duties of which, though their exact nature is not known, would appear to be somewhat inconsistent with the ministerial calling.' He gained the confidence of the 'Ministry of the day by important communications and services in the secret department,' and his son was advised by Lord Chesterfield—'*Patrisare*'—to do as his father did before him. There seems to be no record of his scholarship or literary works, and his only distinction seems to be that he 'assisted Ducarel in his plan for the endowment of vicarages.' He was apparently rather a secular-minded and successful prelate. He died at his house in Hill Street,

Berkeley Square, London, and was buried with his wife in Westminster Abbey.

Some other Bishops are included in the Rev. F. L. Colvile's 'Worthies,' from which many of the facts and quotations in this summary have been borrowed, but their connections with the county are too slight, or too remote, or of too little general interest, to be introduced into this necessarily brief survey of Church 'Worthies.'

JUDGES, with Warwickshire connections, are not numerous, nor perhaps important, but three deserve some place in this record.

Sir Edmund Anderson (1530-1605) was born at Broughton, in Lincolnshire, but he was associated with Warwickshire by his purchase of Arbury, near Nuneaton, which he afterwards exchanged with the Newdigates for Moore Hall and Harefield, in Middlesex. He was a fierce Churchman, severe on Brownists and other schismatics, but he was bold enough to resist royal interference, and stood firmly on statute law. In 1586 he sat in judgment on Mary Queen of Scots. At Arbury he pulled down the house and church and built a mansion with the ruins. He entertained Elizabeth at Harefield, and was buried at Eyworth, Bedfordshire, in 1605, leaving no printed works except 'Reports.'

Sir John Willes (1685-1761) was born at Bishop's Itchington, and was educated at Lichfield and Oxford. In 1722 he was M.P. for Weymouth, and supported Walpole. In 1733 he was Attorney-General and Chief Justice of Chester, and three years later Chief Justice of the Common Pleas. His ambition and his anger made him many enemies, and he was greatly disappointed that he lost the Lord Chancellorship. He died in Bloomsbury Square, and was buried at Bishop's Itchington in 1761.

Sir John Eardley Wilmot (1709-1792) inherited an estate at Berkswell from the Marrow family, and was Chief Justice of the Common Pleas in 1766. In 1771 he retired from public life and studied medicine and antiquities, and was one of the first members of the Society of Antiquaries. He died in London, but was buried at Berkswell, where a monument records his birth and death, his official appointments, and the names of his children.

MARTYRS.—The proto-martyr of the Reformation was probably a Warwickshire man, although recent researches have thrown grave doubts on the popular story. *John Rogers* (*circa* 1509-1555) is claimed by Fuller as a native of Lancashire, but has long been regarded as a son of John Rogers of Deritend, Birmingham—a part of the town in the parish of Aston—where he is said to have been born in 1509. Colonel Chester, an excellent authority, allows that it is 'possible' that the proto-martyr was born in Deritend, but tradition and popular feeling have gone further, and a tablet has been placed on the outer wall of the present St. John's Church, Deritend, in honour of the memory of John Rogers. Whether born in Birmingham or not, Rogers does not seem to have had any special connection with the town in his later life. He graduated B.A. in 1526 from Pembroke College, Oxford. He went abroad, and was chaplain to the English merchants at Antwerp, where he met Tyndale and Coverdale, and became a Protestant; and about 1531 to 1535 he was at Wittenberg, and he is said to have had a large share in the translation of the 'Matthews' Bible, published in 1537. He was afterwards a prebend of St. Paul's, reader of Divinity lessons, and 'held for a time the Rectory of St. Margaret and the Vicarage of St. Sepulchre's, both in London. On the accession of Mary he advocated what he had taught under Edward VI., was cited and dismissed, but was afterwards examined before Gardiner, Bishop of Winchester and Lord Chancellor, and having refused a pardon if he would recant, he was burned at the stake in Smithfield.

The 'Mancetter Martyrs,' so called from their connection

with Mancetter, near Atherstone, have long been famous in the ecclesiastical records of Warwickshire. *Robert Glover* and his brother *John Glover* suffered persecution, and Robert was burned at the stake. Their family had lived at Mancetter from 1432 to 1677, and another brother, *William*, also lived at the same place. When the Mayor of Coventry had received the Bishop's warrant for the arrest of John Glover, he sent timely warning, but John and William had just left the house when the officers arrived, and forthwith arrested Robert, who was sick in bed, and who was imprisoned. John Glover afterwards returned, concealed himself in the woods, died of ague at Mancetter in 1558, and was buried in the churchyard. Six weeks afterwards, Dr. Draycott, the Chancellor of the Diocese, sent for the Vicar of Mancetter, and demanded to know why the body had been buried in the churchyard. The Vicar answered that he was ill at the time, and did not know of the burial, and he was then ordered to return home, to exhume the body, and to throw it over the wall into the highway. The Vicar protested, and was then ordered to read the curse on heretics over the grave, to take up the bones (after twelve months), and 'cast them over the wall, and then I' (the Chancellor) 'will come and hallow again the place where he was buried.' *William Glover* sought safety at Wem, Shropshire, and died there soon after his brother. His principles were known, and the Bishop who had condemned Robert to the flames forbade the rite of burial to William, and his body was drawn by a horse into a field and buried.

Robert Glover (*circa* 1513-1555) was born at Mancetter, and in 1533 he was elected from Eton to King's College, Cambridge, and became B.A. in 1538 and M.A. in 1541. He returned to Warwickshire, and led a quiet and studious life; receiving instruction from Bishop Latimer (whose niece he had married) and who sometimes sought and found retirement at Merevale Abbey and at Baxterley

Hall, then secluded places in the Forest of Arden. When apprehended in place of his brother John, he was first taken to Coventry, removed on horseback to Lichfield, where he 'inned at the sign of the Swan,' but after supper was removed to the 'church-prison, where he was confined in a dark, narrow room, adjoining the dungeon, with straw instead of a bed, and allowed no chair, stool, or anything else to sit on.' Soon after he was taken to Coventry, and burned with one Cornelius Bongey, a capper, 'without the city, at a place called "The Hollows," on September 14th, 1555, and on the 16th of the same month his friend and pastor, Bishop Latimer, was burned at Oxford in the eighty-fifth year of his age. A friend and fellow-martyr, *Mrs. Joyce* (or *Jocasta*) *Lewis*, also lived at Mancetter. She was a Roman Catholic, like her husband, but was converted by the arguments of John Glover, her neighbour, and clung steadfastly to the Protestant faith. On the delivery of the Bishop's citation, her husband held a dagger to the officer's throat, and compelled him to swallow the writ, and then sent him away. A month's respite was allowed, but she resisted all arguments of her husband, and she was taken to prison, brought up several times for examination, and was condemned to the stake, but twelve months passed because the Sheriff was unwilling to put her to death during his year of office. She was burned at Lichfield in December, 1557. A memorial tablet to the two martyrs was placed in the church at Mancetter in 1833. Full details of the lives and death of these 'Mancetter Martyrs' are given in Foxe's 'Acts and Monuments,' in Riding's 'Mancetter Martyrs,' and in other works, as revelations of the barbarities of those troublous times. Another Warwickshire martyr was *Julius Palmer*, the son of a Mayor of Coventry, who was educated at the school of Magdalen College, Oxford, Fellow of the college in 1549, B.A. in 1547, Reader in Logic in 1550. His 'heretical' opinions were so clearly shown that he was expelled before the reign of Edward VI. had closed ; but his devotion to the Roman Catholic faith, soon after the accession of Mary, restored him to his Fellowship. The study of Calvin's 'Institutes' and the witnessing personally of the heroic faith of Ridley and Latimer, when burned at Oxford, led to a great change. He renounced Romanism, went to the Grammar School at Reading, afterwards to Evesham to ask his mother's blessing, but was repulsed with maledictions, was seized and imprisoned, hung up by hands and feet in the stocks for ten days, refused the high preferment promised, if he would recant, and was burned at Reading in 1562.

PHYSICIANS.—Many men of far more than merely local fame have been associated with Warwickshire, and some have been so illustrious as to deserve fuller notices than the limits of this record will allow.

John Ash, *M.D.* (1723-1798), was born at Coventry in 1723, and educated at Trinity College, Oxford. He settled at Birmingham, and soon became the chief physician of the town and neighbourhood. He was the founder of the General Hospital in Birmingham (1765), and he built a large house, which has given its name to the neighbourhood—Ashsted—which was transformed into St. James's Chapel. In 1787 he removed to London, and was elected F.R.C.P., and he won all the high honours of his profession in his day. It is reported of him that when he found his brain seemed to be affected by his numerous and arduous professional duties, he recovered by intense devotion to mathematics. In his retirement he wrote a valuable work on the waters of Aix-la-Chapelle and Spa, with full discussions of the discoveries of Cavendish, Priestley, Bergman and Lavoisier. His personal appearance has long been familiar through a life-size, full-length portrait by Reynolds—one of his finest works—engraved by Bartolozzi in 1761. His nephew, *Edward Ash, F.R.S.* (1770-1829), was born in Birmingham, was M.D. of Oxford in

1796, Physician-extraordinary to the King, and his large fortune and leisure enabled him to devote much energy and knowledge to literary and scientific pursuits.

James Cooke (died 1688) was, during all his later life, a resident at Warwick as a 'practitioner in physick and chirurgery,' and was successful and popular all round Warwick for many years. His principal claim to fame and honour, and to a record here, is that he had the good fortune to find some of the fast-perishing records relating to Stratford-on-Avon in the days of Shakespeare. Soon after the death of John Hall, M.D., the son-in-law of Shakespeare, James Cooke was surgeon to a detachment stationed near Stratford Bridge in the Civil War days. He was invited to see Mistress Hall (Shakespeare's daughter Susannah), and he gives the following account of his interview: ' Being, in my art, an attendent to parts of some regiments to keep the pass at the Bridge of Stratford-on-Avon, there being then with me a mate allyed to the gentleman that writ the following observations in Latin, he invited me to the house of Mrs. Hall, wife to the deceased, to see the books left by Mr. Hall. After the view of them, she told me she had some books left, by one that professed physick, with her husband for some money. I told her, if I liked them, I would give her the money again. She brought them forth, among which was this, with another of the author's, both intended for the presse. I, being acquainted with Mr. Hall's hand, told her that one or two of them were her husband's, and showed them to her. She denyed; I affirmed, till I perceived she began to be offended. At last I returned her the money.' The manuscript is written in a neat hand and in Latin, and Cooke published a translation of it into English under the title of ' Select Observations of English Bodies; or, Cures both Empiricall and Historicall performed upon very Eminent Persons in Desperate Diseases. First written in Latin by Mr. John Hall, physician, living at Stratford-on-Avon in Warwickshire, where he was very famous, as also in the counties adjacent, as appeares by these Observations, drawn out of severall hundreds of his choicest.' The importance and interest of this case-book, so remarkably saved from loss, can scarcely be overstated, and Cooke deserves all praise. Unfortunately there is no reference to the death of Shakespeare, nor even to his last illness, but the little volume is full of quaint and curious facts, professionally and popularly readable. Cooke also published 'Mellificium Chirurgiæ; or, The Marrow of Chirurgy' (1662), and dedicated to Lord Brooke; and a later edition with a chapter on anatomy; and another work entitled the 'Marrow of Physic.' Cooke died in 1688, and was buried in St. Mary's, Warwick.

Nehemiah Grew, M.D. (1644-1712), was born at Atherstone, and probably educated at Pembroke College, Cambridge, where, at any rate, someone of his name was B.A. in 1661. He received his professional instruction abroad, and on his return to England with a doctor's degree he settled at Coventry, where he wrote his 'Anatomy of Plants,' or at least the first part, which he dedicated to Dr. Wilkins, Bishop of Chester. In 1672 he removed to London and was elected F.R.S., and on the death of the secretary in 1677 he was appointed his successor, and devoted the larger part of his life to the work. He pre-prepared a 'Catalogue of the Natural and Artificial Rarities' in 1681, was elected honorary member of the College of Physicians in 1680, and he died in 1712. He had formed a fine library—divinity, medicine and history—but his chief work was given to the Royal Society. He published several works, learned and popular in his own time, and valued even now, such as the 'Anatomy of Vegetables,' the 'Physiological History of Plants,' 'Cosmologia Sacra; or, A Discourse of the Universe as the Creature and Kingdom of God,' and other works of minor importance, but all showing much acute observation, wide research, minute industry, and remarkable power of description.

John Hall, *M.D.* (*circa* 1575-1635), as the son-in-law of Shakespeare would be sure of some recognition and some fame, while his knowledge as a physician and his large practice in the Midland counties gave him many means of observation, which unfortunately he only partially used. He might have saved the world endless speculations if he had left only a few notes on Shakespeare's life at Stratford after his retirement from the stage. He might have gratified a reasonable world-wide curiosity if his case-book had contained only a few words on the poet's latter days, illness and death. He might have ensured for posterity a few scraps of Shakespeare's handwriting and a few notes on his private life and personal friends. He seems to have done his best to honour the poet's memory by the bust and the epitaph, but he should have done more, and have spared the present generation the endless wrangles about doubtful 'facts.' John Hall seems to have settled in Stratford early in the seventeenth century as a physician, and in 1607 he married Shakespeare's daughter Susannah, then in her twenty-fifth year. In 1617 he was chosen a member of the Corporation of Stratford, but he declined to serve. In 1623 he was chosen Chief Burgess, but was again excused. In 1632 he accepted office, but in 1633 he was displaced, and seems not to have been on good terms with the Corporation. On the coronation of Charles I., and having sufficient property and income, he paid a fine of ten pounds *not* to be dubbed a knight! He died somewhat suddenly in 1635, and left his books and manuscripts to his son-in-law Nash, and all trace of them has long ago been lost. Dr. Hall was a zealous Protestant, and apparently held Puritanical opinions, as some of the other members of the Shakespeare family did, so, possibly, the papers and plays of the great poet may have been deliberately destroyed. As a physician, however, he commanded respect, and was evidently a man of great ability. Dr. Bird, the Linacre Professor, speaking of him in 1657, said: 'And this I take to be a great sign of his ability, that such who spare not for cost, and they who have more than ordinary understanding, nay, such as hated him for his religion, often made use of him.' His only literary work —that entirely professional—has already been mentioned (*s.v.* Cooke, p. 177), and its entries do not begin till 1616, the year of Shakespeare's death. Dr. Hall was evidently a prominent person in Stratford life for more than fifty years, and could have recorded, if he had kept a diary of general, as well as of professional, facts, a record which would have enriched English history. He lies buried with his wife and their daughter, and Shakespeare and his wife, in the chancel of Stratford Church.

Edmund Hector, M.D. (1709-1794), was born at Lichfield in the same year as Samuel Johnson, and they were schoolfellows, between whom an unclouded friendship existed till Johnson died in 1784. Hector was honoured by his friend, who always spoke of him and wrote to him in the kindest words. He said of him: 'We passed through the school together; we have always loved one another.' Hector removed to Birmingham in early life, and began to establish himself as a physician. He lived with Thomas Warren in an old half-timber house, where Johnson was his guest for six months. Warren was the printer of the first newspaper in Birmingham, of which only one solitary copy has survived; and as it has some Johnsonian sentences, there is little reason to doubt that Johnson assisted Warren, who certainly gave him his first commission to translate the 'Travels of Father Lobo in Abyssinia' from the French. The indolence of Johnson 'stopped the press,' and Hector at last wrote down the words from Johnson's dictation as he lay abed. Hector began to prosper, and afterwards occupied a large house in the 'Old Square,' where Johnson was often a guest in later years. Boswell has left a graphic sketch of his visit with Johnson to Hector's house. Hector survived Johnson ten years, and died on the 2nd of September, 1794. He was a true friend to Johnson when friends were few, and he greatly helped him in his early struggles. Very few of the friendships of history are more pathetic and more honourable than that of Johnson and Hector for nearly seventy years.

Edward Johnstone, M.D. (1757-1851), was the third son of Dr. James Johnstone, of Worcester, the friend of Pope and Thomson, and of George, Lord Lyttelton of Hagley, of whom he wrote an excellent biography; and he was also famous for the use of muriatic acid fumes in arresting the progress of contagion. Edward became M.D. of Edinburgh, and settled in Birmingham, where he soon became the first physician of the Midland counties. He was much younger than his contemporaries Ash and Withering, but he succeeded them at a very early age. He served the General Hospital for twenty-two years, and acquired the highest professional and social position. He retired early, and enjoyed a ripe old age at Edgbaston Hall. His principal works were on puerperal fever and hydrophobia. He died at the great age of ninety-four, in 1851.

John Johnstone, M.D. (1767-1836), his brother, also held a high position as a Fellow of the College of Physicians and of the Royal Society, and as physician to the General Hospital for thirty-two years. He was not only professionally famous, but scientifically too. He was a personal friend of Dr. Parr, whose life and works he wrote and edited—a monument of industry and learning, of great historic value, but now neglected, except by the few students who have taste and time for the elaborate records of learning which were fashionable sixty or seventy years ago. His works on 'Mineral Poisons,' on 'Medical Jurisprudence,' and on 'Madness: hereditary and partial,' are excellent proofs of his skill and knowledge. He died near Birmingham in 1836, aged sixty-nine.

Richard Pearson, M.D. (1765-1836), was born in Birmingham, and was a brother of Thomas Aris Pearson, proprietor and editor of *Aris's Birmingham Gazette*. He received his early education at the Grammar School, Sutton Coldfield, and afterwards at Chiswick. He graduated as M.D. at Edinburgh in 1796, and then travelled for two years in Germany, France, and Italy with Mr. Knox, afterwards Lord Northland, and then settled in his native town in 1792, succeeding Dr. Withering as physician to the General Hospital till 1801, when he removed to London. After some years in London and Reading and Sutton he returned to Birmingham, where, with Mr Sands Cox, he assisted in the foundation of the Medical School, which finally expanded into the Queen's College, chiefly through the munificent gifts of the late Dr. Warneford. Dr. Pearson was a ready and prolific writer. He wrote many reviews in the *British Critic.* He contributed many articles to 'Rees's Cyclopædia.' He was the associate of Dr. Shaw and Dr. Hutton in the 'Abridgments of the Philosophical Transactions.' He gave special study (after his master, Dr. Cullen) to the analysis and classification of drugs, and his researches resulted in an important work, long regarded as authoritative, in 1808. He died in Birmingham in 1836, and was buried in the graveyard of St. Paul's, in his native town.

William Withering, M.D. (1741-1799), was not merely a local worthy, but a man of science, whose studies and researches and writings have secured him fame wherever the science of botany is known. He was born at Wellington, Shropshire, and was chiefly educated by the Rev. Henry Wood, of Ercall. At Edinburgh he took his M.D. degree in 1766, and afterwards became a Fellow of the Royal and of the Linnæan Societies. His first professional work was at Stafford, where the banks of the

Trent, the North Stafford hills, and the vast area of the wildest untrodden parts of Cannock Chase, gave him the fullest opportunities of studying his favourite science of botany, and of collecting the mass of material for his future famous work. In 1775 he removed to Birmingham, where a professional career seemed open to him by the death of Dr. Small, the life-long friend of Matthew Boulton, of Soho. The venture proved to be a great success; and on the retirement of Dr. Ash the practice of Dr. Withering increased, till it surpassed, or at least equalled, that of any physician in the country. In 1786 he went to live at the largest house near Birmingham, Edgbaston Hall, where the second edition of his 'Botany' was completed. The fine park and pool and rookery, his Newfoundland dogs, his herd of French cattle, afforded him continual relaxations among his heavy professional work, and his ever-delicate health was greatly benefited. In 1791, however, a storm-cloud burst over his prospects and peaceful pursuits. The terrible four days' riots of that year, when a furious mob held possession of the town, and wrecked and burned some of the best houses, unchecked by public opinion or by main force, threatened his house, although he had taken no part in political matters, and was himself a 'good Churchman.' He was obliged to leave his home, as an attack was threatened, and to hide his books and specimens in hay and to hurry them away; but fortunately the forced march of soldiers from Nottingham alarmed the rioters, and Edgbaston Hall was spared. Curiously enough, Dr. Withering afterwards removed to Fair Hill, Dr. Priestley's house, which had been wrecked at the same riots, and all its countless treasures—the apparatus, the notes and experiments of years—ruthlessly destroyed. Dr. Withering's few leisure hours were fully and methodically employed. He was one of the pleasant company of men of science whose presence irradiated Birmingham's social life. He was the friend of Boulton, Watt, Priestley,

Keir, Murdoch, Darwin, Day, Edgeworth, Galton, Banks, Smeaton, and many others who were resident-members or visitors of the famous Lunar Society, so called because its meetings were held so as to enable the members to have a moonlight ride home after dinner at each other's houses—all round Birmingham—where philosophical questions had been discussed. His own house, like that of Boulton at Soho, was the guest-house of all distinguished, and especially of foreign, visitors. A long-standing and serious malady of the lungs greatly limited his work, and he spent two winters at Lisbon, where, true to his studies, he analyzed and described the hot mineral waters at Caldas da Reinha, and published the results in the 'Transactions of the Lisbon Academy,' and afterwards in the 'Philosophical Transactions.' His physical weakness never impaired his intellectual vigour, nor repressed his ardour of research. He was slowly dying of consumption, and all hope of recovery was fading. It was gracefully said of him, 'The flower of physicians is indeed Withering.' He died in his own house in Birmingham in 1799, honoured by all who knew his works, and mourned by those who knew all of his gentle and genial life and devotion to science. He was buried in Edgbaston Church, near to the hall and park where some of his happiest days had been passed, and six of his own servants bore his body to the grave. He left a valuable library to his son, and his works have won him universal fame, from his 'British Plants' (1776)—through numerous editions—down to his 'Foxglove' and 'Scarlet Fever' treatises, and his name is preserved in botany by 'Witheringia' for a *genus* of American plants, and in chemistry by 'Witherite,' the native carbonate of barytes, which he first discovered. The two volumes of his 'Life and Correspondence' are highly interesting, and far too rarely read.

Francis Willughby, F.R.S. (1635-1672), was born at Middleton, near Kingsbury, and was in 1653 entered as a

Fellow Commoner at Trinity College, Cambridge, where he first met the celebrated botanist John Ray, who became his friend in life, and his biographer when he died. In 1661 the two friends made an excursion through the northern counties to Scotland, and in the following year to the south-western counties of England—accounts of which are given in Ray's 'Itinerarium.' The journeys were not merely pleasant excursions, but careful surveys, not only of Natural History, but whatever of science or art was to be found. In 1663 another journey, and with a larger party, was made to several parts of Europe, which Willughby extended, alone, to Spain. Unfortunately, the written records were lost, but most of the specimens collected have been preserved at Wollaton. In 1665 another 'Itinerary' was undertaken to the western and south-western counties, and with equal or even greater care. In 1665 Willughby succeeded, on the death of his father, to the Middleton and Wollaton estates—at one or other of which he lived till his death in 1672. He prepared a paper for the Royal Society on his scientific researches into the nature of vegetation in 1669; but his great work on 'Ornithology' was edited and published only after his death by his good friend Ray in 1678, and gained for him the title of the 'Father of British Natural History'—the first scientific treatise and the basis of the Linnæan system. No more honourable and blameless, no more modest or useful life has ever deserved the loving memory in which Ray held his worthy friend—a genuine Warwickshire worthy of the rarest type.

POETS.—Ben Jonson classified those who are recognised as poets under four great headings, poetaccios (or great poets), poets, poetasters, and poetitos. Warwickshire has produced some of all these four classes, and certainly two who are deservedly ranked among the great poets of their own times, and one of them as the 'poet of all time'— Michael Drayton and William Shakespeare. All that the space of this record allows must be limited to the chief outlines of their lives as connected with Warwickshire, and to references to the character of their works. Both were born in Warwickshire, and lived in the county for many years, so that they are both emphatically 'Warwickshire worthies,' of whom the county has good reason to be proud.

Michael Drayton (1563-1631) was born at Hartshill, near Atherstone, but belonged to a Leicestershire family, and in his early days was a page to Sir Henry Goodeve, of Polesworth; but he seems to have been 'nobly bred and well ally'd.' He was remarkable in his boyhood for his good looks, modesty and pleasant temper. He is not proved, but is supposed, to have been sent to Oxford by his patron, Goodeve, whose kindness he acknowledges, and who introduced him to Lucy, Countess of Bedford, sister to Sir John Harrington, of Combe Abbey. He was also a close friend of Sir Aston Cokain, of Polesworth, and of Sir Walter Aston, to whom, 'in the spring of his acquaintance,' he dedicated his 'Barons' Wars.' His connection with such persons is a sufficient proof that he was no mere courtier, but a man of scholarly attainments and refined tastes, and this is more fully proved by his earliest works. Little else is known of his personal or local life, except that, before he left Warwickshire for London, he had paid his addresses to a Coventry-born lady, who lived near the river Anker, and in 1594 he published fifty-one sonnets under the title 'Idea's Mirrour: Amours in Quatorzains' —the lady being 'Idea,' and receiving his homage for many years, although she never became his wife. In his 'Collection,' in 1609, he had 'A Hymn to my Lady's Birthplace,' and one magnificent sonnet, 'Since there's no help, come let us kiss and part.' All these early poems were in the Petrarchian style, but in robust and brilliant English. His adoration of his lady lasted thirty years, but he died a bachelor in 1631, and had the honour of burial in Westminster Abbey, with a monument erected by the Countess of Dorset, and an epitaph, 'Doe, pious marble, let thy readers know,' traditionally assigned to Ben Jonson, and worthy of his pen. His stature was short, his complexion swarthy, his expression sad; and his personal character was beyond reproach. He corresponded with Drummond, of Hawthornden, and was a friend of most of his great contemporaries. There is no positive evidence of his personal friendship with Shakespeare, but there is Ward's later record that 'Shakespeare, Drayton and Ben Jonson had a merry meeting,' and still more definitely that Drayton was cured of a 'tertian' by Shakespeare's son-in-law, Dr. John Hall. His first work, in 1501, was the 'Harmonie of the Church,' a metrical version of various passages in the Scriptures, which was dedicated 'To the godly and vertuous Lady, the Lady Jane Devoreux, of Merivale,' with a reference to the 'bountifull hospitality' she had bestowed upon him. For some unknown reason Archbishop Whitgift ordered that the work should be destroyed, but that 'forty copies should be preserved at Lambeth Palace'—of which only one copy has survived, and is now in the Museum Library. In 1593, in the 'nine eglogs' of the Shepherd's Calendar, he wrote excellent lyrical verse, but many rugged lines, which he afterwards revised, for he was a severe critic of his own works. In the same year he produced his first historical poem, the legend of 'Piers Gaveston.' In 1596 he issued in his 'Mortimeriados' the first draft of the famous history poem, 'The Barons' Wars' of 1603, first written in seven-line, and afterwards in 'ottava rima,' followed in 1597 by 'England's Heroicall Epistles,' one of the most important and popular of his works. These history-poems were soon to be superseded by history-plays, but they were great works of their class, full of fire and life and interest, in most poetical and almost dramatic form. Between 1597 and 1602 he followed the fashion and wrote some plays; some alone, but others with Chettle, Dekker, and other dramatists, and with marked originality and effect even in that prolific play-writing age. In 1605 his 'Poems Lyricall and Pastorall,' etc., showed far higher powers; and among the 'Ballads' was his famous 'Battle of Agincourt,' a most brilliant and patriotic martial lyric. In 1613 his greatest and most famous work appeared as 'Poly-Olbion; or, A Chorographicall Description of all the Tracts, Rivers, Mountains, Forests, and other Parts (etc.) of Great Britaine.' In each 'Song' (or book), full and fanciful, mythological and topographical, historical and descriptive details were given in rich, high-sounding lines, of the legends and history of all parts of Britain, with copious antiquarian annotations by John Selden. Such a work must necessarily be monotonous in form and style, however varied in subject, and not even the numberless passages of high poetic beauty could make the work welcome to the readers even of that day. It is, however, a marvellous work, full of poetic fire, brilliant description, minute observation, graphic record, unrivalled imagination and fanciful power. Its magnificent metre and lofty imagery were bestowed on facts, and often on legends, and it wanted the human interest and sympathy which alone could raise it to the rank of the highest poetic art. Isaac d'Israeli said of it, that 'it was without a parallel in the poetic annals of any people,' and that we might derive its birth 'from Leland's magnificent view of his designed work on Britain,' and 'that hint expanded by the "Britannia" of Camden, who inherited the mighty industry without the poetical spirit of Leland: Drayton embraces both.'

John Freeth (1730-1808) is a descent from a poetaccio to a poetaster, or poetito, but alphabetical arrangement necessarily brings strange folk together. He was born in Birmingham, and scarcely left the town all his life. He was probably unique as an example of a publican-poet, for he kept nominally a coffee-house, but really an old-fashioned sort of club-inn, where the men of Birmingham met constantly to talk over the news of the day. He was a bright and genial man, fairly well read, and remarkable for ready wit and rough humour. He 'wrote songs, found tunes, and sung them too.' His house was a Whig club, before Liberals or Radicals were known. He wrote songs and catches on the topics of the day. His regular visitors were known as the 'Jacobin Club,' and there was a rival house of Tory fame, which announced, 'No Jacobins admitted here.' Most of Freeth's songs were in a free-and-easy style—short, sharp, 'catchy,' and emphatic; but the other house had no poet to attract its 'company.' Freeth began to write and sing about 1750, and continued to do so for more than thirty years. He had the honour of having his first 'poems' printed by John Baskerville in 1771, and in his later years he published others. His songs are literally stainless as to phrases and words, and while full of genial satire and political feeling, were always in good taste. He was honoured by all who knew him, was a 'power' in his way, and a 'celebrity' in his own town. He died, aged seventy-eight, and his own words formed his epitaph:

> 'Free and easy through life 'twas his wish to proceed,
> Good men he revered, be whatever their creed.
> His pride was a sociable evening to spend,
> For no man loved better his Pipe and his Friend.'

Huckell, John (1729-1771), was another of the minor poets, who once was popular by his poem 'Avon.' He was born in Stratford, educated at the Grammar School under the Rev. Joseph Greene, a scholar and antiquary, who was the master (1735-1772), and who left many now valuable sketches of old buildings and copies of old manuscripts, which are preserved in the museum at Shakespeare's birthplace. In 1750 Huckell graduated B.A. at Oxford, and after ordination was a curate at Hounslow. As an old Stratfordian he took part in the Garrick Jubilee celebration of 1769, and wrote several of the songs for that festival, and a poem to Garrick (on his receiving the 'freedom of Stratford'), which appeared in the *Gentleman's Magazine*. His 'Avon' is one of the historico-topographical poems, then very popular, and it has much merit as a record of the scenes on the banks of the 'classic stream.' This poem, an early work, had the honour of being printed by John Baskerville in a handsome quarto in 1758. Huckell died in 1771, and was buried at Isleworth.

Richard Jago (1715-1781) was another of the local poets of the then popular class. He was of a Cornish family, but born at Beaudesert, Henley-in-Arden, near Stratford. He was at school at Solihull, in the same county, and there a life-long friendship with William Shenstone began, and also with a neighbour poet, William Somerville, another of the three famous friends. At University College, Oxford, he was elected a servitor, took M.A. degree in 1738, and became curate of Smitterfield, near Stratford, in 1737, and vicar in 1771. Like his friend Shenstone at the Leaseowes, he amused his leisure by landscape gardening, but on a much smaller scale. His principal poem was 'Edgehill,' another historico-topographical poem, in which he introduced some graceful lines in memory of Shenstone. These friends—Jago, Somerville and Shenstone, with Lady Luxborough, who lived near Henley-in-Arden—formed a pleasant county *coterie* of literary tastes, and the letters of Shenstone, and of Lady Luxborough especially, are deeply interesting records of Middle England life a hundred years ago.

John Jordan (1746-1809) can be regarded only as a pseudo-poet, pretentious and fraudulent, for he certainly fabricated many of his 'facts' in connection with Shakespeare and Stratford. He was born at Alveston, over Avon, from the Stratford side, and was ignorant and presumptuous. He published one poem—'Welcombe Hills,' a lovely scene close to Stratford, with charming park and gentle hills, and remains of old earthworks of British days.

He was a constant correspondent of Malone, who helped him liberally, and he contributed topographical and antiquarian papers to the *Gentleman's Magazine;* but most of his 'facts' require very careful scrutiny. He prepared in a rough and illiterate style a 'History of Stratford,' the MS. of which is preserved at the museum there, with a volume of original letters from Malone from 1790 to 1799. His numerous drawings are poor, and at least, *in*exact, and his help to Ireland's 'Avon,' especially as to Shakespeare's house (New Place), cannot be accepted as genuine. He died at Stratford in 1809, and was buried near the site of the charnel-house, which was destroyed nine years before, together with the College near the church—two relics of mediæval Stratford which would have had extraordinary interest now.

William Shakespeare (1564-1616) was born at Stratford-on-Avon, and his baptism is recorded in the church register on April 26, 1564. The custom of the time was to baptize on the third day, so that the day of birth is traditionally accepted as April 23, and at the house now known as Shakespeare's birthplace, which was bought by public subscription, and afterwards restored to its form as it originally existed at the end of the sixteenth century. His father was for some years a prosperous man, and in 1568 High Bailiff. Scarcely any definite facts are recorded as to the early days of Shakespeare, but his father certainly occupied and purchased the house as it now remains, and within its walls the boy Shakespeare lived. There can be no doubt that he was sent to the Grammar School originally founded by Thomas Jollyffe in 1482, and refounded in the reign of Edward VI. (1553). The school buildings still remain as in Shakespeare's time. On the ground-floor under the upper school is the Gild-hall, where, when his father was High Bailiff in 1568-69, and the poet was a boy of five, he saw his first dramatic performance, as the Queen's and the Earl of Worcester's players visited the town. As a confirmation of the fact that young children were present at such performances, a contemporary account of a play at Gloucester records the presence of a boy of the same age as Shakespeare, and the details of such a play as the young Shakespeare must have seen, and which must have impressed his mind and have influenced his after-life. In the absence even of traditions which have any value, all that can be done is to look to the surroundings and influence of Stratford life in Shakespeare's boyhood, and this has been accomplished with remarkable knowledge and graphic power by the late Professor T. Spencer Baynes, but a mere reference to his researches must suffice. In *Fraser's Magazine* of November, 1879, and January and May, 1880, he wrote three remarkable papers on 'What Shakespeare Learnt at School,' giving the fullest and clearest details now available of the books used, and the teaching given in all similar schools of that period, of which any accounts have been preserved. The results are singularly interesting and valuable, for they are pictures of school life as to masters, books, and scholars, and are strangely realistic in showing the school life of the Elizabethan age. They still more clearly show that the boy Shakespeare must have had within easy reach, and for several years nearly, if not all, that was needful to explain the numerous classical allusions in his poems and plays. These examples of circumstantial evidence very clearly show the *curriculum* of a country school, and there is still more direct evidence as to the Grammar School at Stratford between 1570 and 1580, when Walter Roche for two years, Thomas Hunt for five years, and Thomas Jenkins for three years, were the masters of the school. In another, and unhappily his last work, Professor Baynes has contributed an invaluable help to the study of the local influences on Shakespeare's life. It appeared *s.v.* 'Shakespeare' in the ninth edition of the 'Encyclopædia Britannica,' of which he was chief editor. It is a most scholarly and brilliant survey of the influences which surrounded Stratford and Shakespeare, and which combined to mould his character and genius. It consists of a minute study of all the facts, physical and moral, ethnological and historical, topographical and social, which affected his ancestry, his home, his friends, his neighbours, and the state of social life in Stratford. Every detail of general and local history, every physical feature of the country around, every subtle impression from the varieties of scenery, or ancient legend, or exciting story, is carefully weighed, and shown to account for most of the references in Shakespeare's poems and plays. Even in his life in London the surroundings are shown to have been such as would have influenced his tastes and genius, such as—to take only one example—his associations with John Florio to explain the Italian plots and allusions in his plays. These careful studies by Professor Baynes are most original and most valuable, for they throw a flood of light on many of the darkest scenes of Shakespeare's personal as well as professional life. In the absence of special details, such a methodical and thorough survey of the 'environment' of Shakespeare is the more valuable as a series of sidelights on history; and these papers ought to be collected and published in one volume in justice to the memory of their author, and as an original and learned summary of the great facts of Shakespeare's life and times.

Warwickshire, and especially Stratford, are necessarily closely associated with the whole of Shakespeare's life. His mother, Mary Arden, was of an old yeoman family who had held land for several generations, and she was an heiress when John Shakespeare married her in 1557, from Wilmecote, near Stratford. The poet's boyhood days were mostly passed among the pleasant Stratford scenery of gentle hills and soft-flowing Avon, as the many and minute references in his plays and poems show, and many of those allusions are clearly Warwickshire. In 1582 he married Ann Hathaway, but where is not known, and only the 'Bond' at Worcester records the fact. Their first child, Susannah, was baptized at Stratford in 1583, and two others, Hamnet and Judith, were baptized, in 1585. Soon after, when between twenty-one and twenty-two years old, Shakespeare went to London, and tradition records, through a quarrel with Sir Thomas Lucy, but the facts are mostly doubtful, and the real reason has never been discovered, while the sarcastic references in the 'Merry Wives of Windsor' indirectly support the tradition. Several years of Shakespeare's life in London are blank, but certainly he had some connection with the theatres, first, probably, in some humble office, when his Stratford friends, Burbage and Greene, doubtless helped him, and he began to edit and alter old plays, and afterwards to write his own. In 1593 his 'Venus and Adonis' was published, and in 1594 his 'Tarquin and Lucrece'—two poems worthy of the fame of any author of his age. As early as 1592 he was known as a rising actor, and he doubtless had some share in the 'Henry VI.' plays about that time, but the chronology of his plays is very uncertain. 'Love's Labour's Lost,' the 'Comedy of Errors,' and the 'Two Gentlemen of Verona,' are certainly his earliest works. In 1596 'Romeo and Juliet' was produced at the Curtain Theatre; and in August of the same year his only son Hamnet died in the twelfth year of his age. In 1597—twelve years after his arrival in London—he showed his interest in his native town by the purchase of New Place—the 'Great House' of Stratford—which was in 'great ruyne and decay and unrepayred,' and it was close to the Grammar School and Gild Chapel. It was described by Leland (1540) as 'a prety house in brick and timber,' and it was also described as of 'timber and brick with stone foundations, gabled, and with bay window on the east or garden side.' In this house Shakespeare passed his latter years, and there he died in 1616. After his death it was pulled down to the ground, and its successor was in due time removed by the Gastrells, so that now only the gardens of Shakespeare's freehold remain. They were purchased through the energy and liberality of the late J. O. Halliwell-Phillipps, and are now included with the Birthplace Trust.

Although Shakespeare became so famous in London, it is remarkable how greatly he was attached to his native town. Tradition records that he visited it every year, and certainly in the height of his fame he left London for the retirement of Stratford during the last years of his life. In 1607 his daughter Susannah was married to Dr. John Hall; and in the same year his brother Edmund, described as 'a player,' died, aged 28, and was buried at St. Mary Overy Church, Southwark. In February, 1608, his granddaughter Elizabeth Hall was born; and in September of the same year his own mother, 'Mary Shaxspere, widow,' died, seven years after her husband. In 1609 his famous 'Sonnets' were published, to puzzle every succeeding generation of critics, and they have never yet been satisfactorily explained. In the same year the poet is seen as a practical man of business by the Court record of his suing a debtor for the sum of six pounds, and afterwards the debtor's surety — one of the few survivals of any mention of Shakespeare's personal life. Early in the next year he bought more land from the Combe family, and thus held one hundred and twenty-seven acres in and around Stratford. In March, 1613, he bought the house in the Blackfriars, on the mortgage of which is one of the only five authentic signatures of Shakespeare—now in the British Museum—the others being one on a similar document at the Guildhall, and the other three on his last will at Somerset House.

No other scrap of Shakespeare's handwriting has been discovered, and only one letter addressed to him has been found, the letter from Quiney, now in the Birthplace Museum. His life at Stratford was uneventful. He lived in the 'Great House.' He bought land and sold malt.

He wrote some of his latest and grandest plays. His name is sometimes mentioned in the numerous local records, but never with more than some merely official fact. He was consulted as to the enclosure of some 'common fields' at Welcombe, but whether he favoured the enclosure or not, depends on whether a crabbed letter in a manuscript is to be read 'I' or 'he,' and as the experts differ, it is difficult to decide. In the spring of 1614 an itinerant preacher was a guest at New Place, and the Corporation accounts show that twenty pence were spent on 'a quart of claret and a quart of sack' for his entertainment, but there is no record whether Shakespeare was present, or the hosts were Dr. and Mrs. Hall. In 1616 his younger daughter Judith was married to Thomas Quiney, and two months later the great dramatist was stricken with fever, died on the 23rd of April, 1616, and was buried in the chancel of Stratford Church. His last will was elaborate and precise, but makes no mention of his poems or plays, and even the inventory of his household goods has been lost. The provisions of the will have been fiercely discussed with very little practical result, and the impenetrable veil which has hidden all the details of his private life has never been lifted to disclose the facts.

Seven years after Shakespeare's death his 'friends and fellows,' John Heminge and Henry Condell, collected his plays and published them in the 'First Folio' of 1623. It was a labour of love, and, as a whole, was well performed. The plays were nominally printed from his own 'papers,' in which they 'scarce received a blot,' but there are many proofs that they sometimes used some of the 'diverse, stolene and surreptitious copies,' which they formally denounced. While the numerous quarto plays issued before 1623 occasionally contain passages not included in the folio text, which all editors gladly accept as being unquestionably Shakespeare's work, the 'First Folio' has the immortal honour of having preserved copies of eleven

plays which might have been lost to the world. These are
'The Tempest,' 'Macbeth,' 'Twelfth Night,' 'Measure for
Measure,' 'Coriolanus,' 'Julius Cæsar,' 'Timon of Athens,'
'Antony and Cleopatra,' 'Cymbeline,' 'As You Like It'
and 'The Winter's Tale,' for all of which the 'First Folio'
is the sole authority. The 'Folio' contains thirty-six plays.
It was originally published at twenty shillings, but a
perfect and fine copy is now worth £500, since the volume
is the most interesting and important work in all English
literature, as the treasury of all the greatest works of the
'greatest name in our literature, and in all literature.'
The Droeshout portrait of Shakespeare is the only one
which has contemporary and positive claims to be accepted
as genuine and faithful, and the second, with any complete
authority, is the bust in Stratford Church.

William Somervile (1692-1730), already referred to, was
born at Edstone, near Stratford, and inherited a large
estate from a long line of ancestors. His great-grandfather
is said to have been a friend of Shakespeare after his retirement from the stage, and the family possessed the
Hilliard portrait, said to be that of Shakespeare—a charming miniature, but 'not proven' to be an original and
contemporary portrait from life. Somervile was a Fellow
of New College, Oxford, but had few literary tastes. He
was a warm friend of Shenstone, who wrote his epitaph in
Wootton-Wawen Church, and who greatly admired his
only literary work, the poem long popular as 'The Chase'
—a lively picture of the sport to which he gave his whole
life, and lost his large fortune, and which helped to close
his career while in middle life. His fox-hunting fame and
social qualities made him many friends, and he had most
of the virtues and vices of the country squires of his age.
'The Chase' was written late in his life, when physical
infirmities had prevented his following the hounds, and is
certainly a good example of the sort of poetry which was
popular at the end of the last century.

William Warner (――――1609) was a poet, now nearly forgotten, but one whose memory deserves some mention. He was born in Warwickshire, and was probably a son of Dr. Warner, Rector of Radway, near Kineton. He was educated at Magdalen Hall, Oxford, where his favourite studies were history, poetry, and romance. He left without a degree, and went to London, where he won some fame as a minor poet. In 1592 he published his 'Albion's England,' a careful epitome of English history in a folio volume, containing thirteen books. After his death his poems were highly praised, and Antony à Wood says: 'As Euripides was the most sententious among the Greek poets, so was this Warner among the English poets; and as Homer and Virgil among the Greeks and Latins were the chief heroic poets, so Edmund Spenser and this our Warner were esteemed by scholars living in the reign of Queen Elizabeth our chief heroical makers. But since such is the fate of poets and poetry, that Warner is esteemed by some persons now or lately living, only a good honest plain writer of moral rules and precepts in the old-fashioned kind of seven-footed verse, which yet is sometimes is use, though in a different manner, that is to say, divided into two; and though he was not reckoned equal with Sir P. Sydney, M. Drayton, and S. Daniel, yet he was not inferior to George Gascoigne, G. Turbervile, Thomas Churchyard, Henry Constable, Sir Henry Dyer, etc.' Warner's poem-history is rarely read now, but it has much vigour and learning and many fine lines. He died in 1609.

INDUSTRIAL.— Foremost in the record of industrial worthies and their works the name of Matthew Boulton must necessarily come as the great 'captain of industry' at the world-famous Soho. The site of the works is outside the county of Warwick—in Staffordshire, and Boulton did not begin to build there till 1765. He was, however, so closely associated with Birmingham by birth and residence, and had offices in Birmingham in connection with Soho, that he may properly be placed among the local worthies.

Matthew Boulton (1728-1809) was the son of a Birmingham button-maker, and was born in the town and educated in Deritend. He began business as a maker of those 'steel toys' from which Edmund Burke described Birmingham as the 'toy-shop of Europe,' for these toys were the sword-hilts, and shoe-buckles, and brooches, and chatelaines, which were fashionable, and were largely imported from France. When quite a young man he made many improvements in their manufacture and design, and he left his works in Snow Hill, Birmingham, for the vast building of Soho—nearly two miles away—in 1765. The site was a wild heath, and was taken chiefly to utilize the water-power, as being then the best known source of 'power.' His mental qualities, wide culture, business capacity, and vigorous enterprise soon extended his transactions, and Soho became one of the wonders which all foreign visitors went out to see. When Boswell visited the works, Boulton gave him his famous phrase: 'Sir, I sell here what all the world desires to have—Power.' This was literally true after the happy accident which brought James Watt to Soho with his improvements in the 'fire-engine' of Newcomen, which used steam only to be condensed and create a vacuum, and not as a source of power. The partnership of Boulton and Watt was simply perfect. Each supplied what the other lacked. Watt was a patient, studious inventor, but nervous and anxious, and readily discouraged by failures of a business sort. Boulton was bold, adventurous, undaunted, and ready to face the most serious risks. The union of these two made the fortunes of both, and each of them lived to an advanced age and reaped the rewards of their genius and industry, and Soho became famous the wide world over. It was not only in the making of steam-engines that the success of Soho was won. Boulton had very large and varied scientific knowledge, as well as business sagacity, indomitable energy, and patient skill. He designed a new form of press for medals and coining, and this was so complete and useful that it has remained almost unaltered down to our own day. He had also great good taste in art. He sought out the best artists, and surrounded himself with designers, and modellers and medallists like Flaxman, Küchler, Pidgeon, and the best men of the day. The Soho mint sent forth not only coins of the realm, but medals of the very highest class of art as to design, and of the most perfect beauty as to delicacy and clearness of execution. Not only in this line, but in another, he showed his taste and love of art. He bought from his friend Wedgwood the delicate blue and white cameos which Etruria was pouring forth, and 'mounted' the scent-bottles in silver and the brooches in the 'steel-toys'—the 'cut' and 'fretted' steel pins—which have long been prized by the curious collector. He was ready to manufacture anything which good taste demanded. He led the way, he set the fashions, and the world crowded to his works. Crowned heads from all parts of Europe, notables from remote regions, became not only his visitors, but his guests, in the famous hostelry ('l'Hotel de l'Amitié,' as he called it) on Handsworth Heath. He was on friendly and even intimate terms with all the most famous men of his time — Benjamin Franklin, Josiah Wedgwood, Dr. Erasmus Darwin, Dr. Priestley, R. L. Edgworth, Thomas Day, and all the celebrities of the age. His personal manners are described as princely, courteous, refined, hearty, and he made friends wherever he appeared. His long association with James Watt, who survived him, was alike honourable to both. Boulton had risked his fortune and run into debt, almost to bankruptcy, before the steam-engine began to pay; but he never lost heart or hope. His indomitable energy never flagged, while Watt was often in the depths of despair over the worries of life. 'The Story of Soho' in full detail is almost romantic in its variety, and is literally charming as to the details, even apart from its historical interest. Mr. Smiles has given an excellent account, but even he has scarcely realized its great significance, or had the opportunity to do full justice to its memorable growth and working during those eventful years.

Another of the heroes of Soho deserves a passing word of praise and honour. *William Murdock* (1750-1839) looks like a minor star when Boulton and Watt are ascendant, but he was almost as prolific an inventor as Watt, and almost as bold an adventurer as Boulton. He was the first to use coal-gas for lighting purposes. He made and ran the first model of a locomotive steam-engine, which still remains intact in the possession of Mr. Richard Tangye, and is the most interesting memorial and relic of the first road-engine—the prophetic forerunner of all railway lines. Another name associated with Soho should not be forgotten—that of the second son of *James Watt*, who bore his father's name, and was one of the first to use a steam-engine on a vessel and to cross over to the Continent. He was the second son of Watt—the first son was the gifted *Gregory Watt*—a young man of varied attainments and great promise, who died in early manhood, to the great grief of all who knew him. The Soho heroes of industry were united for many years of active life, and in death they were not divided. They rest together at Handsworth, almost in sight of where Soho once stood (for the last buildings were removed in 1853), and Matthew Boulton, James Watt, William Murdock, and Francis Eginton repose in honour in this 'Campo Santo' of illustrious dead. James Watt has a memorial in a life-like statue, by Chantrey, in a chapel in Handsworth Church, and another in the heart of Birmingham by Alexander Munro. Boulton and Murdock have only mural monuments and busts in the same church, but must some day have the honour their memory deserves of public memorials in the town where their busy and useful lives were passed. The closing words of Lord Brougham's fine epitaph on James Watt may justly be applied to these three great industrial heroes—Boulton, Watt, and Murdock—that 'they enlarged the resources of their country, increased the power of man, and rose to an eminent place among the most illustrious followers of science and the real benefactors of the world.'

Edward Thomason (1769-1849) was one of the numerous examples of the permanent and widespread influence of Matthew Boulton and Soho. He was born in Birmingham, and his father, like Boulton's, was also a button-maker. When he was sixteen young Thomason was articled to Boulton, and he learned at Soho the arts which he used so successfully in his after-life. When he was twenty-one he began to make gilt and silver buttons, and afterwards undertook medal-work, tokens, coins, bronzes and gold and silver plate. His works became extensive, and he placed over the front copies of the famous horses from the façade of St. Mark at Venice, and a statue of Atlas, and succeeded in attracting all distinguished travellers to visit his works. He issued a great variety of medals—some being medallic summaries of scientific facts—but his principal work was sixty large medals of Bible history, copies of which he sent to all the monarchs of Europe, from many of whom he received honours and medals in return, which he highly valued. His greatest art-work was his full-size copy in bronze of the great Warwick Vase, which was found at Hadrian's Villa, near Tivoli, and brought to England by Sir William Hamilton, and is now in the Orangery at Warwick Castle. His works were a sort of smaller Soho as to show-rooms, etc., but none of his productions had any marked merit as to originality or taste. He became High Bailiff of Birmingham—the highest honour at the time—and was very proud of the orders of knighthood and gold medals which he had received from foreign powers. He left—unfinished it is said—two volumes of Memoirs, which are amusingly egotistical, and which seem to show that he was quite as 'diligent in business' as devoted to art.

GENERAL.—Under this heading some of the 'worthies' who could not be included under any of the previous classifications, but who deserve some mention either from their associations with Warwickshire, or from their personal or public merits, will now be briefly described.

Thomas Arnold, D.D. (1759-1842), was connected with Warwickshire only as headmaster of Rugby School, but his influence there, generally as well as locally, requires some notice. In 1827, after a distinguished career, he became a candidate, and in August, 1828, his new career began as master of Rugby School. 'The prediction,' says Mr. Colvile, 'of Dr. Hawkins, of Oriel, that "if elected he would change the whole face of education throughout the public schools of England,"' was soon to be realized, and during the fourteen years of his administration and example the 'ancient foundation' has risen to a height never attained before. Most of this was accomplished, not so much by reforms and changes, as by the new life and tone and spirit of the master. Indeed, so great was his personal influence that it is reported that some of the boys used to say, 'It's a shame to tell Arnold a lie, for he always believes you'—a remarkable instance of influence on boy-life, fully supported by the later history of the school. 'The principal changes,' Mr. Colvile continues, ' were the transference of the boarding-houses to the sole charge of the masters, the assumption by the headmaster of the pastoral and ministerial office over the boys, and the infusion into school instruction, not only of a larger religious element, but of copious measures of English composition, modern languages and modern history.' His strong personal character, his singular power of attracting or impressing, his stern justice and considerate tenderness, and his readiness for every emergency, combined to secure a kind of power and influence which produced the most beneficent results on the moral as well as intellectual growth of the school. He died the day after the school summer 'half' of 1842, the day before his completion of his forty-seventh year, and was buried in the school chapel, honoured and mourned by all who knew him.

Thomas Cartwright (1535-1603), an eminent Puritan divine, was born in Hertfordshire, but was appointed by Leicester master of his hospital at Warwick, in 1585, with a house and a stipend of £50 a year. His life in Warwick was earnest and active, and he won every honour; but his restless spirit carried him into serious trouble, and he was sent to prison, in the Fleet, for two years. On his return to Warwick he resumed his active work in the neighbouring churches, and he became generally popular by his charities and blameless life. He was especially bountiful to poor scholars, and apart from his controversies he made troops of friends. His principal opponent on Church government was Whitgift, and he vigorously maintained his principles. He died in 1603, and was buried in St. Mary's, Warwick.

Robert Catesby (1573-1605) was born at Bushwood Hall, near Lapworth, and belonged to one of the 'first families' in England. In 1592, during his minority, he married a daughter of Sir Thomas Leigh, of Stoneleigh, and he was then probably a Protestant. He supported the rebellion of Essex, and purchased his pardon by a fine of £3,000. He was afterwards engaged in many treasonable plots, and is generally held to have been the proposer of the famous Gunpowder Plot, in the conclusion of which he lost his life in 1605, having been shot at Holbeach while attempting to escape when the plot had failed. He is described as having been six feet in height, and as having a noble and expressive face, very attractive manners, and great personal influence over all around him.

William Croft (1677-1727) was born at Nether Eatington,

Warwickshire, and educated under Dr. Blow, at the Chapel Royal, Windsor, and was afterwards organist of St. Anne's, Westminster. In 1704 he was joint organist, with Jeremiah Clarke, at the Chapel Royal, and on Clarke's death in 1707 he became organist, and in 1708 he succeeded Dr. Blow as Master of the Children and Composer to the Chapel Royal, and as organist of Westminster Abbey. In 1712 he published his ' Divine Harmony,' anonymously, words without music, and giving a brief account of Church Music. In 1724 he published his ' Musica Sacra ; or, Select Anthems in Score '—' the first engraved and stamped on plates,' and afterwards several other works of secular music for violins and flutes. He died in 1727, and was buried in Westminster Abbey.

George Dawson, M.A. (1821-1878), was the most worthy of all the ' strangers within the gates ' who have done so much for the chief town in the county, and whose name and fame will ever have the highest honour. He was born in London, was for some years a teacher in his father's school, went first to Aberdeen and afterwards to Glasgow, where he took his M.A. degree, and after a brief ministry at a Baptist Chapel at Rickmansworth, he accepted a similar charge in Birmingham. His presence was soon felt ; his earnestness, eloquence, and originality attracted crowds from all sorts of congregations. He soon outgrew the narrow limits of mere creeds as a bond of Christian union, and boldly preached that no theological creed should be the basis of a Church, but the good works of mercy, charity, and care for the neglected. On this basis the Church of the Saviour was founded, and became a city of refuge for all creeds, united for educational and charitable work. The results were remarkable; the old narrowness of some Nonconformists was supplemented by larger and more spiritual life and practical work, not merely in their principles, but in their public worship and private life. For thirty years the leaven extended to other places : light and colour were introduced, chants and anthems were sung, outdoor social gatherings were arranged, and new life, new work, new hopes were developed. The personal charm of Dawson won all hearts; the congregation was large and united, the services bright, hearty, genial, and impressive, and George Dawson became a great power. No man ever did more to elevate the tone and taste of great masses of people. 'The common people heard him gladly.' To hear him merely read the Scriptures was worth many sermons. To hear his sermons, full of the loftiest teaching, touching eloquence, human interest, tender sympathy, and generous feeling, was a memory for life. Old and young, orthodox and heterodox, rich and poor, listened with breathless interest to his golden words, and went forth to practise the lessons he had given, in the ordinary work of life. He was intensely English all round, and outside his own people his influence was deep and lasting. He took part from the first in all public work. He was an eloquent speaker on all great public questions. He urged the duty of sacrifices for public life. He was the friend and helper of the humble poor, and of the refugees of Poland and Italy in the troublous times. He did more than any other man to raise the tone of life in the town—private, public, social, literary, and political. His brilliant lectures sent all his hearers to read the books he praised. He conducted, without fee or hope of reward, English Literature classes for several years—a series of lectures unhappily not preserved. He advocated physical training and manly exercises, and they became the fashion. He was first and foremost in all that could refine and elevate the tastes of the people. He fought for Free Libraries against great opposition. He popularized the study, not the mere reading, of Shakespeare by lectures all over the kingdom, and has left memories in the minds of all who heard him which will never die. His personal influence was wonderful wherever he went. All were the better for his visit, his example, and his teaching. He was 'at home' in Birmingham. He worked incessantly and successfully for her truest interests and highest culture, and the news of his sudden death, after thirty years of manly devotion to public duties, saddened all hearts, and left a blank in local life which has never been filled. The results of his teaching and work will ever remain, for every part of local life—political, religious, philanthropic, social—owes an eternal debt to his memory for his unrivalled help in raising the standard of private life and public duty in his adopted town.

Two others—his fellow-workers and devoted friends—well deserve a few words in connection with his honoured name. They also worked in the same spirit and on the same lines, but in different departments of public work, and both were also 'strangers within the gates.' *John Henry Chamberlain* was born at Leicester, but lived and laboured in Birmingham for nearly thirty years. As an artist and architect he enriched the town with its finest buildings as to design and usefulness, and was the most devoted and eloquent teacher of the greatest principles of art. His knowledge, taste and skill, his brilliant intellect and unsurpassed eloquence, as well as practical mind, were generously devoted to every great public work, and his memory will ever be honoured by all who knew him. *William Costen Aitken* came from Dumfries, and for forty years gave his untiring energy and splendid services to art and the industries of Birmingham, of which some record remains in his history of the various trades in the 'Hardware' volume of 1866. These three friends—Dawson in all social and literary work, Chamberlain in the highest interests of all real and true art, and Aitken as the scientific and artistic teacher of art applied to manufactures—will ever be honoured as worthies, whose full merits have never yet been adequately praised, in the history of a great town.

Thomas Wright Hill (1763-1853) was born at Kidderminster, but passed nearly all his long life—eighty years—in Birmingham. His earliest tastes were scientific, largely influenced by Ferguson's lectures, when he was only nine years old, and of which he left a curious account in a remarkable autobiography, privately printed in 1859. He was first apprenticed to a brassfounder in Birmingham; but the work was uncongenial, and his experience as a Sunday-school teacher under Dr. Priestley led him to devote himself to teaching, and to the unsurpassed successes of his life. He established first the Hill Top School in Birmingham, and afterwards the Hazelwood School at Edgbaston, where many eminent men received their early training—for he was no mere teacher—and pupils came to him from all parts of Europe. He had a very remarkable and original power of interesting boys. He made his school a small republic, and trained the boys for the work of life.. He encouraged manual labour, as well as games and sports. He not only proposed a magazine, but the boys printed and illustrated it also, and many excellent etchings and early lithographs were produced. The best proof of the success of his system is found in the lives of his five sons. The eldest, Sir Rowland Hill, was for several years his helper in his work; and all his sons, without influence or patronage, won high places: Rowland at the Post-Office, Matthew Davenport as a jurist (on criminal reform), Edwin at the Stamp Office (with many inventions), Frederick as inspector of prisons, and Arthur, who carried on the school at Bruce Castle, Tottenham, after Hazelwood was closed. As late as 1849 the venerable schoolmaster discussed philological and other questions *vivâ voce*, and in public, and in clear and eloquent words. He died in 1853, full of honours as well as years, and has been remembered by three generations of pupils and friends, who owe to his teaching and example the culture and success of their lives.

Mary Linwood (1755-1845) was born at Birmingham, but her parents removed to Leicester when she was six years old. About 1782 some mezzotint plates sent to her attracted her attention, and she resolved to imitate them in needlework. 'She took some ravellings of black and puce-coloured silk, and with these copied pictures so accurately on white and sarcenet as to astonish those who witnessed the effect produced.' Her first attempt to imitate painting was in 1785, and with great success. Her exhibition of her works in 1798 was very attractive, and was removed to Edinburgh, Glasgow, and Dublin, and finally into Leicester Square. It included one hundred works, one of which, the Judgment of Cain, occupied her needle for ten years, and was completed in her seventy-fifth year, when her eyesight failed and her labours ceased. She died at Belgrave Gate, Leicester, and her gallery of pictures, sold by auction, realized only a small sum.

William Thomas, D.D. (1670-1738), although not born in the county, was Vicar of Exhall, and often a resident at Atherston-on-Stour. His special work was his edition of Dugdale's 'Warwickshire,' which he issued in two volumes in 1730, and to which he added many facts, the results of long and wide researches. He claimed that he had visited all the churches, and he took great care to give the later monumental inscriptions after Dugdale's days, and thus increased the value of his work for genealogical purposes. He commenced a history of Worcestershire, and he collected much material, but his death in 1738 left it unfinished. He was buried in the cloisters at Worcester Cathedral, whose history he wrote.

CHAPTER VIII.

FOLK-LORE AND DIALECT.

Warwickshire and Leicestershire.—Old Popular Legends.—Superstitions. — Curious Customs. — Pronunciation and Dialects. — Glossaries of Local Words and Phrases.—Examples from Sharp's Glossary.—Comparisons with Neighbouring Counties.

WARWICKSHIRE is far less famous than many other counties for the number and variety of its superstitions, folk-lore, and dialect. Its central position among the English counties has not isolated it in such respects, or preserved so many fables, phrases, and words as might have been expected from the influences to which coast-counties or border-counties have been exposed. Perhaps, indeed, on the whole, it has lost many of its ancient characteristics by the influences of the surrounding counties—Worcester, Stafford, Leicester, and Gloucester—and to a smaller extent as to Oxford and Northampton. No very clearly-marked boundary separates Warwickshire from the surrounding counties so far as folk-lore and superstitions, and even dialect, are concerned, except that as to pronunciation the speech of Worcestershire and Gloucestershire, the voices and accents, 'bewray' readily, and differ materially from the 'common talk' of Warwickshire. This is most notable, of course, in rural districts, but even in a large town like Birmingham the Worcestershire and Gloucestershire accent is readily detected, and often survives for many years in the 'mixed dialect' which becomes common in large towns. In Birmingham, among the less educated people, the 'common talk' is more influenced by Stafford than Worcester, and sundry peculiarities are very difficult to trace back to their origin among so many sources of influence, not merely from neighbouring, but even from distant counties. Neither the folk-lore nor the dialect of Warwickshire have ever had full and careful study, such as Dr. Sebastian Evans and his father gave to 'Leicestershire Words and Phrases,' or Miss Jackson to her 'Shropshire Word-Book,' or the Dialect Society to some of the Worcestershire phrases and words and traditions. Warwickshire has so long a Leicestershire border on the north-east, that it is not surprising to find many of the words and phrases familiar in Leicestershire are common to both counties, while in the south of Warwickshire the influence of Gloucestershire, and on the west that of Worcestershire, are very marked. In all references and examples given it must not be assumed that they are exclusively of Warwickshire origin, but only that they exist in the county, although they may be found elsewhere. Indeed, it is practically impossible to prove that any word, phrase, or superstition is peculiar to any county without so complete a knowledge as no expert is likely to possess. It is only possible by some corporate effort on such a basis as the 'Folk-Etymology' of the Rev. A. Smythe Palmer, supplemented by the 'Dictionary of Archaic and Provincial Words' by the late J. O. Halliwell-Phillipps, in which, in many cases, the names of the counties are added to the descriptions and origin of the words, that any really trustworthy record of county facts and phrases can be secured. Even in Dr. J. A. Murray's unrivalled 'New English Dictionary on Historical Principles,' while the literary history of every word is fully and carefully given, it has been found impossible to mark to any great extent those which are peculiar to the English counties. It is, perhaps, scarcely possible to secure such a work of comparative county folk-lore and phrases, so that any of the examples cited must be accepted only *valeant quantum*, and not as final, either as to origin or use.

In a paper read to the Archæological Section of the Midland Institute, Birmingham, in November, 1875, Dr. J. A. Langford collected from literary sources, and gave from personal knowledge of over fifty years, some of the most remarkable of the superstitions current in Warwickshire, but now slowly dying out. From this paper and from other sources, personal and special, the following examples are given, necessarily without any formal classification. The country districts are, of course, the principal places where old folk-lore lingers, but even in large towns like Birmingham many of the strange superstitions are still cherished by the older people, especially those whose early life was passed in rural places. Curiously, too, many of these old phrases and superstitions are preserved in fiction; and 'George Eliot' (Mrs. Cross) has garnered in 'Adam Bede' and other stories more of the most life-like and remarkable sayings and proverbs of the Warwickshire folk, especially of the northern part of the county, than can be found in any other records of half a century ago.

Rural Warwickshire is rich in phrases and superstitions about weather and birds and garden-lore. A good crop of hawthorns is held to be not only a sign of a severe winter, but as a provision for the birds in the time of frost and snow. A wet Friday and a wet Sunday are always followed by a wet week. 'Rain before seven, fine before eleven,' is a popular jingle, if not a faithful prophecy. The generally common oak and ash leaf prophecy is well known and generally believed: 'The oak before the ash, a summer of splash; the ash before the oak, a summer of smoke'—a hot, dry summer. If the robin is heard in the morning, it means rain before night; if in the evening, it will be fine next day. The common augury of bees runs in Warwickshire:

> 'A swarm of bees in May
> Is worth a load of hay;
> A swarm of bees in June
> Is worth a silver spoon;
> A swarm of bees in July
> Is not worth a butterfly.'

Names—popular names—of birds are curious, and probably special. The woodpecker = hickle; the goldfinch = proud taylor; the wood-pigeon = queecer; the water-hen = dipchick; the black-cap = black-a-top; the swift = jack-squealer; the fly-catcher = hewsick; the chaffinch = pie-finch, and sometimes pink; and the yellow-hammer = Grecian, from the supposed Greek letters on its eggs.

The superstitions are very numerous and nowadays absurd, but are often still believed in, and probably have had some reasonable origin, and in some cases have had a good preservative effect. The robin is almost sacred, and the most unlettered clown would never dream of killing one. If you burn egg-shells, the hens will cease to lay; and if you burn milk, the cows will run dry. If a death has occurred, unfasten every lock in the house. If the palm of the right hand itches, 'rub it on wood; it will come to good.' If the right eye itches, it means joy; if the left, tears; but 'left or right, good at night.' If the nose itches, you will be kissed, cursed, or vexed—by a fool. Magpies are famous augurs. If you meet one, cross yourself or lift your hat, or you will have bad luck. To see one means sorrow; two, mirth; three, a wedding; and four, a birth. If you see a shooting-star, whatever you wish during its flight will happen, but—you will repent it. If a grave is left open on Sunday, there will be another death before the month is out. It is a common practice to shroud a looking-glass before a funeral. If you look into a mirror with a corpse in the room, you will see the corpse looking over your shoulder. It is unlucky to carry a baby down, instead of upstairs, the first time after its birth. As recently as 1869 old women were seen near Rugby catching the falling rain on Ascension Day and bottling it for future use, with the belief that the water would prevent 'heavy bread,' by adding a teaspoonful to the leaven. It is a common belief that the clock will stop when anyone in the house dies. When the master of the house dies, the bees must be told, or they will leave the hive. When you lose a tooth, you should put salt on it and throw it into the fire. If this is not done with children, the second set of teeth will be bad. If a pig is killed in the wane of the moon, the bacon will shrink in boiling; if at the full, the bacon will swell.

Many of the superstitions are preserved in clumsy but effective rhymes :

'If in your house a man shoulders a spade,
For you or your kinsfolk a grave is half made.'

'If your bees fall sick and die,
One of your house will soon in churchyard lie.'

The following are curious, but possibly common :

'Sneeze on Monday, sneeze for danger ;
Sneeze on Tuesday, kiss a stranger ;
Sneeze on Wednesday, have a letter ;
Sneeze on Thursday, something better ;
Sneeze on Friday, sneeze for sorrow ;
Sneeze on Saturday, see true love to-morrow.'

Another is also curious as a day-of-the-week 'forecast' for birthdays :

'Sunday's child is full of grace ;
Monday's child is fine of face ;
Tuesday's child is full of woe ;
Wednesday's child has far to go ;
Thursday's child's inclined to thieving ;
Friday's child is free in giving ;
Saturday's child works hard for his living.'

In 'Adam Bede,' when he is at work all night at the coffin which his father had neglected, the howl of a dog disturbed him, and realized the popular superstition that the howling of a dog means death—a very common belief. Another Warwickshire superstition is also preserved in the same story—

> 'Happy is the bride the sun shines on;
> Blessed is the corpse the rain rains on'—

when old Martin Poyser, opening the farm-gate for the family to go to church at the funeral of Thias Bede, says: 'They'll ha' putten Thias Bede i' the ground afore ye get to the churchyard. It 'ud ha' been better luck if they'd ha' buried 'im i' the forenoon when the rain was fallin'; there's no likelihoods of a drop now, and the moon lies like a boat there—dost see? That's a sine o' fair weather; there's many as is false, but that's sure'—an excellent example of Warwickshire dialect and sound. This forecast from the moon is universally believed; and, further, that when the 'crescent' form seems nearly upright, that the moon is so tilted that the rain can run out. Another common bit of moon-lore is to turn your money the first time you see the new moon; and others are: to bow (or curtsey) nine times to the new moon to secure good luck for the month; never to see the new moon through glass; always to bow nine times to the first new moon of the new year, and to turn your money in your pocket, to secure good luck for the year.

Superstitions about witchcraft have nearly died out, but in September, 1875, a 'survival' remained at Little Compton, in South Warwickshire, where a labourer named Haywood killed Ann Tennant, a woman eighty years old, by piercing her with a two-pronged fork, and gave as his reason that she was the 'properest witch [he] ever knowed;' that there were 'sixteen more in the parish as should be done away with;' and, further, that many more of the villagers had the same belief.'

Many other superstitions far less harmful exist still—*e.g.*, that fern-seed gathered with certain rites on Midsummer Day can render persons invisible, especially young women; and Mr. J. R. Wise, in his charming volume ('Shakespeare: his Birthplace and Neighbourhood'), says: 'A maiden takes some of this fern-seed into a garden at midnight, scatters the seed about, and repeats:

' "Fern-seed I sow, fern-seed I hoe.
In hopes my true love will come after me and mow."'

Other forecasts are found in the 'coming stranger' seen in the red-hot patch in the wick of the candle, or the thin, flickering leaf which hangs on the bar of the fire-grate, and which not merely foretells the coming of a 'stranger,' but also how many 'strangers,' if carefully watched before it falls. Another candle-omen is found in a sort of 'winding-sheet' seen in a candle, and which means a certain and early death in the family. The cuckoo has a sort of lore: if you hear the first cuckoo of the year on your left, you will have bad luck; if on your right hand, good luck. And the same results follow in the case of young lambs: if you see their faces towards you, good luck follows; if their tails, bad luck is certain. Many curious forms of charms are still sometimes heard of—as, for example, in the power of healing which 'Silas Marner' had, and his cure of 'Sally Oates,' and the references to the 'wise woman at Tarley.' Dreams are, of course, prolific sources of wonder and fear. Dr. Langford mentions 'one very curious superstition. A Warwickshire girl once said to me, "Ah! now you have broken my dream." On asking what she meant, she replied: "If anyone dreams of any person, or of an event of any kind, and someone the next day mentions the name of the person or the circumstance of the dream, then it is broken, and you need take no further notice of it, for it will not come true."' The cures of rickety children are by drawing them through a cleft in a tree, or through a twin or double ash, and many believed that the health and life of the infant were involved in the preservation of the tree; and a case is given in the *Gentleman's Magazine* of October, 1804, in which Thomas Chillingworth, of Shirley, carefully preserved an ash through which he had been passed as a child.

Among the customs which are probably peculiar to Warwickshire, two are worth special mention. The memory of the massacre of the Danes on St. Brice's Day, in 1001, was long kept as a festival. Dugdale records that when Elizabeth visited Kenilworth in 1575, 'and that there might be nothing wanting that these parts could afford, hither came the Coventre men and acted the ancient play, long since used in that city, called "Hocks-Tuesday," setting forth the destruction of the Danes in King Ethelred's times, with which the Queen was so pleased that she gave them a brace of bucks and five marks in money to bear the charges of a feast.'

Another Martinmas custom is especially curious, and is continued every year without fail even now. This is also described by Dugdale; but Mr. W. G. Fretton, F.S.A., Coventry, one of the local secretaries of the Society of Antiquaries for Warwickshire, has recorded a recent celebration, of which the following are the principal facts: A relic of old village life and land tenures is celebrated in the Knightlow Hundred 'Moot' on Martinmas Day at Knightlow, five and a half miles north-east of Coventry, on the old London road, just within the parish boundary of Ryton-on-Dunsmore, on the high ground at the top of Knightlow Hill, where the base of an old cross still remains with a hollow, of basin-shape, which stands on a mound of raised earth. 'Here at this stone is annually collected for the Duke of Buccleuch, by his steward, on Martinmas Eve, at sun-rising (November 11), what is called "wroth-money" or "ward-money," from the various parishes in the Hundred of Knightlow. The tumulus on which the cross rested is about thirty or thirty-five feet square, with sides running parallel to the road, having a large fir-tree at each angle, of which the people round about say that the four trees represent the four knights who were killed and buried there. The portion remaining of the cross is thirty inches square at the top, with a hole in the centre to receive the shaft; and the whole structure corresponds with those at present in existence at Meriden and Dunchurch. Its date was probably *tempore* Edward III. There is a mason's mark on one side in the shape of a cross, six inches long, which shows that it was set up by a master-mason of his trade-guild. The "wroth-money" has been collected from time immemorial, excepting for a few years at the beginning of the present century; but the Scott family subsequently revived it, or "kept up the charter," as it is locally called. In 1879, at 6.45 in the morning (November 11), the "wroth-money" was collected. There were thirty-four persons present to witness the ceremony. The steward, having invited the party to stand round the stone (the original custom was to walk three times round it), proceeded to read the "charter, or assembly," which opens thus: "Wroth-silver collected annually at Knightlow Cross by the Duke of Buccleuch, as lord of the manor of the Hundred of Knightlow." The next proceeding was the calling over of the names of the parishes liable to the fee, and the amount due from each, when the parish, by the representatives present, cast the required sum into the hollow of the stone. The amounts collected were: Astley, Arley, Burbery, Shilton, Little Walton, Barnacle, and Wolfcote, one penny each; Whitley, Radford - Semele, Bourton, Napton, Bramcote and Draycote, three-halfpence each; Princethorpe, Stretton-on-Dunsmore, Bubbenhall, Ladbrook, Churchover, Waverley, and Weston, twopence each; Wolston, Hill Morton, Hopsford, and Marton, four-pence each; Leamington Hastings, twelvepence; Long Itchington, two shillings and twopence; and Arbury, two shillings and threepence-halfpenny—a total of nine shillings and threepence-halfpenny. Ryton pays nothing, although the stone is within that parish. The fine for non-payment was in olden time one pound for every penny not forthcoming, or else the forfeiture of a white bull with a red nose and ears of the same colour. The fine has not been paid within man's memory. No one seems to know (not even the steward of the Duke himself) why or for what purpose the money was originally collected, nor why one parish should pay more than another.' The custom is supposed to be of prehistoric origin (confirmed by Saxon charters), and to have some connection with the primitive Aryan customs of fabulous times.

Many old customs have survived only as 'sayings' and proverbs, the origin of which is now unknown. In out-of-the-way country places these abound, and while some have lost all meaning, others are intelligible and in common use. It is common among boys to emphasize a promise by linking their little-fingers together, often with the words, 'Ring finger, blue-bell, Tell a lie and go to hell;' sometimes varied to 'Ring finger, ring bell,' etc. Mr. C. G. Prowett suggested that this custom may probably refer to the origin of Lady Percy's words to Hotspur:

> 'In faith, I'll break my little finger, Harry,
> An' if thou wilt not tell me all things true.'

Among other couplets are:

> 'If the sage-tree thrives and grows,
> The master's *not* master, and that he knows.'

> 'A whistling woman and a crowing hen
> Will frighten the devil out of his den '—

which in Warwickshire is (for the second line), 'Are neither good for gods nor men.' Other well-known Warwickshire lines are:

> 'A gift on the thumb is sure to come;
> A gift on the finger is sure to linger.'

> 'When Easter falls on Lady Day's lap,
> Beware, old England, of a clap.'

> 'March will search, and April try,
> But May will tell you if you live or die.'

> 'Even-leaved ash, or four-leaved clover,
> You'll meet your true love before the day is over.'

And this horse-test is curious:

> 'One white foot, buy a horse;
> Two white feet, try a horse;
> Three white feet, look well about him;
> Four white feet, go away without him.'

It is now fashionable to throw a handful of rice after a newly-married pair, but in some parts of Warwickshire wheat as well as rice is thrown, and in others the traditional 'old slipper' is flung for 'luck.' Fortune-telling by cards or omens is little known except from gipsies, but even in towns of considerable importance foolish girls, and still more foolish women, are constantly found having their 'planets ruled.' Fairy-lore is rarely heard of now, but there are many remarkable 'survivals' of the 'old beliefs' still to be found in 'place-names.' The Will-o'-the-wisp is known as 'Hobady's Lanton,' or 'Hobany's Lantern'; 'Hob Lane' at Sheldon and Yardley; 'Hob's Hole' at Barcheston; 'Hobbin's Close' near Alcester, and at Copt Heath; 'Hob's Moat' at Solihull; and 'Hobgoblin's Lane' at Fillongley.

A careful analysis of the origin and history and changes of words, and especially of comparison with those of other counties, would throw much valuable light on many dark and doubtful questions; and the work of the English Dialect Society, and of such patient students as Miss Jackson and Miss Burne on 'Shropshire Folk-Lore,' with the full details of all old customs, the careful map of the variations in even parts of a single county, should have the support and personal work of all who can help to preserve some records of the fast-fading customs, and superstitions, and proverbs, and phrases which have been interwoven in our national life, and without which no real history of our strangely-mixed people can ever be completely written.

The dialect of Warwickshire has never yet had due attention, and so few are the materials available in a literary form, that only long and patient personal researches in the nooks and corners of the county can save much invaluable material from irretrievable loss. The 'Leicestershire Words and Phrases,' previously referred to, began in 1848 by a small volume (12mo., 116 pages), by the late Rev. Dr. A. B. Evans, of Market Bosworth, and was expanded by his son Dr. Sebastian Evans to a large volume of rare excellence, for the English Dialect Society in 1871— a rare and notable example of what may be found by systematic and careful researches, and an example well worthy of imitation by every county in the kingdom. Warwickshire, unfortunately, has only one attempt at a Glossary, that compiled by Thomas Sharp, of Coventry, early in this century, and which was fortunately preserved in a few privately-printed copies by the late Mr. J. O. Halliwell in 1865, whose interest in the M.S. arose from the facts that its contents 'curiously illustrated the phraseology of Shakespeare.' This unique authority for Warwickshire words, dialect and pronunciation will be the best available means of illustration, generally in Sharpe's own words. The diphthong 'ea' is generally pronounced as a long 'a,' 'plase' for please, 'mate' for meat, 'pase' for pease, 'wake' for weak. The vowel 'o' is sounded as 'u,' 'sung' for song, 'lung' for long, and 'wunst' for once. In many cases the final consonant is also dropped, as 'grun' for ground, 'fun' for found, and 'pun' for pound. The vowels 'o' and 'a' are very often interchangeable, as 'drap' for drop, 'shap' for shop, 'yander' for yonder, and *per contra* 'hommer' for hammer, 'rot' for rat, 'gonder' for gander. The letter 'd' is softened into 'j,' as 'juke' for duke, 'jed' for dead. The letter 'd' or 'ed' is added to some words, as 'drownded' for drowned, and 'gownd' for gown. The vowels 'e' and 'a' are interchanged, as 'fatch' for fetch, 'laft' for left, 'bally' for belly. The nominative and accusative cases are perpetually confounded, as 'They ought to have spoken to *we*,' 'Her told him so,' 'He told *she* so,' '*Us* won't hurt her, will *us* ?' Many other similar perversions of plain spelling might be mentioned, and the fringes of the county are necessarily affected to some extent by the Staffordshire, Leicestershire and Worcestershire pronunciations of words. All the words in the Glossary are especially Warwickshire, but sometimes not exclusively. Only the more remarkable words, or variations of meaning and use, need be noted here. In many examples only the word or phrase need be given, in others some description may be necessary.

'All along of,' 'an end,' an upright ; 'arsy-versy,' topsy-turvy ; 'arter,' after ; 'aw,' yes ; 'ax,' ask ; 'back-stone-iron,' for baking cakes ; 'badger,' a seller ; 'bad,' ill or sickly ; 'bulks,' cross strips or ridges over fields ; 'batter,' to cohere, as snow in hoofs ; 'barm,' yeast ; 'blench,' a glimpse ; 'blown on,' blossom on trees ; 'blowsy,' untidy ; 'brass,' copper money ; 'breed and seed,' birth and parentage ; 'cap,' to excel ; 'chewer,' a narrow road ; 'clemmed' or 'clammed,' hungry, starved ; 'clean,' wholly ; 'colly,' black ; 'cows and calves,' bloom of *arum maculatum*, and 'bulls and cows,' lords and ladies flower ; 'deaf nut,' no kernel ; 'denial,' injury ; 'dither,' tremble with cold ; 'ditless,' stopper for oven ; 'in dock, out nettle,' a charm when nettle-stung ; 'doddered,' a pollarded tree ; 'dowl,' down or feather ; 'dumble,' a small wood in a hollow ; 'easens,' eaves ; 'egg,' to instigate ; 'etherins,' rods on top of hedge ; 'faggot,' a female ; 'favour,' to resemble a parent ; 'fligged,' fledged ; 'footing,' foot-ale, on working at a new place ; 'flew,' shallow ; 'glir,' to glide on ice ; 'gloom,' fat or greasy ; 'god-cake,' gift of sponsors to

Examples from Sharpe's Glossary.

children on New Year's Day; 'goslings,' bloom of willow; 'greats,' groats for puddings; 'haunty,' of a horse full of spirit, *not* restive; 'hay-gob,' buck-weed; 'hike,' to swing or throw; 'hob,' side of fire-grate; 'hocketimon,' cut sides of a rick; 'hull,' shell of walnuts; 'housen,' houses; 'insense,' to inform; 'jack-bannell,' a minnow; 'jack-sharpling,' a stickle-back; 'jee,' crooked; 'just-now' or 'just-nows,' soon; 'kank,' gossip; 'lace,' to beat; 'lawter,' lay of eggs; 'leif,' or 'as leif,' willingly, or as willingly; 'louk,' to strike; 'mawkin,' long-handled mop; 'mawks,' a slattern; 'mort,' a great number; 'next way,' directly; 'nor,' for than, 'sooner nor do it;' 'nope,' bull-finch; 'on' for 'in '—' her cut a bit out on it,' 'two on 'em;' 'othergates,' otherwise; 'peelings' or 'pillins,' parings of apples, etc.; 'pelf,' rubbish; 'pikel,' pitchfork; 'plash,' to cut and bend down hedges; 'rake,' to cover up a fire; 'ramel,' rubbish; 'ran-pike' or 'rennpike,' the decayed top of a tree and dead branches; 'reckling' or 'wreckling,' the last-born; 'reasty' or 'reasey,' bacon; 'recks,' smoky; 'render,' to melt down; 'rick-staddle,' supports of rick; 'sad,' heavy as bread or sad-iron; 'sag,' to hang heavily or swag, weighed down; 'scour,' rapid turn in brook; 'scrattle,' to scratch; 'seam,' fat or lard; 'shackling,' idle, loitering; 'shog,' shake or throw off; 'shoul,' a shovel; 'sliving' or 'slinge,' lazy, lubberly; 'sneyd,' the handle of a scythe; 'sprunt,' a struggle; 'stodge,' cram full; 'stunker' or 'thunker,' arable land separated; 'stye,' pimple on eyelid; 'swarm,' to climb a tree; 'swatched,' loosely-dressed women, or 'daggled,' 'welly-swatched,' dirty; 'sword,' the skin of bacon; 'terry,' sticky; 'tether,' to marry; 'thack,' thatch; 'thrall,' stand for barrels; 'tick' and 'tag,' game of bowls; 'toot,' to pry; 'tot,' small cup; 'trig,' narrow path, also a game of quoits; 'unked,' melancholy; 'up and told,' related a narrative; 'urchin,' a hedgehog; 'us,' our; 'varsal,' universal; 'wangle,' to totter; 'wattle and dab,' plastered house; 'whamp,' to beat a child; 'whittle,' to cut; 'wig,' cake or bun; 'wizzened,' shrivelled; 'yaup,' loud noise; 'yawnups,' ignorant fellow.

Another partial Glossary of Warwickshire words is that appended to Mr. J. R. Wise's delightful little volume 'Shakespeare: His Birthplace and its Neighbourhood,' first published in 1861, and now extremely scarce. His Glossary includes only the words which are found in Shakespeare's works, but are still common in Warwickshire; and although its range is therefore limited, it is valuable as a record historically as to Warwickshire, and also as to Shakespeare's frequent use of his own 'mother tongue.' Mr. Wise notes in his short preface to his Glossary 'how very strongly the different dialects are marked in England, and the wide difference there is not only in the meaning, but in the pronunciation, of the same words in Dorsetshire, where the Saxon element is most marked, and in the Eastern and Midland counties, where the Anglian is more prominent. Thus in the "Venus and Adonis" Shakespeare rhymes "juice" as if spelt "joyce" —a thoroughly Midland pronunciation of the word. . . . And again, in the very next stanza, as Dr. Farmer also remarked, "ear" is rhymed, as it is to this day pronounced in Warwickshire, as if it were "air."' He then gives a list of fifty-seven words, which he has himself noticed as still in use among the peasantry of Warwickshire, premising only that the chief value is in the fact that they are spoken still by breathing human beings—the same sort as those from whose lips Shakespeare learnt his mother-tongue. All the words are here given, but the explanations are abbreviated:—'Batlet': a beater used in washing, sometimes called a 'dolly,' 'maiden,' or 'maid' ('As You Like It,' ii. 4). 'Bavin': the scrapings of chips of a faggot, easily lighted; 'Rash bavin wits, new kindled, and soon burnt' ('1 Henry IV.,' iii. 2). 'Bottle': a 'bottle' of hay, which Bottom pined for ('Midsummer Night's Dream,' iv. 1). 'Bow': which still means a yoke for cattle; 'As the ox has his bow, sir' ('As You Like It,' iii. 4). 'Biggen': a child's cap; 'Whose brow with homely biggen bound' ('2 Henry IV.,' iv. 4). 'Bravery': finery, etc. ('Taming of the Shrew,' etc., p. iv. 3). 'Brize': gad-fly, pronounced 'breeze' or 'bree' ('Antony and Cleopatra,' iii. 8). 'Broken tears': tears suddenly stopped, but sometimes tears with sobs ('Troilus and Cressida,' iv. 1). 'Childing': pregnant (beautifully applied in 'Midsummer Night's Dream,' ii. 2). 'Claw': to flatter; 'Look how he claws him' ('Love's Labour Lost,' iv. 2). 'Cob-loaf': a badly-set-up loaf, or sometimes cake (Ajax to Thersites in 'Troilus and Cressida,' ii. 1). 'Commit': to commit adultery; 'What! committed!' ('Othello,' iv. 2). 'Customer': a common woman ('Othello,' iv. 4). 'Dout': a corruption of 'do out,' very commonly used for putting out a candle, used metaphorically ('Hamlet,' iv. 7). 'Dup': from do up, fasten, or 'sneck' the door ('Hamlet,' iv. 5). 'Doxy': 'neither maid, wife, nor widow' ('Winter's Tale,' iv. 2). 'Eanlings': young lambs just 'eaned,' or dropped ('Merchant of Venice,' i. 3). 'Feeders': idle, good-for-nothing servants ('Timon of Athens,' ii. 2). 'Fore-wearied': very tired; 'This fore-wearied flesh' ('King John,' ii. 1). 'Fardel': a faggot, or 'kid,' or bundle of sticks ('Winter's Tale,' iv. 3; v. 2; and 'Hamlet,' iii. 1). 'Gib cat': a tom cat ('1 Henry IV.,' i. 2). 'Honey stalks': white clover ('Titus Andronicus,' iv. 4). 'Jet': to strut ('Twelfth Night,' ii. 5). 'Inkles': cheap tape, 'beggars' inkle' ('Winter's Tale,' iv. 3). 'Irk': to make uneasy ('As You Like It,' ii. 3). 'Keck' or 'kex': umbelliferous plants in ditches and hedges ('Henry V.,' v. 2). 'Kindle': birth of rabbits, to litter ('As You Like It,' iii. 2). 'Lief': soon; 'as lief do so-and-so' (sixteen examples in various plays). 'Lated': belated, benighted ('Macbeth,' iii. 3). 'Lifter': a thief ('Troilus and Cressida,' i. 1). 'Lodge': beaten down or 'laid' corn ('Macbeth,' iv. 1). 'Loggatts': an old English game, similar to skittles ('Hamlet,' v. 1). 'Loon': a stupid scamp, sometimes 'lown' ('Macbeth,' v. 3; 'Othello,' ii. 3; and 'Pericles,' iv. 4). 'Mammet': a doll or puppet ('I Henry IV.,' ii. 3). 'Master': still used as a prefix; 'good Master Fenton,' etc. ('Merry Wives of Windsor,' iii. 4). 'Mortal': extreme; very 'mortal in folly' ('As You Like It,' ii. 4). 'Nine men's morris': a game on the turf on a marked 'court' ('Midsummer Night's Dream,' ii. 2). 'Noul': the head; 'ass's noul' ('Midsummer Night's Dream,' iii. 2). 'Pash': a rough head, sometimes 'pash-head' ('Winter's Tale,' i. 2). 'Patch': a fool, a simpleton ('Midsummer Night's Dream,' iii. 2). 'Pick thanks': tale-bearers, also 'pick-thanking work' ('I Henry IV.,' iii. 2). 'Pun': to pound or crush ('Troilus and Cressida,' ii. 1). 'Quat': a pimple, pustule, boil ('Othello,' v. 1). 'Race': a stick, as a stick of ginger ('Winter's Tale,' iv. 2). 'Ravin': to devour ('Measure for Measure,' i. 3). 'Rid': to destroy; 'The red plague rid you' ('Tempest,' i. 2). 'Sagg': to sink down, to tire ('Macbeth,' v. 3). 'Salt': applied to Cleopatra (ii. 1), and still used of loose women, but origin unknown. 'Shive': a slice; 'A shive of a cut loaf' ('Titus Andronicus,' ii. 1). 'Shog': to jog off or make off ('Henry V.,' ii. 3). 'Shovel-board': a long board, marked, on which large metal disks were played ('Merry Wives of Windsor,' i. 1). 'Squash': an unripe pea-pod ('Winter's Tale,' i. 2; and 'Midsummer Night's Dream,' iii. 1). 'Statute-caps': woollen caps ordered to be worn by statute of 1571, for the encouragement of the woollen trade ('Love's Labour Lost,' v. 2). 'Tills': the shafts of a waggon ('Troilus and Cressida,' iii. 2). 'Urchin': a hedgehog ('Titus Andronicus,' ii. 3). 'Wench': a young maid, still used as a term of endearment ('Taming of the Shrew,' v. 2). 'Whip-stock': a carter's whip-handle; 'Malvolio's nose is no whip-stock' ('Twelfth Night,' ii. 3).

Another interesting but limited contribution to Warwickshire provincialisms is found in Mrs. Francis's paper on 'South Warwickshire Provincialisms,' in the 'Transactions of the English Dialect Society, Original Glossaries,' Series C, No. VI., 1876. This list refers only to words collected in the village of Tysoe, near Kineton, whose remoteness from external influences has secured the survival of many words and phrases which have become obsolete in other parts of the county. As Tysoe is only fifteen miles from Stratford-on-Avon, many words and phrases found in the works of Shakespeare are found in this list, thus either confirming the notes of Mr. J. R. Wise, or in some cases adding to his list. Eight only of the words quoted by Mr. Wise are in Mrs. Francis's Glossary, but these are still in use in Tysoe; and some few words common at Rugby, in the north of the county, are also commonly used in Tysoe. Mrs. Francis's Glossary includes three hundred and forty-eight words. Many of those are, doubtless, common to other counties, and some even to Leicestershire and Worcestershire; so that her list may reasonably be accepted as a summary and series of examples of the dialect of the middle counties generally, as well as of Warwickshire specially. Quotations of some of the more remarkable words will be interesting, as showing the meaning and pronunciation of Warwickshire words and phrases, and all are given as they appear in the Glossary, with occasional omissions or abbreviations:

'Abeare,' to like or endure—'I can't abear it.' 'Adone,' have done, leave off—'Adone, will ye?' 'Agreeable,' willing —'Well, I'm quite agreeable.' 'Aince a while,' now and then, at intervals (sometimes 'wunce in a while'). 'Anointed,' wicked—'He's an anointed young rascal.' 'Arter,' after. 'Bangles,' the larger pieces of wood in faggots. 'Batch-loaf,' a fresh-baked loaf. 'Becall,' to speak against a person. 'Bee-skep,' a beehive. 'Bisnings,' the first milk from a cow who has just calved; sometimes, also, 'beistings.' 'Brevet,' to sniff about like a dog. 'Cade,' tame, as a 'cade lamb.' 'Casualty' (pronounced 'kaszhulty'), feeble, shaky— 'He's very old and kaszhulty now.' 'Cheeses,' the unripe seed-vessels of the common mallow. 'Codger,' a miser. 'Dag,' dew—'A nice drop o' dag.' 'Daglocks,' the wool cut from round a sheep's tail. 'Dishabil' (pronounced 'dish-abil')—'I'm all of a dishabil.' 'Dubersome,' doubtful. 'Hisn,' 'shisn,' 'ourn,' 'yourn,' 'theirn,'. for his, hers, ours, yours, and theirs. 'Housen' for houses, still very commonly used. 'Hugger-mugger,' disorder. 'Hurden,' windy, drying. 'Ill-convenient,' inconvenient. 'Innards,' inside of body, entrails. 'In,' used for 'of'—'They be just come out in school.' 'Jack bannial,' or 'bannell,' a tadpole; a very common word, but in some parts used for 'stickleback.' 'Joistings,' the keep of an animal out at grass. 'Judge,' to suspect. 'Kiver,' the tub which butter is made in. 'Knag' or 'nag,' to tease—'Always a-knagging at me.' 'Maunt' (sometimes pronounced 'mohnt'), for may not. 'Middling' has two meanings, according as it is preceded by 'pretty' or 'very'—*e.g.*, 'I'm pretty middling,' or 'We gets on pretty middling,' means tolerably well, or doing well; but 'I'm very middling,' or 'He's going on very middling,' means he is doing very badly as to health, or conducting himself very badly. 'Moikin,' or 'moukin,' a scarecrow. 'Moil,' to work hard. 'Mothering Sunday,' Mid-Lent Sunday, when girls pay their mothers a visit—a custom fast dying out. 'Mummock,' to pull about, to worry. 'Odds,' to alter, to make different—'It'll all be odds'd in a bit.' 'Ooman,' woman; generally applied to wife—'my old ooman.' 'Out-asked,' asked in church. 'Outs,' leavings; 'orts' in many counties. 'Padded,' dried at top, applied to land. 'Paddle,' to cut with a spud, as thistles. 'Peel,' long-handled flat shovel for baker's use. 'Pither,' to snatch, pet, or fondle. 'Raggle,' to succeed—'I can manage to raggle on.' 'Rimming,' removing to another house. 'Riz,' gone up in price. 'Roomthy,' roomy. 'Sad,' heavy — said of bread. 'Sarment,' a sermon. 'Sated,' tired, wearied. 'Scribe,' a poor puling thing.

'Sen,' since. 'Share,' a wooden sheath in waistband to rest a knitting-needle in. 'Shut on,' rid of—'I shall be glad to get shut on her.' 'Sight,' a great many—'There was a sight o' folk.' 'Slom,' right over—'He turned it slom over the road.' 'Slommock,' an untidy person. 'Slop,' a short white frock, gathered into a band at the waist, worn instead of a coat, and sometimes used for a labourer. 'Smock-frock,' the long loose, white, 'worked' over-dress, now rarely seen, but which survives in the new word 'smocked' as to the present fashion in ladies' bodices, etc. 'Spinney,' a small wood.' 'Staddle,' the framework on stones on which ricks are built. 'Swagger,' to satisfy or surpass—'Yo was wantin' to see some big dale-yos (dahlias); now, if yo'll come into my garden, I'll swagger you.' 'Tageous,' a mispronunciation of 'tedious,' or perhaps the original pronunciation of the word 'tewer,' a narrow passage. 'Thack,' to thatch. 'Thomasing': to 'go a-Thomasing' is to go round on St. Thomas's Day begging for Christmas gifts. 'Tisiky,' delicate in the lungs. 'Token,' a death-sign—'Summut 'as cum to my son, for I saw his token last night: it was a white dove flew out of the bed-curtains, and was gone in a minute.' 'Tot,' a small mug. 'Turn,' time, season. 'Unaccountable,' very unusual—'It's unaccountable weather. 'Unbeknownt,' unknown. 'Unked,' (1) lonely, dull, solitary; (2) terrible, ghastly—'His leg is an unked sight.' 'Wops,' a wasp. 'Warm,' to thrash or beat—'I'll warm you.' 'Watch-ed,' wet-shod, wet through—'He came home watch-ed and famelled.' 'Wevver,' however. 'Whum,' whom. 'Wizen,' dried up, withered. 'Worrit,' to tease or worry. 'Wratch,' a weak old person. 'Wuts,' oats. 'Yarbs,' herbs. 'Yed,' head. 'Yent' or 'yaint,' is not, often 't'ain't.'

Many of these examples are also found in Worcestershire and Gloucestershire, but all help to show very clearly the principal characteristics of the Midland dialects; and as all such phrases are rapidly becoming obsolete, such Glossaries deserve the highest praise.

The dialect of Warwickshire is, in fact, far less marked by local characteristics than that of the adjoining counties. It may fairly be claimed that it well represents the old English, say, of the sixteenth century, and has suffered fewer changes than in other counties which surround it. It has fewer eccentricities of pronunciation—fewer modern words—than many of its neighbours. Its form and style are more nearly those of the English Bible and of the works of Shakespeare than those of other counties. It is more easily read and understood by foreigners who have learned English than is generally supposed. The county has for many centuries been the scene of the holiday spectacles, the May-Day celebrations and rites and games, and many of these have retained their old forms till very recently. The morris-dancers died out only some sixty years ago. The statute hiring-fairs, or mops, still survive in remote places, but are dying out, and leaving few traces of their origin and fame, and 'strange, eventful history.'

CHAPTER IX.

CASTLES, MANSIONS, AND OLD HOUSES.

Castles, Mansions and Old Houses, and Deer Parks,—Warwick Castle, Kenilworth Castle, Maxtoke Castle, Tamworth Castle, Astley Castle. — Baddesley Clinton, Compton Wynyates. — Ruins of Brandon, Caludon and Coventry Castles.—Temple Balsall Hall and Church.—Combe Abbey, Guy's Cliff, Warwick Priory, Charlecote Hall, Clopton House, Stoneleigh Abbey, Ettington Hall, Merevale Abbey, Arbury Hall, Ragley Hall, Coughton Court, Pooley Hall. — Weston Park, Wormleighton. — Deer Parks : Charlecote, Stoneleigh, Ragley, Warwick, Arbury, Maxtoke, Packington.

TWO of the most famous castles connected with English history are within the lines of Warwickshire. The county castle, *Warwick*, has a long and interesting history, and although some of its finest rooms were burned a few years ago, it has been restored successfully, and now ranks as one of the most picturesque of English castles—a history of seven centuries in stone. Its site, on a lofty rock overhanging the Avon, with a richly wooded park along the river, forms a scene never to be forgotten. From the fort, or castle, or dungeon in the courtyard, built by Ethelfleda a thousand years ago, it has grown to its present vast proportions and impressive grandeur. The castle at the Norman Conquest was granted to Henry de Newburgh, but was destroyed by the Barons in the reign of Henry III. and levelled to the ground. Under Edward III. the walls were restored and a stronger gate built. The famous Guy's Tower was built under Richard II., and under Edward IV. many additions were made. Richard III. laid the first stone of a new tower, but Sir Fulke Greville restored far more effectively, making the castle more like a mansion than a fortress, and forming the great area of park and 'pleasaunces.' Robert Lord Brooke was a zealous Parliamentarian, and during his absence in August, 1642, an unsuccessful attack was made by the Earl of Northampton, and the military history of the castle was closed. So much has been preserved, and with so few changes, that the castle is exceptionally interesting as an example of the series of stages in the growth of military architecture. Its great extent has been carefully surveyed and its details fully examined and described by the ablest men of our age. To the mere sight-seer it is especially interesting from its contents and its works of art, ancient relics, superbly furnished rooms, extensive park and magnificent trees, all readily accessible and 'a joy for ever.' As an early fort, a Norman keep, a baron's castle, a lordly mansion, the attractions and historic interest of Warwick are almost unrivalled, and its great gardens, its famous huge marble vase, its long line of picturesque river and splendid range of park can scarcely be over-praised.

Kenilworth, only six miles distant, is a wonderful contrast in every way. Its great halls are ruinous, its great park cut up, its tilt-yard scarcely traceable among the trees, its 'pleasaunce' desolate and now mere kitchen-garden ground, its great lakes long ago dried up, its once impregnable keep with a battered and broken wall. As another example of the evolution of military architecture, as an object-lesson to vivify the dry bones of English history, it is curiously interesting. From Geoffrey de Clinton, the Chamberlain of Henry I., and Simon de Montfort—the Father of Parliaments—and John of Gaunt —'time-honoured Lancaster'—and Richard II., who built walls and turrets and the great hall and adjoining tower; from 'the favourite' Leicester and Elizabeth's famous visit; from babbling Laneham's story of the festivities down to the troublous times of the great Civil War, when the castle was destroyed, never to be restored, is a stirring series of chapters in English story; but far less interesting to the crowds of visitors than the little incident some sixty years ago, when 'a tall lame old gentleman, who leaned on his stick,' rambled among the ruins, chatted with the old custodian, and seemed loth to depart, became the 'Wizard of the North,' and awoke more than the ancient echoes of the castle, and re-peopled the ruins with characters and incidents which the world 'will not willingly let die.' The seer of Abbotsford, with his magic pen, gave a new and exciting interest to the gray and crumbling walls. The story of Amy Robsart and the famous Leicester, 'all made out of the dreamer's brain,' almost eclipsed the visit of the 'Virgin Queen,' and Kenilworth Castle became the great attraction to romantic readers from all parts of the world. 'The pen' has been 'mightier than the sword;' the brave fights of Simon de Montfort are forgotten; the reckless extravagance of Leicester is almost unregarded; the long siege of the castle is 'ancient history,' and too dull to read; the Civil War contests are scarcely thought of, and the old hall and the tower where Amy took refuge (according to Scott *only*) are the great centres of attraction and interest to the modern visitor to the picturesque old ruins and the wrecks of the history of seven hundred years.

Maxtoke Castle, near Coleshill, is in many ways more interesting than either Warwick or Kenilworth, for its moat and outer walls and its old iron-bound gate and gatehouse are scarcely changed during six hundred years, and it is the most complete castle in Warwickshire. It was built by a Clinton in the reign of Edward III.; was granted to the Comptons by Henry VII., who sold it to the Lord Keeper Egerton, under Elizabeth, and was afterwards bought by the Dilke family, in whose hands it now remains. It is in form a parallelogram, with hexagonal towers at each corner; is surrounded by a moat with borders of flower-beds; has a stone bridge, where the old drawbridge once hung; and the iron-work on the massive old gate bears the arms of Humphrey, Duke of Buckingham. A noble hall, dining-room, curiously carved door and chimney-piece, an ancient chapel and kitchen escaped the effects of a great fire; and the casernes for the garrison, the old wheel-timber beams supporting the floor of one of the towers—an example almost unique—make Maxtoke Castle one of the most interesting 'survivals' of the ravages of time among old English castles. Its lovely situation, on low ground, in a fine old park, and the care of successive owners—especially the Fetherstones and Dilkes—have happily preserved this curiously interesting and almost perfect relic of English military architecture.

Tamworth Castle is another of the ancient castles which have remained almost unchanged for many centuries. It is just in Warwickshire, although the town is in Staffordshire. It stands on a lofty mound alongside and overlooking the Tame, and although showing little more than one great tower, when seen from a distance among the trees, its walls are unharmed and its interior very interesting. It was given by William the Norman to Robert Marmion, one of his followers, and remained in that family till 20 Edward I. (1291), when it passed by marriage to the Ferrers and Compton families, and afterwards to the Townsends. The larger part of the mound is artificial, and probably dates from the early Saxon times, as some 'herring-bone' work is still visible near the base of the road leading up to the castle. Many of the rooms are large and lofty, and it forms an early example of the old 'keep' tower, adapted for residence as well as defence.

Vestiges of large and deep trenches, called the King's Dyke, remain to show that it was considered an important post, and was ready to receive and resist successfully even a serious attack. It is partially protected by the river Anker, as well as the Tame. As the home of the Marmions and as an ancient castle, it has considerable interest, but it has no important historic record, and is now let to, and occupied by, an inhabitant of the town.

Astley Castle, near Nuneaton, is the only example in the county of one of the castles of the thirteenth century (Edward I.), when a castle was a fortified house with a moat. Astley Castle is a small building, almost unaltered as to exterior and surrounding walls, with a picturesque moat enclosing house and garden, and a stone bridge in place of a drawbridge. Its walls are embattled, and it has a good gateway from the bridge, but the interior has been modernized. The walls are ivy-covered, and the pile has an old-world appearance. The Duke of Suffolk, the father of Lady Jane Grey, lived in the castle, and after concealment in the woods near the moat, he was discovered and finally beheaded on Tower Hill. A contemporary portrait, a chair and table used by him in his concealment, are preserved as heirlooms in the house. The castle and manor passed from the Astleys, by marriage, to Lord Grey de Ruthin; then to the Duke of Suffolk, and afterwards, by an exchange of lands, to the Newdegate family, to whom, with the neighbouring Arbury Hall—the 'Cheverel Manor' of 'Scenes of Clerical Life '—it now belongs.

Brandon Castle and *Caludon Castle*, both near Coventry, were formerly important places, but little more than the ground-plan of the ruins of Brandon and some fragments of Caludon are now left. At *Beaudesert*, near Henley-in-Arden, the foundations of a large castle, erected soon after the Conquest by Thurstane de Montfort, are known only by mounds of ruins and the lines of a moat, and its history is unknown.

Among the fortified manor-houses which followed the military castles in more (or less) peaceful times, Warwickshire has several examples of exceptional interest. *Baddesley Clinton*, near Knowle, is the finest example, but it is comparatively unknown, as it lies in a remote park distant from road and rail. It is charmingly picturesque, for it has a fine ancient moat surrounding its gray walls, and quaint gables and chimneys, and its pretty garden parterres surrounded on three sides by the rooms of the house, most of which belongs to the end of the fifteenth century, with some additions of later date, which, however, are so venerable and harmonious with the older parts that it is really an old-world house, even to the rooms and furniture. Early in the fifteenth century it was the property of the Bromes, but soon afterwards it passed to the Ferrers family, with whom it now remains—an unbroken line of thirteen generations. It is beyond all doubt one of the two most interesting old houses in the county, perfect as a mere picture of old life and times, picturesque to an unsurpassed degree, and historically memorable as the home of one of the early antiquaries of Warwickshire—Henry Ferrers, of Baddesley, the friend and fellow-worker of Sir William Dugdale and of Sir Symon Archer, to whom, as has been noted in an earlier chapter, the lovers of Warwickshire are eternally indebted for ' materials of history.'

The other great and famous historic house of Warwickshire is *Compton Wynyates*, six miles from the site of the Battle of Edge Hill. From the 7th Edward I. (1278) to our times it has been a cherished treasure of the Compton family. The house, unlike Baddesley Clinton, has only a part of the old moat left; but it is far more lofty, extensive, and picturesque. It was built in the early years of Henry VIII. (*circa* 1510), and in the best style of that time. It is a marvellous and harmonious combination of the best and most artistic work in brick, stone, and wood. Its variegated colours of brick, its richly-moulded brick chimneys, its exquisitely carved gables and beams and wainscoting, its bold and vigorous and delicate stone carving, its noble rooms and great hall, with minstrels' gallery, its ninety rooms, with a secret chapel in the roof, its long lines of dormitories for soldiers, its venerable, moss-covered, and picturesque quadrangle, combine a series of charming views which are unequalled in Warwickshire and unsurpassed elsewhere. It stands in a secluded 'combe' among fine trees, which conceal it from view till it comes suddenly into sight, and impresses the visitor so as to be a memory for life. For several years it had a strange charm as an almost deserted, but not neglected, house, but it was carefully repaired (not restored) a few years ago, and is certainly the most quaint, original, and picturesque old-world house in Warwickshire.

Among the smaller castles in Warwickshire, some, once famous, but now in ruins, are worth passing mention. *Brandon Castle*, near Combe Abbey and Coventry, has only some grassy slopes indicating the place and lines of its old walls. Its builder and its destroyer are alike unknown; but it was a large and important fortress early in the thirteenth century, and is supposed to have been attacked and ruined by the friends of Simon de Montfort, in consequence of its then owner (John de Verdon) raising troops for Henry III. to attack Kenilworth Castle. After this wreckage, it is supposed that Theodore de Verdon rebuilt the castle. At the Conquest it was given to Turchill de Warwick, and remained in the hands of Norman holders till 7 Richard I. (1195), when it was fully garrisoned; and in 2 Henry III. (1226) the formation of a great pool, probably a defensive moat, was opposed by the monks of Combe. In Dugdale's time (*ante* 1656) 'nothing remained thereof but the moats and heaps of rubbish' of the once famous castle.

Caludon, three miles from Coventry, although the few remains show a castellated mansion rather than a castle proper, has many marks of an early work of the fourteenth century—a large moat and important earthworks still showing the extent of the site. Its remaining ruins are singularly picturesque, although little known. It has considerable historical and some literary interest, as in the reign of Richard II. it was held by Thomas Mowbray, Duke of Norfolk, who went forth from it to Gosford Green, Coventry, to meet the Duke of Hereford (the famous Bolingbroke) before Richard II., each 'to appeal the other of high treason,' and to 'throw down his gage' for single combat. In the third scene of the first act of 'King Richard the Second' Shakespeare has given a vivid dramatic picture of the historic scene of the rebuke and banishment of Bolingbroke.

Among other remains of the smaller castles, of which only little is known as to their origin, history, or ruin, *Beaudesert*, near Henley-in-Arden, which was held in Simon de Montfort's time and had been built soon after the Conquest by Thurstane de Montfort, was the principal residence of the family for several generations. During the Wars of the Roses it was dismantled, and scarcely a trace of its site now remains except the mound which marks the keep. *Brinklow*, seven miles from Coventry, has a lofty tumulus, on which tradition records that a castle once stood; but the earthwork, largely artificial, is probably only an early British fort, which the Romans may have utilized, as the Foss Road passes close by, and Roman intrenchments are found around the tumulus. *Coleshill* has some traces of an early castle or mansion almost unknown in history. *Coventry*, or rather *Cheylesmore*, has some highly interesting remains. It is supposed that Coventry itself was originally built by Leofric, Earl of Mercia, and his Countess Godiva, for a convent of nuns, about 1043, but the early history is very obscure. 'Cheylesmore' (or Coventry) Castle, of which very considerable relics remain, was originally the manorial residence of the Earls of Chester, and its earliest known state is rather that of a fortified mansion than of a feudal castle. It has, however, much latent interest, and although much has been done to destroy its original form, some remarkable discoveries have been made during the summer of this year (1889). In another of the series of alterations which have been so often in progress during several generations, some of the most important and valuable wall-paintings ever found in Warwickshire have been discovered. On removing the plaster from one of the walls, a very large fresco in colours, singularly clear and perfect, has been found. A modern flooring (probably a century or so old) divided a lofty hall, or probably chapel, into two parts, and the lower part shows about half of an exceptionally large 'rood,' with the lower part only of the cross, and various figures and inscriptions (one especially interesting) of very early date. The best authority (Mr. J. A. Cossins, of Birmingham) is doing all he can for the preservation of these rare relics, and it is to be hoped that when these lines are read, these ancient and valuable remains of ecclesiastical art may at least have been carefully copied, if not reverently preserved. So far as is known at the time of writing, they are more than equal in interest, because of earlier date, than those once in the Guild Chapel, Stratford-on-Avon, which were whitewashed over early in the present century, but whose quaint scenes and vivid colours have been fortunately preserved in Fisher's careful drawings of the 'Frescoes at Stratford-on-Avon,' in 1810. 'Cheylesmore,' now known as 'The Charterhouse,' was rebuilt by Hugh, son of Ranulph, Earl of Chester, in the twelfth century, and it has so much interest in many details of early work that, even after its many changes, it ought to be carefully preserved.

Another remarkable relic of the best days of British art still remains at *Temple Balsall*, near Knowle, almost unaltered, as to the church and some of the buildings erected by the Knights Templars, who built the church and the preceptory in the reign of Richard II. Under Edward II. the fraternity was dissolved, and the possessions passed to the Knights Hospitallers, who held them till the Dissolution. Elizabeth granted the manor to her favourite, Robert Dudley, whose granddaughter, Lady Catharine Leveson, bequeathed it as a hospital for thirty alms-women, who are still liberally supported by the trust. The ancient hall or refectory, 140 feet long and of very fine proportions, has been spoiled by internal divisions; but the church remains so nearly as it was built by the Templars, that it is thought, at the first glance, to have been recently restored. It is 104 feet long, 39 feet wide, and 57 feet high, and without any aisles to spoil its noble proportions. Its floor slopes upwards from the west door, and there is no division of the chancel except by three low steps across the floor. On the south are three stone seats with a canopied recess and a small niche. The lofty east window has five lights, and in the side-walls are three windows, with three or four lights alternately, and the tracery of all greatly varied and exquisitely designed and carved. Over the west door is a fine window of five lights, with a Catharine wheel or marigold window of twelve compartments. As an example of a preceptory and church of the twelfth century, of which neither restoration nor neglect have changed any important feature, Temple Balsall (or Balsall Temple) is unrivalled in Warwickshire, and not surpassed in any part of England.

Combe Abbey, near Coventry, is another fine example of the substantial preservation of an old monastic foundation, although a few years ago it was almost rebuilt in a French Gothic style from Mr. Nesfield's designs. Some parts of the old Norman building, the quadrangle and cloisters, have been preserved, and the famous gallery of portraits, and the fact that they were bequeathed by Elizabeth of Hungary, sister of Charles I., and that the abbey was so closely connected with the Gunpowder Plot, have given the place far more than local fame.

Guy's Cliff, near Warwick, is not only famous as the reputed retreat of the legendary Guy when he became a hermit, and lived in the cave still shown, but is the most picturesque house in Warwickshire. All that is old has been carefully preserved, and even the later additions and alterations are in excellent taste. The pleasant house on the lofty cliff, the fine avenue of trees, the picturesque mill, have been too often photographed to need description; and nearly opposite the house the rude stone which marks the place where Edward's favourite, Piers Gaveston, was beheaded in 1312, by the arts of Guy de Beauchamp, Earl of Warwick, 'the black dog of Arden,' has given the scene historic fame.

The Priory at Warwick is another fine example of an ancient and picturesque house long ago secularised, but retaining many of its original characteristics as a monastic building. As the Priory of St. Sepulchre (the Holy Sepulchre), it was founded by Henry de Newburgh, Earl of Warwick, and his son, in the reign of Henry I. (*circa* 1100-1135), and was granted to one Thomas Hawkins at the Dissolution, and after many vicissitudes and the destruction of many parts, it was bought by the Great Western Railway Company and afterwards sold. It is now in private hands, and its venerable remains are carefully preserved.

Charlecote, near Stratford-on-Avon, is well known the wide world over as the seat of the Lucys, one of whom has been famous as associated with the tradition of Shakespeare's deer-stealing exploits, *valeat quantum*. The house is in a fine park, with a stream meandering through the grounds, and the building is an excellent example of an Elizabethan house. The family succession runs back from the twelfth century, when Walter de Cherlcote took the name of Lucy, and the family have been lords of Charlecote ever since. In the early part of the reign of Elizabeth, Thomas Lucy was knighted, soon after the house was built. The house, built mainly of brick, with stone quoinings, and the fine gatehouse and garden, are exceptionally interesting, and the interior has been practically unchanged —except as to some fashions of furnishing—and some of the old portraits and furniture are carefully preserved. Near the house is the little modern church, in which some remarkable and interesting monuments to members of the Lucy family may be seen, and are well worth seeing.

Clopton House, also near Stratford-on-Avon, belonged to a family of very ancient date, and is chiefly famous for the munificence of Sir Hugh Clopton, Lord Mayor of London, at the end of the fifteenth century, who lavished his wealth upon his native town. He built the Great Bridge over the Avon, and greatly helped in Church and other work, and although his own monument has perished, and its site is marked only by a modern altar-tomb, his *monumentum ære perennius* is seen in all parts of the old town where he was born. Clopton, as a name, was assumed *tempore* Henry III. by a family one of whose descendants was married to Sir George Carew, afterwards Earl of Totness, to whose memories a double effigy and an imposing monument remain in the Clopton Chapel in Stratford Church. Clopton House, as to some parts, is of the fifteenth century, but little of that date remains, and the family is long ago extinct.

Stoneleigh Abbey, near Kenilworth, is one of the largest and finest of the 'mansions' of the Georgian era, and is placed in one of the great parks of the county. The estates were held by the Crown till the reign of Henry II., when a Cistercian Abbey was founded by the monks from Radmore (Staffordshire), with very extensive privileges as to markets, fairs, and free-warren. Some of the best art of the time was lavished on the abbey-buildings, and many picturesque remains have been preserved. At the Dissolution the abbey-lands went to Charles Brandon, Duke of Suffolk, on whose attainder they passed to others, and in 3rd Elizabeth (1560) were bought by Sir Thomas Leigh, who erected a mansion among the monastic buildings, and partly on the site of the abbey; but this, in its turn, made way for the great mansion built by Edward, Lord Leigh—a great square brick building, behind and under which the old relics—except the gate-house of Robert de Hockele (1349), and with the arms of Henry II.—have practically been lost.

Eatington (or Ettington, as now spelled) is another picturesque house of various dates and great antiquity, in the southern part of the county, four miles from Shipston-on-Stour. Dugdale notes with great pleasure that this is 'the only one in the county which glories in an uninterrupted succession of its owners for so long a tract of time.' Henry de Ferrers held it at the Conquest, and it has remained in the same male line ever since. Until the reign of Henry III. (*circa* 1250) it was the principal seat of the family, but they afterwards fixed their seat at Shirley (co. Derby), and thence took their present name. Eatington Hall is of various dates as to building, with some few fragments of very early date. The late Mr. Evelyn Philip Shirley took great interest in the house of his fathers, and preserved all that remained. In 1795 'the church was desecrated,' and a new one built at Upper Eatington, but the tower and some parts of the nave and chancel remain, covered with ivy, and are not likely to be 'desecrated' again.

Merevale Abbey, near Atherstone, is another survival of the 'ages of faith,' and of the admirable art which was lavished on the church-work of centuries ago. Robert, Earl Ferrers, in 13 Stephen (1147), founded and largely endowed a Cistercian monastery among the pleasant, sunny slopes of North Warwickshire, and many curious memorials still survive the wreck of the Dissolution days,

16—2

when the site was given to Sir Walter Devereux, Lord Ferrers of Chartley, one of whose successors sold it to one of the Stratford family, in which line it came, by maternal descent, to the Stratford-Dugdale family, with whom it now remains. The mansion stands on a commanding height in a richly-wooded park, and contains some of the relics—books and papers—of Sir William Dugdale, the historian of the county. The remains of the abbey church are especially interesting, and a great east window—a very fine example of a 'Jesse' window—is quaint in design and rich in colour; and there are also several sepulchral monuments in alabaster and stone. As connected with the present owners, the house of Sir William Dugdale must be mentioned here. *Blythe Hall* takes its name from the small river Blythe, near Coleshill. In 1625 the famous antiquary, historian, herald and genealogist purchased the manor of Blythe in the parish of Shustoke, and in 1626 he removed to Blythe Hall, where he passed the rest of his busy and useful life over his 'History of Warwickshire,' which is generally admitted to be the greatest county history which English knowledge and research and industry have ever produced. He died at Blythe Hall February 10, 1686, in the eighty-first year of his age, and was buried in Shustoke Church, where others of his family repose in peace.

Arbury Hall, near Nuneaton, is chiefly a building of the last century, and although not level with modern taste and better knowledge of art, is a remarkable proof that the love of Gothic art (as Sir Charles Eastlake has shown) never wholly died out, nor was its true spirit lost even in the darkest days of Georgian ignorance of the principles and practice of art. A monastery *tempore* Henry II. fell in due course, at the Dissolution, to the Duke of Suffolk, 30 Henry VIII. (1538), and under Elizabeth to Sir Edmund Anderson, who 'totally demolished the fabric of the house and church,' which he afterwards handed over, for a considerable consideration, to John Newdigate, Esq., to whose successor, Sir Roger Newdigate (says the late Thomas Sharp) 'we are indebted for that architectural gem, the "Strawberry Hill" of Warwickshire.' This was done with a lavish expenditure and very remarkable good taste — for that age. Imitations of the groinings of Henry VII.'s Chapel at Westminster were introduced, and various classic remains were brought from Italy, so that Horace Walpole had an earnest rival in his classic tastes. The park is well wooded, and even in the full light of modern æsthetics and art-knowledge Arbury deserves much praise as a link in the chain of love of Gothic art. Modern readers, however, will be more interested in the fact that Arbury is the 'Cheverel Manor' of George Eliot, and therefore very widely known.

Ragley Hall, at the other end of the county, was built by Lord Conway about a century ago, and is a good example of Wyatt's 'classic' style. The estates have come down through Marmions, Camviles, Botelers, Rouses, Brownes, and Conways to the present Marquis of Hertford, who has a truly lordly park and a fine gallery of pictures on the pleasant banks of the Arrow, near Alcester; and close by is another famous old 'Court.'

Coughton Court, near Alcester, was noted by Leland on his visit: 'Mr. Throgmorton hath a fayre mannour place moated at Coughton'—a manor which came to the family in the reign of Henry IV. (*circa* 1399-1413), and has remained in the same hands. The fine turret-gateway is said to have been removed from Evesham at the Dissolution, but Dugdale merely records (and he does not often give so much building detail) that it 'was intended that the house should be finished in the same style.' Some of the windows, probably, were brought from Evesham, and the principal parts of the house are of the best years of Henry VIII., but with numerous alterations of the worst period of Charles II. The gate-house is a specially fine example of the early Tudor style, and the stone selected was so excellent that the details seem as fresh and clear as any work of recent date.

Pooley Hall, near Tamworth, was held by the Marmions, of Tamworth, in the time of Stephen, with other lands at Polesworth, but passed to the Cokain family by marriage, and the 'Mannour-house' at Pooley was built by Sir Thomas Cokain in 22 Henry VII. (1506). It is a remarkable survival of the castellated mansions which began to replace the castles and fortalices of the more troublous times. The remains are singularly picturesque, but have suffered many changes and are almost ruinous, but enough is preserved to be greatly interesting.

Kenilworth Castle is not only remarkable as a Norman fortress and as still showing the ruins of the Great Hall of John of Gaunt and the Leicester buildings erected by the favourite of Elizabeth, but it has one well-known portion which is a rare and fine example of 'evolution' in architecture—the great gate-house. It was also the work of Robert Leicester, *circa* 1565, and its turret corners are massive and handsome, but about a century later the two Gothic gables were added, to finally de-militarize the building and to add residential rooms. The Rev. E. H. Knowles, the learned historian of the castle, estimates the date as about 1656, as Dugdale's print shows the gate-house before the addition of the gabled rooms.

Kingsbury Hall (or Manor-house), between Coleshill and Tamworth, marks the site, according to Dugdale, of a seat of the Mercian kings, where Bertulf held a great council in 891. The Countess Godiva held this and many other manors near, and in the reign of John (1199-1216) it came by marriage to Peter Bracebrigge, whose descendants lived there till Elizabeth's reign, when they sold it to the Willoughbys of Middleton. The present farmhouse hall has some walls and windows probably not earlier than the reign of Elizabeth, but the remains of a moat and the choice of the site—a cliff above the Tame—indicate clearly, that many centuries earlier Kingsbury was an important position.

Weston Park, near Shipston-on-Stour, has no traces of the great sixteenth-century house described in Thomas's Dugdale, which was levelled and a new house built about a century ago. The Sheldon family had 'a park' of three hundred acres, which was to be 'called Weston Park for ever.' The present house, large and stately, has no special merit, but the builder of the old house—William Sheldon, who died in 1570 was the first to introduce tapestry-weaving into England. He possessed a series of maps of the counties of England on a very large scale, and with many curious details. They were woven under his direction, and he hung them on the walls of his great hall at Weston. In 1781 the library and furniture at Weston were sold, and the tapestry-maps were bought by Horace Walpole for thirty guineas. Walpole presented them to Earl Harcourt, who built a special room for them at Nuneham Courtney, but some of them (at least) were given to the Museum at York, where they were hung some years ago. 'The maps are so well executed that the rivers, hills, clumps of trees, churches, and even windmills,' are clearly shown. Those at York represent principally the Midland counties, of which they would be a very interesting record, if they should prove on examination to give facts and details not noted in the maps of the sixteenth century, which were generally on a small scale, and from which many local sites and places were necessarily omitted.

Wormleighton, also in South Warwickshire, is so remote as to be rarely visited and little known. From the Earl of Mellent at the Conquest, and Geoffrey de Clinton, it passed in 22 Henry VII. (1506) to John Spencer (afterwards Sir John), and is now the property of Earl Spencer of Althorpe, the Spensers of Wormleighton having settled later in Northamptonshire. The manor-house at Wormleighton

dates from the later years of Henry VIII., but is a very
fine specimen of the best architecture of that time, and
before the decadence under Elizabeth and James. Although
now only a farmhouse, there are many interesting and
striking portions of the old house left. Some portions
must have been removed, as Dugdale describes the place
as 'a fair mannour house, wherein he [Sir John Spencer]
had his residence with sixty persons of his family, being a
good benefactor to the Church in ornaments and other
things.'

Many other ancient or notable houses exist in various
parts of the county, and some of them singularly complete
and interesting after the chances and changes of two or
three hundred years. Any old house merely architecturally
or archæologically remarkable has been purposely omitted,
and only those which have some historical or biographical
associations have been included in this summary. The
'Bibliography' appended to this volume will include the
titles and some notes of the works concerning Warwickshire in which fuller details and descriptions may be
found.

DEER PARKS in Warwickshire are neither so numerous
nor so famous as in some other counties, but as their principal historian (the late Evelyn Philip Shirley) was a
Warwickshire 'gentleman,' and has left some account of
them, a few details may reasonably be given here as supple-
mental to the 'ancestral homes' already described. Seven
only of the forty 'shires' of England have any famous
deer-parks, but Warwickshire has some twelve or fourteen
of more or less interest. The time of Elizabeth was most
noteworthy for the formation or preservation of deer-parks,
and it has been estimated that they were seven hundred in
number in England during her long life. Many parks,
like Charlecote, were formed during her reign; but now,
probably, not more than half that number, all told, could
be found. The Civil War was one great source of

the destruction of deer-parks, and an anonymous writer ('J. P. B.') of a very interesting paper records that Charles II. found, on his accession, that deer were so scarce, even in the royal parks, that he bestowed a baronetcy on a gentleman in the Isle of Ely who sent him some deer. The extravagance of the gentry and nobles under Elizabeth, the large sales of land for cultivation, and the troubles of the Civil War time, combined to reduce the deer-parks generally; and in Warwickshire, while Charlecote flourished, parks like Fulbroke and others were neglected and opened for farms. Some of the oldest parks were connected with Warwick Castle, such as Haseley, Wedgenock, and Grove; and the latter two still remain, but Haseley was disparked some two hundred years ago. *Sutton Coldfield Park*, another very old one, is still preserved almost unaltered, but has long lost its deer, and is now only a vast woody paradise for the thousands of Birmingham residents and the teeming population of South Staffordshire; while the northern portion of that county has the vast area of Cannock Chase, in which a few wild red deer still remain. *Kenilworth* had a Great Park when Elizabeth paid her famous visit to her favourite Leicester, and there were nearly eight hundred acres devoted to red deer. 'The circuit of the castle, manors, parks, and chases lying together contain at least nineteen or twenty miles, in a pleasant country, the like for strength, state, and pleasure not being within the realm of England.' During the Civil War the park was divided and cut up into farms, so that the ruins of the castle stand in a very limited area, and the visitor gets no adequate idea of the former magnificence and extent of the possessions of Robert Dudley, Earl of Leicester, when he entertained his Queen with such lavish hospitality and splendour for seventeen days in July, 1575. The historian Dugdale, who never indulges in elaborate description or exaggeration, gives a graphic account; and Gascoigne's 'Princely Pleasures of Kenilworth,' and the amusing details given in Robert Laneham's ('gentleman mercer, of London') 'Letter' are too well known and too well worth reading at length to require any of the details to be quoted here. There can be scarcely a doubt that Shakespeare, then a lad of eleven, saw some of those 'Revels,' and they seem to be clearly referred to, with other local incidents, in the brilliant lines of the 'Midsummer Night's Dream' (Act i., Scene 2), in the courtly conversation of Oberon and Titania.

Among other deer-parks in Warwickshire were a park near Astley Castle, to which ninety acres were added in 1497, but, except some few fine trees, no remains exist; the Great Park of *Stoneleigh*, of nearly six hundred acres with nearly five hundred fallow deer, which, with its grand trees, although not one of the oldest, is the most famous in the county; *Shuckburgh*, with a hundred and twenty acres and about two hundred fallow deer; *Charlecote*, with two hundred acres and four hundred red (or fallow) deer; *Compton Wynyates*, emparked *circa* 1520, but of which few traces remain; *Weston Park* (*circa* 1546), but, like Compton, disparked about a hundred years ago; *Eatington* (or Ettington, as Mr. Shirley preferred to call it in his later life), which existed in 1653, and was emparked long before, but no date can be given—a park of which Mr. Shirley was very proud, for it covered over four hundred acres, with two hundred light and dark coloured fallow-deer; *Fulbroke*, originally a royal hunting preserve, emparked *circa* 1418, but disparked *circâ* 1600, when portions of a splendid gateway and other buildings were pulled down and some of the wreck removed to Compton Wynyates, and in 1615 the park was purchased by Sir Thomas Lucy, who did not empark Charlecote till later; so that if Shakespeare did steal deer, it would have been from Fulbroke, and not Charlecote; and the late Mr. Charles Holte Bracebridge showed very clearly that the whole deer-stealing story was extremely doubtful.

Ragley Park (Marquis of Hertford) is not of very ancient date, but finely timbered and well stocked with deer; and a neighbouring park at *Arrow* is of very ancient date, as it was emparked by Sir Robert Burdett in 1334, and when Edward IV. was hunting there he shot a favourite white buck, and Thomas Burdett, 'openly wishing the horns in his belly that moved the king so to do, being arraigned and convicted of high treason for those words, upon inference made that his meaning was mischievous to the king himself, he lost his life for the same.' One of the oldest parks now remaining in the county, and still stocked with deer, is that around *Maxtoke Castle*, near Coleshill, which probably dates from early in the fourteenth century, and which was considered an old park in 1522, when its owner, Edward Stafford, Duke of Buckingham, was attainted of high treason. *Packington*, near Hampton-in-Arden and Coleshill, was emparked by Sir Clement Fisher early in the reign of James I. (*circa* 1605), with five hundred acres and large herds of deer; but it is better known in the county for its large number of most ancient and picturesque oaks, which have attracted artists and delighted patrons of art for more than fifty years. *Arbury* has a fine park, dating from about the middle of the last century; and *Merevale*, which lost all its deer in 1656, has been restocked during the last twenty-five years with about one hundred 'head' in its nearly two hundred acres of magnificent park. The latest-formed park is *Clopton*, near Stratford-on-Avon, enclosed *circa* 1850. *Aston Hall*, close to Birmingham, had a large park around its fine old hall from 1610, and was well stocked with deer as late as *circa* 1818; but only forty acres around the hall now remain as a People's Hall and Park.

CHAPTER X.

CITIES, TOWNS, ETC.

Old and New Cities : Coventry and Birmingham.—Historic Coventry, St. Michael's Church and St. Mary's Hall, Charterhouse and Recent Discovery, Changes of Industries.—Birmingham : Early History, Antiquities, Gilds, St. John's Chapel and Popular Vote, Civil War Time, Restoration Days, City of Refuge, Growth of Manufactures, Social and Political Progress, Incorporation and Rapid Development, Free Public Libraries and Municipal School of Art, Educational Institutions, Political History, Varieties and Extent of Trades.—Leamington ; Stratford-on-Avon.

COVENTRY.—Warwickshire contains two cities, one being one of the oldest, and the other the very newest, in English annals. Coventry, the 'city of the three tall spires,' has held the title of an episcopal see (Lichfield and Coventry, sometimes alternated Coventry and Lichfield) almost from the time of Leofric, eight hundred years ago. Birmingham became a 'city' only in January of the present year (1889). The city of Coventry, as a 'see,' arose from the monastery founded by the Earl Leofric and his Countess Godiva early in the eleventh century, and a century later the monastery rose to the rank of a cathedral and its Prior held the position of a mitred abbot and sat in Parliament as a spiritual peer. 'Coventre' and 'Coventria' were the ancient names of the city from the foundation of a religious house, of which Sancta Osburga was the Abbess, as early as the seventh century ; but this was destroyed *circa* 1016 by Edric, who had overrun Mercia and destroyed many of the villages and towns. On the site of the ruins of the abbey, Leofric and Godiva founded a monastery *circa* 1043 (Edward the Confessor), which they endowed and decorated munificently, as noted in an earlier page (p. 19). Leofric died in 1057, and the couplet in the stained glass window—

> 'I, Luriche, for love of thee,
> Do make Coventre toll free'—

is enough to show how baseless is the later legend of his barbarous condition of Godiva's ride through the city, which was first publicly celebrated as a procession so late as the reign of Charles II. Although the affix 'tre' is supposed to be British, there is little doubt that a Roman vicinal way passed through the place. In 1337 the lordship of the manor, as that of Cheylesmore, was annexed to the Dukedom of Cornwall (Edward the Black Prince), but under George IV. the manor was sold to the Marquis of Hertford. In 1344 the town was incorporated, having previously obtained various charters for paving, for a common (public) conduit, and for an exemption from toll in all England. In 1335 the walls were begun, and Richard II. gave stone from Cheylesmore Park for the walls and the two principal gates; and in 1397 he appointed Coventry as the place for the Dukes of Hereford and Norfolk to fight out their quarrel, and he came in person to Gosford Green, outside the city, attended by all his peers and an army of 10,000 men. In 1404 a Parliament was held in the Great Chamber of the Priory, and as the writs which summoned it required that 'no lawyer or person skilled in the laws should be returned,' it became famous (and unique) as the *Parliamentum Indoctorum*: the Legislature of the Unlearned. Henry VI. and his Queen made several visits to Coventry, and in 1451, as a mark of favour, Henry made the city, with certain hamlets and villages adjacent, an entire and separate 'county,' and raised the Bailiffs to the rank of Sheriffs.

In 1459 another Parliament assembled in Coventry, when the Duke of York and others were 'attainted,' and some chronicles have called that assembly the *Parliamentum Diabolicum*. In the contest between Henry VI. and Edward IV. the citizens were loyal to Henry, and when Edward reached Coventry in 1470 the gates were closed against him, and he afterwards, when safely seated on the throne, withdrew the privileges of the city, and restored them only on the payment of a fine of five hundred marks. In 1485 Henry VII., victorious from the Bosworth Field, arrived in Coventry and be-knighted the Mayor. In 1565 Elizabeth, in her summer 'progress,' visited the city. In 1569 Mary, Queen of Scots, was brought to Coventry, from Tutbury, for greater security, and is traditionally said to have been lodged in the Queen's Chamber—part of St. Mary's Hall. In 1617 her son James was warmly welcomed at Coventry; but in 1642 the citizens closed their gates against his son (Charles I.); and when, at the Restoration, Charles II. came into place and power, he employed five hundred men for twenty-four days in dismantling the walls and gates—the walls three miles in circumference, and with thirty-two towers and gates. James II. was in Coventry in 1687, and William III. passed through the city in 1690—altogether such a royal record as few cities can surpass or even rival. This mere outline of facts and dates will suffice to show that the ancient city has had a 'strange, eventful history,' and happily few cities have a more complete and perfect historical record, so far as old documents, charters, gild-books, letters, seals, and account-books can throw light upon the dark places of the past. The records and muniments, long neglected, but left unharmed except by time, have, thanks to several generations of Coventry citizens, been preserved, and still later overhauled and cared for.

The labours of Thomas Sharp, fifty years ago, and of John Fetherston, twenty years ago, have left the record-wealth of Coventry unrivalled as to extent and condition—a wondrous treasury of the priceless memorials of English life and progress for many centuries.

Although so much manuscript history has been preserved, vast masses of monumental history have been destroyed or buried beyond recall. The wild revenge of Charles II. broke down relics of the old times which would have been appreciated and understood as 'history in stone' with the greater lights of later days. The Dissolution and the Restoration alike have much to answer for, as well as the ever-maligned Cromwell and the Civil War. Even the exact site of the Cathedral was uncertain till some thirty years ago, when the removal of some buildings disclosed some of the foundations, and indicated the lines of the place. These fragments, with excellent and praiseworthy taste, have been left uncovered now, and help to show how important and interesting a building disappeared at the Dissolution, and how bright a light is thrown on the reports of the Commissioners of Henry VIII. during their visitations of the religious houses. The old remains of Coventry, which are so frequently uncovered during excavations for new buildings, are interesting enough to be a national trust. The preservation of 'ancient monuments' should not be limited to 'schedules' of prehistoric remains; but a public officer should examine and report, and a public fund should provide for the preservation or record of many of the surviving relics of the 'good old times.'

St. Michael's Church is not only the most conspicuous, but one of the most interesting relics in Coventry, and, with one exception, the largest parish church in England. Its grand tower and graceful spire are landmarks for miles around, and the details of its carving are still charming, although sadly worn and crumbling during its long four hundred years. Not only the height and grandeur of its tower and spire, but the fine proportions of its interior, are universally appreciated and admired, and the citizens of Coventry, with some help from the county of Warwick, have formed a munificent fund for the restorations, now nearly completed, with excellent judgment and good taste. The other two of the 'three spires'—*Trinity Church* and *Greyfriars*,—have also some notable history, but no details can be given here, nor of the many other picturesque historic remains in the city—with very few exceptions.

St. Mary's Hall, close to St. Michael's, in a picturesque old 'lane,' is full of interest to historian, architect, and artist. It is a superb example of the domestic, as contrasted with ecclesiastical, architecture of four centuries ago. It was built *circa* 1400 as the house of the Gild, and except from the 'corroding tooth of time,' it remains untouched. Its exterior is massive, grand, and impressive; its great window a superb work of art in stone, with its rich mullions, worn niches and exquisite 'tone' of darkred sandstone. Its Great Hall, with the large ancient tapestry (probably of the time of Henry VII.), is an 'old-world' study, and every nook and corner is artistic and historic. The old manuscripts and merchants' marks, seals, trade insignia, and volumes full of rare autograph letters, of all dates, are marvellous illustrations of four centuries of English life.

Ford's Hospital, in Greyfriars' Lane, is a wonderfully picturesque, half-timber house, around a small court of sixteenth century date, also unchanged, since it was founded as a home for poor women by Richard Ford in 1529. *Bablake Hospital*, too, founded by Thomas Bond in 1506 for forty poor men, and later for twenty-four boys, who are fed and clothed and educated, has also much interest. The *Free School* (1572), which was formerly the Hospital of St. John, is another of the many charities (or foundations) of the city, which has also its ancient look. Another peculiarly interesting relic of old Coventry is the *Old Palace Yard*, which still retains most of the external forms which were seen by the royal and noble visitors to the city generations ago. This quaint and curious series of buildings, surrounding a long, large yard or court, has just been sold by auction. Its future is unknown; but if it cannot be saved from destruction, plans and measurements and photographs should be taken as a record of what so ancient a building was four hundred years ago.

Grey Friars monastery is now represented by little more than the spire (which forms one of the famous three), but originally it was a very important place. It was founded in 1324, and the church in 1358, but only the fine octagonal tower survived the Dissolution, and it stood in lonely dignity till the modern church was built. The *White Friars* monastery was founded in 1342, and many and extensive remains of its former dignity are mixed up in a union workhouse—notably, part of the cloisters over which is the old dormitory. The gate of the chapter-house and the lines of the old church are among the remains of the once famous 'house.' *The Charterhouse*, founded in 1381, has no important remains, except a piece of the work of the bridge, and of some other parts, which have been used up in the numerous changes during many years, but, as already mentioned in a previous page (239), some discoveries of fresco work on the walls have given some hope that still further discoveries may be made. One remarkable example of the losses of old relics and of the laudable attempt to secure a record of their existence, site, and purpose is worth quoting. On a corner of the building now called the Pilgrim Inn, in Ironmonger Row, is the following inscription:

'Upon this site stood the large and very ancient edifice called The Pilgrim's Rest. It was supposed to have been the Hostel or Inn for the Maintenance and Entertainment of the Palmers and other Visitors to the Priory of Benedictine Monks which stood to near the Eastward. It became ruinous, and was taken down A.D. MDCCCXX., when this house was erected.'

No formal remains, except in manuscripts, are now found of the religious dramas—mysteries and moralities—for which Coventry was famous in the Middle Ages. Most of these were played on portable stages; but one especially local—the old Coventry play, 'Hock Tuesday,' founded on the massacre of the Danes—was played before Elizabeth at Kenilworth in 1575; and the costs of such performances were generally paid by the numerous Gilds which abounded in Coventry, and of whose 'books' and 'records,' unhappily, too few now remain.

Coventry is, in fact, full of the quaintest and most picturesque old buildings, and even houses which have no special history have all the charm of age. Even now, when so much has been done, new discoveries of old facts may be fully expected, and history may yet be enriched by the patient and unselfish care and research of antiquaries like Mr. W. G. Fretton, F.S.A., who knows every nook and corner of the ancient city.

Coventry Cross has long been so well known by tradition and history that it must be mentioned as once 'one of the chief things in which the city most glories,' and which for 'workmanship and beauty was inferior to none in England.' It was begun in 1541 and finished in 1544, and it replaced an earlier one of 1423. It was hexagonal in plan, fifty-seven feet high, in three stories, and seven feet wide at its base, with eighteen niches adorned with Saints and Kings, some of which had been saved from the White Friars. In 1760 only the lower and part of the second story, with a statue of Henry IV., remained, all much defaced, and all these remains were removed in 1771. Several early drawings confirm the report that Coventry Cross was a very exceptional example of late Tudor style in stone and metal work.

At the Dissolution, the City of Coventry bought large quantities of the old Church lands, buildings, etc., from the Crown, including the Priory buildings, the Mote House, the Grey Friars, and later, in the reign of Edward VI., the lands and possessions of the many Gilds and Chantries which were then dispersed. The Dissolution had, however, caused the rapid decrease of the city, and in 3 Edward VI. (1548) the population had fallen from 16,000 to 3,000 persons, with a general decay of trade, so that additional fairs were established to attract the masses of the people to the almost deserted city. The list of Mayors is complete from 21 Edward III. (1347). The Gilds were very numerous—the Merchants, Trinity, St. Katherine's, the Sheremen and Taylors, Corpus Christi, and many others; and the chantries, almshouses, pensions and indemnities, hospitals and schools, show how great and important a place the city of Coventry was during the Middle Ages.

The modern history of Coventry is principally industrial. For many years it had been famous for its ribbon manufactures, but the French treaty seriously affected its prosperity and paralyzed its trade. One department, however, became a new departure, and has held its ground—the use of the Jacquard loom for the production of pictures and letters on ribbon with perfect clearness and artistic style, at very low prices; so that a large demand has been secured, and a permanent novelty seems to have been added to the industries. One branch of this supply—book-markers—is well known, and not only the originator, Mr. Stevens, but others, have for many years secured a large and increasing demand. Another branch of textile productions in trimming has been developed by Messrs. Cash, and practically the textile industries have not only been revived, but greatly extended, during the past ten or fifteen years. Even cotton-spinning, which was first accomplished by machinery in Birmingham about the middle of the last century by John Wyatt and Lewis Paul, has obtained a place in Coventry, and also weaving; but while the cotton-mill built in Birmingham was turned into a rolling-mill about ninety years ago, and the Lancashire mills and looms still stand supreme, some extensive factories exist at or near Coventry, and have been more or less successful during the past ten or twelve years. The manufacture of elastic webbing, which rose so rapidly, and which is a great industry at Nottingham, had also become an important manufacture in Coventry in 1862, and is still continued under the very severe competition of other places. Woollen and worsted goods, court-lace, and carriage-trimmings are also made in great quantities, but even silk-dyeing is an important trade. The watch manufacture has long been famous as a Coventry industry, and Coventry watches of the best class have probably never been surpassed. It is curious that the 'movements' or 'materials' of watches are principally made at or near Preston (Lancs.), and the cases in Birmingham; but the 'Coventry watches' still hold their own, even against the severe competition of the French, Swiss, and American importations, and the machine-made watches with interchangeable 'movements,' which are made in Birmingham as well as imported from the United States. Many efforts have been made to keep abreast of the competition by the careful study of horology and the more formal and definite technical instruction in the schools. There are, even in the present depressed state of the trade, about one hundred and fifty makers in the city.

The vicissitudes of manufacture are remarkable, and the universal introduction of machinery has had a curious advantage in enabling manufacturers to change their produce by re-arranging their machinery. In Birmingham cases have occurred where elaborate and costly machines made for producing gun-locks and furniture have, when demand has varied and other articles have been required, been adapted to turn out, successively, sewing-machines and bicycles, and hereafter, when wanted, to supply large quantities of any article which can be made wholly or principally by complex machines. About twenty years ago sewing-machines were made in large quantities at Coventry; but when the market was becoming overstocked and the demand declining, the 'cycle' rage commenced, and all available machinery, or all new machines, were 'adapted' to satisfy the new demand. The sewing-machine industry has, in fact, been swamped by the cycle demands, and Coventry now ranks among the principal 'seats' of bicycle and tricycle production. The Coventry Machinists Company (Cheylesmore) were the first to begin the manufacture, and were followed by many others—'Rudge,' 'Premier,' 'Singer,' 'Fleet,' 'Centaur,' 'Meteor,' 'Excelsior,' 'Wellington,' 'Victoria,' and others, which have become famous throughout the cycling world.

Another very notable manufacture was established about thirty years ago—the Skidmore Art-Works in Metal, which was conducted for many years with the help of the late William Costen Aitken, whose refined taste, large knowledge, technical skill, and devoted labour, produced some of the finest art metal-work of modern days, and whose loss, in the best interests of artists and artisans, will ever be mourned by all who knew his genius and worth.

Since the preceding pages were written the discovery of an ancient charter by Mr. Walter de Grey Birch, F.S.A., has thrown additional light on the early history of Coventry, and has helped to confirm rather than to correct the details already given. This charter is an Anglo-Saxon MS. of King Edward the Confessor to the Abbey of St. Mary, Coventry, for the reception of an Abbot and twenty-four monks of the Order of St. Benedict, thus converting the nunnery into the monastery, as previously shown. The other charters—that of Leofric (1043), the Bull of Pope Alexander (1043), and the Conqueror's (1084) —were known to Dugdale, but he and others had overlooked this Anglo-Saxon charter, which was found and added to the British Museum two years ago. It is on a single sheet of parchment, $9\frac{1}{2}$ inches high by $7\frac{1}{2}$ inches wide, written in twenty-three lines, with the sharp, upright letters of the period, and with ink (now) of a dark-yellow tint, so that it is a remarkable example of eleventh-century palæography. A township certainly existed during the Saxon Heptarchy; a religious house of nuns was destroyed by the Danes in 1016; and Archbishop Æthelnoth, of Canterbury, gave a valuable relic—the arm of St. Augustine of Hippo—in 1022; and Leofric founded the abbey church on the north of the 'vil' of Coventry in 1043, as a Benedictine monastery, which rapidly became extremely wealthy and famous. Mr. Birch has issued a facsimile of the newly-found charter, and has added a translation into English, the substance of which is that :

'Eadward, King, greets Edsie, the Archbishop, and all my bishops, abbots and earls, thagnes and sheriffs, and all my faithful men kindly. Every man it behoves very rightly to love and to highly honour our Lord God, and earnestly and unanimously to follow God's laws, and diligently to incline to alms deeds, whereby he may release himself from the bonds of sin. . . . For which necessary things I make known unto you all that I grant with full permission that the same gift which Leofric the Earl and Godgyuæ have given to Christ and His dear Mother and to Leofwin, the abbot, and to the brethren within the minster at Coventry, for their souls to help, in land and in water, in gold and in silver, in ornaments and in all other things, as full and as forth as it stood themselves in hand, and as they therewith that same minster worthily have enriched, so I it firmly grant. And, furthermore, I grant to them also, for my soul, that they have besides full freedom, sac [jurisdiction in religious suits], toll [exemption from toll], and theam [vouching to warranty], hamsocne [power to enforce fines for personal entry, etc.], foresteall [power to punish for forestealing], blodwite [power to fine for assault and bloodshed], weardwite [power to maintain watch], and numbrice [power to punish breach of the peace]. Now will I henceforward that it ever be a dwelling of monks, and let them stand in God's peace, and St. Mary's, and mine, and according to St. Benedict's rule, under the Abbot's authority. And I will not in any way consent that any man take away or eject their gifts and their alms, or that any man have there any charge upon any things or at any season except the Abbot and the brethren to the need of this minster. And whosoever shall increase this alms with any good, the Lord shall increase for him Heaven's bliss; and whosoever shall take them away or deprive the minster of any thing at any time, let him stand in God's anger and His dear Mother's and mine. God keep you all.'

The spelling of the name of Coventry is noted by Mr. Birch as varied in these early charters. This Anglo-Saxon charter has 'Covæntréé.' In those previously named it is 'Countr';' while in the Conqueror's charter it is 'Coventrea,' and he thinks that probably the name was derived from the early convent of nuns, or from the small river near, according to Dugdale's opinion. He further adds that the Abbot Leofwin was a near relation of the Earl and Countess; that he was Abbot from 1043 to 1056, when he died of fever, brought on by the havoc done to the lands of his church by the Norman Conquest. He further says that the rights mentioned by King Edward are mostly judicial in their bearings, but the Abbot and his brethren had 'full freedom,' and were exempt from 'toll,' probably the tax of setting forth soldiers, building bridges and castles, customary at that time, and more fully alluded to in the King's Latin charter. In neither of the Latin charters is the name of the Countess Godiva mentioned, and Leofric appears alone as the donor. In this Anglo-Saxon charter, however, she is spoken of in conjunction with her husband as a benefactor. While it is clear that the Earl gave part of the 'vill' and twenty-four manors to the church, it does not seem clear that the Countess gave lands of her own, but she certainly gave gold, silver and precious ornaments to the abbey, as mentioned by Vitalis, Malmesbury and other chroniclers, and to do so literally stripped herself thereof. Did she thereby acquire the right of 'freedom' granted in the charter—so that the Earl, as stated in the Coventry legend (mentioned by Dugdale), exclaimed :

> 'I, Luriche, for love of thee,
> Doe make Coventree toll free'?

This Anglo-Saxon charter is certainly very curious and interesting as an example of an early grant, as giving quaint details of the form of devotion, as a collection of Anglo-Saxon words, now almost forgotten except by the learned few, as a picture of the pious deeds of eight centuries ago, and more especially as a scrap of genuine history, which helps to clear the character of Leofric from the libel that he was a 'thankless churl,' and to show that his relations with Godiva were far too tender and chivalrous to justify the later legend of Godiva's heroic devotion to the deliverance of the city from an odious tax—the story which chroniclers and poets have delighted to tell, and which must surely now be numbered among the baseless fables of the past.

BIRMINGHAM, the chief city of the county, has but little written history before the great Norman survey, the famous Domesday Book, in which its description indicates a place of considerable importance. The origin of its name has long been warmly contested, and even the one hundred and thirty-two forms of spelling, collected from old documents, have helped to 'darken counsel.' Dugdale guessed that the final 'ham'—the Saxon for home—denoted that the name of some Saxon owner was the origin of the prefix. Hutton guessed more wildly, and supposed that the word was really Broom (broom), wych (dwelling), and ham (home), ignoring the Domesday spelling of Bermingeham (Berminghà). Dugdale was more nearly right, and modern researches have now practically settled that a tribe or family of ' Beorm,' or ' Berm,' gave the early Saxon name. The name has had many mutations, but all the earlier examples confirm the present form, while the familiar and cynical ' Brummagem ' dates only two centuries ago.

The Domesday record gives: 'Richard holds of William (Fitz Ansculf) four hides in Berminghà. The arable employs six ploughs : one is in the demesne. There are five villeins with four bordars, with two ploughs. Wood, half a mile long and four furlongs broad. It was and is worth twenty shillings. In the time of Edward the Confessor it was held by one Uluuine ' (Ulwin) ; and the place was certainly of some importance in Saxon times, since William de Bermingham, in 1309, proved that his ancestors held a market there before the Conquest. The theory of Stukeley, that the town was the Roman ' Bremenium ' has long since been abandoned, and Richard of Cirencester's ' Bremenium ' was certainly not Birmingham, although the Ikenield Street, which runs through the west of the city to Lichfield, might have had a Roman station near. A castle, or more probably a fortified manor-house, was built by Peter de Birmingham about 1154, and a moat and some traces of old walls remained till 1821. No church is mentioned in Domesday Book, but some early stonework, discovered in rebuilding St. Martin's Church, showed that probably a church existed before the Conquest. Fairs were established in 1166 and in 1251 ; and the town appears in a curious manuscript map (*circa* 1286-1300) in the Bodleian Library, with a church clearly marked and houses also, while many neighbouring towns nominally of greater importance are omitted, and 'Bryrningha'' is given as the name, although Coventry and Warwick are neither indicated nor named. The De Birminghams of Ireland are described by Dugdale as of the Birmingham family, but the local connection ended with the tragic murder of Edward de Birmingham in 1545.

In 1285 a *Priory* was founded, but few traces of it have been preserved except in street-names, and its history is very vague. At the Dissolution (1545) it was valued at £8 8s. 10d., and dissolved, and the exact site of the building is uncertain. The mother church (St. Martin's) is doubtful as to its date, but in the recent restoration, or, rather, rebuilding, Norman remains were found, and it contains several important altar-tombs of the fourteenth and fifteenth centuries, and its registers are very well preserved, and date from 1554. Another church, *St. John's, Deritend*, has a remarkable history. It is a chapel, in Aston parish, and was described by Leland as 'a propper chappell' in 1538, when it was a picturesque early English building, pulled down and rebuilt in hideous Georgian brick a hundred years ago. It was founded in 1375 by thirteen of the inhabitants, who, on account of floods, were sometimes unable to reach the mother church at Aston, and who raised a handsome endowment of land—producing ten marks (£6 13s. 4d., and now £450)—the original Charter of Richard II. and the Licence in Mortmain (1381 and 1383) being now preserved in the Reference Library. The chaplain was, and is, elected by household suffrage—male and female—and in the present year (1889) a fierce contest was continued for more than a month in thorough electioneering style, finally limited to two candidates and one day's polling—an old usage which will probably be known no more.

The Gild of the Holy Cross, founded in 1382, to maintain two priests in the church of St. Martin, was, ten years later, formed into a 'fraternitie' of men and women in the name of 'the Bailiffe and Communaltie of Birmingham and other adjacent places for a Chantrie of Priestes, and services in the Church for the souls of the Founders and all the Fraternitie,' and for other more secular work; but in

1545 the lands were seized by the Crown, and in 1550 were given by Edward VI. for the 'Free Grammar School of King Edward the Sixth, for the Education and Instruction of Children in Grammar for ever.' The lands, then valued at £31 2s. 10d., have been the endowment of the famous school, the income of which was £21,983 in 1880, and will probably rise to £50,000 before this century ends.

Leland's description of his visit to the town in 1538 is graphic and picturesque: 'I came through a pretty street or ever I entred into Bermingham towne. This street, as I remember, is called Dirtey (Deritend). In it dwell smithes and cutlers, and there is a brooke that divideth this street from Bermingham and is a hamlett or member belonging to the Parishe thereby. There is at the end of Dirtey a propper chappell and mansion house of tymber hard on the rype (bank) as the brooke runneth down: and as I went through the forde by the (foot) bridge the water ranne downe on the right hande, and a few miles belowe goeth into Tame *ripâ dextrâ* . . . . The beauty of Bermingham, a good markett towne in the extreame parts of Warwike-shire, is one streete going up alonge, almost from the left rype of the brooke, up a mean hille by the length of a quarter of a mile. I saw but one Paroche Church in the towne. There be many smiths in the town that use to make knives and all mannour of cutting tooles, and many loriners that make bittes, and a great many naylors. Soe that a great part of the towne is maintained by smithes, whoe have their iron and sea-cole out of Staffordshire.'

This description of the town is minute and careful. The 'mansion house of tymber' still remains—now as an inn, the 'Old Crown' House—and, nearly opposite, other half-timber houses of the same period still exist. The 'propper chappell' survives in an ugly brick building, but the descriptions of the various trades are no longer exact, since 'cutlery' has gone to Sheffield, 'bittes' to Walsall, and 'naylors' are located around Bromsgrove and Halesowen. The most remarkable change is that the surface has been greatly altered, the course of the river turned, and the swampy, low ground of Deritend covered with buildings, while the river has long lost its rural beauty as Drayton's ' lively tripping Rea,' and is now a thin and dirty stream, and the watercourses which supplied the mills have long ago been diverted, dried up, or covered with shops and houses of last century date.

In 1642 Charles I., on his way to Edge Hill, had been the guest of Sir Thomas Holte at Aston Hall, near Birmingham, a fine seventeenth-century building, now, with part of its great park, the property of the Corporation of Birmingham, as a museum, gallery and public park. The townsmen were on the Parliamentarian side, and Sir Thomas Holte was unpopular, so that the Hall was cannonaded for three days, and some of the balls and broken balustrades remain as relics. In the next year (1643) the fiery Rupert stormed through the town after a brilliant defence by barricades in Deritend, and fired and plundered eighty houses, and left the town with heavy losses of life and limb, including the Earl of Denbigh. The historian Clarendon, with these facts before him, described Birmingham 'as of great fame for hearty, wilful-affected disloyalty as any town in England,' and the town had supplied the Parliamentary army with 15,000 swords, and was more hostile than ever after Rupert's ' Burning Love.'

The latter half of the seventeenth century was a remarkable era in the history of the town. The extravagances of the Restoration times increased the demand for many of its manufactures, and the demand for fire-arms soon began to develop into an important trade. As a modern town without the dead weight of ancient corporation customs and rules, it become a 'city of refuge' for reformers of all sorts, and a free town for all sorts of manufactures. The 'five mile' and similar Acts drove many worthy and able men out of corporate towns, and in Birmingham they found more elbow-room and more free air, and thus the energies and industries of the town were largely and rapidly increased. These causes continued to develop the town in the next century, and the fullest development was reached in the latter part of the last century, when manufactures of all sorts, especially of hardware, iron, brass, steel, etc., became almost beyond count. A large part of this prosperity was caused by the letting of large portions of land on long leases at low ground-rents, whereby encouragement was given to the building of houses and workshops all over the centre and the immediate suburbs. Early in the century the process of cotton-spinning by machinery had been tried by Lewis Paul and John Wyatt, and about 1780 even a cotton-mill was erected, but proved an unsuccessful speculation, and was turned into a metal-rolling mill, which still remains at work. The greatest of all, however, was the establishment of the famous Soho by Matthew Boulton in 1763. His original business as a 'toy-maker'—the buckles, sword-hilts, brooches, etc., gave Burke's famous phrase, 'the toyshop of Europe'—had increased rapidly through Boulton's unbounded enterprise, energy and taste, and when James Watt, almost in despair that he could not get his new steam-engine carefully and accurately made, came to Soho, the success of the steam-engine was secured. The partnership lasted for many years. Boulton was no mean mechanic, as his coining machinery showed, but Watt, with all his genius, was not a business man, and would have failed like so many other inventors without Boulton's help. Soho is now lost to sight, but its memory will ever be honoured. It was one of the first and greatest of English workshops. It was planned and completed on a magnificent scale. Boulton, as Boswell records, said: 'I supply here what all the world desires to have—Power.' Through years of dangerous and endless speculation he persevered, and secured large fortunes for his partner and himself, and largely helped in the general and rapid progress by the inventions and machinery which 'enlarged the resources of the country and increased the power of man.'

The social and scientific, as well as the industrial history of Soho made Birmingham a famous place a century ago. Boulton had set up a standard of mechanical excellence previously unknown, and never since surpassed. In his personal life, too, he had almost magnetic influence. He attracted to Soho and to his own house the most eminent men of science from all parts of the world. The 'Soho circle'—the Lunar Club—was one of the most famous of its own, or, perhaps, of any age. Boulton was a native of Birmingham, but there were many 'strangers within the gates.' James Watt had come from Greenock loaded with inventions; Priestley from Leeds, with his acute brain and minute care and the germs of great discoveries, for the many advantages which a large town affords. Dr. Darwin—the famous Erasmus—whose merits have never yet had full honour, was another of the famous scientists. William Murdock, another great inventor, next to, and perhaps equal to, Watt himself, if all was known of him, had also won his laurels for gas-lighting for houses, and for steam on roads. John Baskerville was 'astonishing the librarians of Europe' by his unrivalled paper, type and printing. Richard Edgworth and Thomas Day, James Keir, a famous chemist, Joseph Berington, the Roman Catholic historian, Dr. Withering, the great botanist, Dr. Parr, the learned 'Grecian,' John Wyatt, the ingenious mechanic, Edmund Hector, the schoolfellow and life-long friend of Johnson, were among the friends or guests of Matthew Boulton, the heroes of the 'golden age' of Birmingham life in the last century, and the pioneers of the greater advances of these later days.

The progress in the present century has been no less

marked in all departments of public, private, social or industrial life. At the close of the great wars the town suffered as all others did, and popular demands for reform of abuses were loudly made. In 1791, the celebration of the fall of the Bastille by a public dinner early in the day, and with a series of toasts without any Radical or revolutionary proposals, was made the pretext for the disgraceful and disastrous riots which destroyed many of the houses of the most worthy residents, and the meeting-houses where Nonconformists worshipped, in a furious zeal for 'Church and King.' The saddest and most shameful vandalism was in the cases of William Hutton, the bookseller, and of Dr. Priestley, the illustrious chemist and discoverer, neither of whom had any part in the celebration mentioned. Hutton lost all his possessions and almost his life, and Priestley lost all his manuscripts, as well as apparatus and books—the records of his scientific researches during many years—a loss simply irreparable. Happily, however, three-quarters of a century later, a marble statue has been raised to his memory, showing him with lens in hand making his great discovery of oxygen in 1775.

The town was governed by a Court Leet, with a high and low bailiff, two constables, a head-borough, two ale and two flesh corners, two affeerors, two leather sealers, nearly all of whom were officers of the lord of the manor, to look after his manorial rights, until the incorporation of the town in 1838, and even then there was so long a struggle between the 'old' and the 'new' that a bailiff was elected as late as 1854. In addition to the Court Leet, there were six other 'rating' bodies in various districts, and the Street Commissioners had the most important share. The ceremonies of the Court Leet, the proclaiming of the fairs, 'by permission of the lord of the manor,' the processions of the members of the Court Leet, and other old customs, were continued to a very recent date. For several years after the charter of 1838 the local authorities held their own, but finally the Town Council acquired all the powers, including the purchase of the markets and tolls from the lord of the manor. The new Council adopted as a corporate seal the arms of the Bermingham family and the motto 'Forward,' but since January, 1889, a city seal has been adopted with two supporters, an 'addition' on the shield, and a hand and hammer as a crest. The city is now divided into sixteen wards, with 131 polling-stations, and a total of sixty-four aldermen and councillors. The Council was engaged in no very notable or eventful work till the urgent advocacy of the late George Dawson induced many of the more educated classes to look upon municipal life as a great and honourable duty, and one of his famous phrases was, ' Never send a man into the Council whom you would not welcome and honour as Mayor.' In 1875, although much good work had been done, the 'new era' began, when Mr. Joseph Chamberlain, whose energy and ability had already accomplished much highly important work, was elected Mayor. The two great Gas Companies were purchased by the town for £450,000, and the Waterworks Company for £54,491, in perpetual annuities. The former has provided very large sums in relief of the rates, and the latter has supplied large and increasing quantities of water without any large profits, water being held to be a 'necessary' of life and health to be furnished at the lowest rates. In 1875, too, the Artisans' Dwellings Act was passed, and this was adopted by Birmingham—the first applicant—to remove large masses of unwholesome buildings, and to make a fine broad street, on which the numerous and costly buildings have been built, with leases of seventy years, which will finally fall to the Corporation at a greatly increased value under the Improvement Act of 1851. The latest undertaking of the Council is the new Assize Courts—the Victoria Courts, of which the first stone was laid by the Queen—assizes having been held since 1884 in the Council House, in two courts arranged for the purpose. The Council House has also been built at a cost of £150,000, including a room for the Council meetings, Mayor's parlour, reception and banquet rooms, and all the necessary rooms and offices for the Town Clerk, Borough Treasurer, Borough Surveyor, Chief of Police, and others. One half of the site originally intended for Assize Courts has been used for the offices of the Gas Department, and over these is a fine series of rooms as a Public Art Gallery, to which many rare and valuable works of art, and especially of industrial art—a great, rich and rare collection by Mr. John Feeney—have been generously given, and loan collections are formed and the Council offers and receives loans from other municipalities from time to time. The Art Gallery was first started by a munificent offer of Messrs. Richard and George Tangye of £10,000, on the condition that a similar sum should be subscribed. The Gas Committee, with the approval of the Council, built the Art Gallery, and the donations have been used to purchase examples of art—of fine as well as industrial art—of remarkable value.

Another notable public work, in which the Town Council has a large share, is the School of Art. This also was first proposed by an offer of £10,000 by Messrs. R. and G. Tangye, a similar offer by the late Miss Ryland, and a gift of land of about the same value from Mr. Cregoe Colmore. The building is one of the latest and best of the artistic genius of the late John Henry Chamberlain, and is not only perfectly adapted for its purposes in every detail of its interior, but is the most graceful and tasteful building in the town. While its income is largely derived from the fees of students, the Town Council has been the first in England to acquire the power of rating, and is the first municipality which has accepted the claims of art to civic recognition and public support by aid from the rates for this Municipal School of Art.

Birmingham was not one of the first to adopt the Free Libraries Act of 1850, but in 1852 the Council approved of the Act, and a poll being demanded, 534 burgesses voted for the adoption, and 363 against it, but, although there was a clear majority, the proposal was defeated, as the Act required two-thirds of those voting to approve. The minority was very mixed. The publicans naturally did not like such dangerous attractions; the economists objected to any rate, even of a halfpenny in the pound; the Nonconformists stood out strongly on their principle of no State-aid from rates; the religious burgesses feared that a public free library would purchase and circulate books which they did not like; and so the Free Libraries proposal failed, partly from want of knowledge and interest, and partly from interested opposition. It is a curious comment on this vote that now the constant question to a candidate for a ward is: 'Will you vote for a Free Library in this ward?' In 1855 Mr. Ewart amended his Act to increase the rate to one penny in the pound, and to allow the purchase of books as well as the provision of buildings. In 1860 the new Act was adopted, only one member of the Council having opposed it, in the interests of the 'small house-owner!' The first committee consisted of eight members of the Council and eight men of eminence in literature, science, or art, to arrange for the libraries and museums. The rate, originally one penny in the pound under that Act, is now by a Local Consolidation Act absolutely unlimited, and no opposition was offered to this, the only example in the kingdom of an unlimited rate for literature and art. The rate produces £9,500 yearly, and maintains a Reference Library (103,000 vols.), a Central Lending Library (25,000 vols.), a Newsroom (5,000 readers a day), and three Branch Libraries, with 10,000 volumes in each. Nearly 3,000 volumes are issued daily. More than 1,000 periodicals and serials are supplied. The News-rooms are visited by nearly 12,000 readers daily. A disastrous fire in 1879 destroyed the Reference Library during its enlargement, but the public spirit was aroused, and thousands of pounds were given in less than a fortnight, finally rising to £15,000, which sum, with that on the insurance of the books, gave £30,000 for the purchase of books *alone*, the buildings being raised by separate funds. During these ten years no cost nor care has been spared to secure the best works of all classes which have appeared in catalogues or at auction sales, and the Reference Library has now 103,000 well-chosen volumes for all classes, creeds, and ranks, down even to books for children and books for the blind. The great loss of the fire was the Staunton Warwickshire Collection, already referred to, and the next the Shakespeare Memorial Library (which has now been restored, with nearly 9,000 vols.). The Library also contains a fine Cervantes Collection (formed by the late William Bragge), the Byron Collection (275 vols., Richard Tangye), and the Milton Collection (182 vols., Frank Wright); and a rare and invaluable Birmingham and also Warwickshire collection of drawings, engravings, manuscripts, and books. The Reference Library (only) has been opened since 1875 on Sundays from 3 to 9 p.m. Six assistants are necessary, and five of them are Jews and the sixth a volunteer, no officer of the Library being obliged to attend on Sundays except by his own free will and pleasure.

The educational institutions are numerous and important, and mostly of modern date, except *King Edward's School*, founded in 1552, rebuilt in 1707, and again, from Barry's designs, in 1833, in the Tudor-Gothic style. In 1750 branch schools were founded, but closed, as they were found to be *ultra vires*. In 1837 elementary branch schools were first established. In 1878, as the Elementary Education Act of 1870 had provided for such schools, a new 'scheme' was framed by the Charity Commissioners to raise the grade and change the sites of these branch schools. This has resulted in some important and valuable changes. Fees are now charged, as important revenue from the richer classes; but free scholars, after passing examinations, are introduced in large numbers to the high schools, and thus there is an open road from the elementary schools to the exhibitions and Universities for even the poorest children. A high school for girls has recently been established, and is developing rapidly as to *status* and numbers, and promises to be one of the foremost schools in the kingdom. Special attention has also been devoted to science-teaching and physical training of girls as well as boys, so that the high schools have now every advantage from laboratories, apparatus, gymnasiums, etc. The recent policy of the Board—no longer self-elected, but really representative—is well appreciated, and under the new departure and foreseeing management the 'old foundation' has taken a new lease of life and vigour.

Queen's College has grown from a School of Medicine in 1828 to an important College of Medicine and Divinity since the erection of the present buildings, some forty years ago. It was incorporated in 1867, and has class and anatomical rooms, libraries and museums, and the courses of study qualify for the degrees of B.A., M.A., B.C.L., D.C.L., M.B., and M.D., in the University of London and the Royal College of Surgeons and the Society of Apothecaries. The college was founded by the late Rev. Dr. Warneford on the original institution of W. Sands Cox, and is now officered to some extent by arrangements with the *Mason College*, which was founded by the late Sir Josiah Mason on very broad and far-seeing lines, and was opened in 1880. It was founded originally as a science college, but literature and languages were afterwards added by a supplementary deed. Instruction in art as well as science may also be given. As to students, there is no restriction as to sex, creed, or birthplace. All the governors must be laymen and Protestants, but there is no restriction on teachers as to creed. One provision of the trust deed is remarkable and valuable— that the trustees *shall* from time to time revise the constitution of the classes, subjects, and management, so as to keep them abreast of the science of the day; and that thus no 'pious founder's' hand shall check the development of the college by any ancient trusts.

The *Midland Institute* is the lineal but matured successor of the Mechanics' Institutes of fifty years ago, designed to give the masses of the people scientific and literary training for moderate payments. It was founded in 1853 by the late Arthur Ryland, to give the artisans of the town the means of continuing their education after they had left school for work. In 1855 the late Prince Consort laid the foundation-stone. A special Act was obtained for the government of the Institute, and its original programme, which was very advanced and comprehensive, has been almost fully accomplished. It was divided into two sections: General, for subscribers to have reading and news rooms, and scientific and literary lectures, etc.; and Industrial, for cheap classes, in which science in all forms should be taught. Afterwards classes for English literature were formed, the late George Dawson having volunteered a three years' lectureship of a class in English literature, which was followed during that term and afterwards by the present writer, and later by Mr. Howard S. Pearson, whose classes have greatly increased in numbers, and whose students have won many honours in examinations for literature and history. The head of the Science Department, Mr. C. J. Woodward, was himself a student in the Institute, and in many other cases the students have developed into teachers, and carried on the excellent work on the old lines for the new generation.

The Institute is now educating more than four thousand students in its various studies in the parent and branch classes. Its programme has been always to supply any want in any branch of knowledge. In 1860 the fact that the Institute was doing the work it had undertaken was shown by the returns that 33 per cent. of the students were artisans, 33 per cent. shopmen and clerks, and 16 per cent. women of the same ranks. In 1868 the numbers were 45, 29, and 21 per cent., and the numbers have continued to increase. An anonymous gift of £2,500 led to the establishment of classes in the Laws of Health, beginning with a class of four hundred students; and now branch classes are established in many of the Board Schools. In 1878 the handsome and useful buildings designed by the late John Henry Chamberlain were commenced, and were finished in 1881. The architect had been for fifteen years the honorary secretary of the Institute, and he had refounded and extended it with unrivalled energy, judgment, and taste. The development was 'truly marvellous,' and his colleagues, in mourning his death, recorded that 'he had the genius to see the needs of the time and the direction in which the Institute could be developed to meet them. The wisdom of his counsel, the extent and variety of his knowledge, the grace of his eloquence, and the wonderful charm of his personal presence, made him a colleague whom it is impossible to replace.' He died very suddenly, after a brilliant lecture on 'Exotic Art,' in the hall which he had built and decorated; for to art, in all forms and uses, he had given the best years of his illustrious life.

The Political History of Birmingham became of national interest with the Reform Bill agitation of 1830, when the town had no representative in Parliament, while many of the old boroughs sent two members. Under the leadership of Thomas Attwood the famous Political Union was formed, public spirit was aroused and organized, and enormous meetings, often at a few hours' notice, were held with determined ardour and ultimate success. Two members were assigned to Birmingham in 1832, and in 1868 the famous 'three-cornered' contest occurred. Three members had to be returned, but each voter had only two votes. The managers of the Liberal Party ingeniously divided the town into districts, and so arranged the candidates that three Liberals should be returned. So perfect was the scheme, and so complete the organization, and so loyal the voting to the instructions how to vote, that all the three Liberals were returned. In the Anti-Corn Law agitation Birmingham took only a small share, partly through the Chartist agitation; but in the contest for further Parliamentary reform the people again took an active part. The election of the late Mr. John Bright in 1857 without any personal attendance was a notable example, and he remained a member till his lamented death. Excepting the Chartist Riots in 1839, when several houses in the Bull Ring were burned, the agitations have been conducted without physical force. Under the Bill of 1885 seven members were assigned to seven districts of the town, and one to Aston, which is practically part of the town, although legally separate.

The Industries of Birmingham are far too varied and numerous to be even partially described. Every sort of article in iron and brass and other metals, from pins and pens to torpedoes and engines and machines of almost all sorts, is manufactured in Birmingham or within a few miles of the centre. 'The Industrial Resources of Birmingham' in 1865, when the British Association visited the town, were described in a volume of seven hundred pages; and on another visit of the association, in 1886, Mr. C. J. Woodward, B.Sc., compiled a careful and elaborate account of the changes during twenty years for the 'Handbook of Birmingham,' now out of print. The following figures, collected by Mr. Woodward, will give some notion of the extent, but by no means of the varieties, of the trades. The figures give the weights of the Exports of 1885 in tons: Bedsteads, 34,976; brass and copper ingots and wire, 4,697; galvanized wire and ware, 11,705; glass, 6,151; hardware and lamps, 110,597; iron and metal tubes, 13,570; iron wire and sheets, 2,999; iron castings, 9,166; nails, 18,936; rolled metal, 7,619; paper and stationery, 9,490; machinery, hides, and leather, 3,375 tons. The Imports of materials are on a similar scale, and the details of the various trades would seem incredible if not thoroughly authenticated by trustworthy returns. As one example, nearly twenty tons of steel are cut up for steel pens every week; and while the best possible steel pens are made and sold at high prices, some are made at less than twopence-halfpenny per gross (twelve dozens) for foreign markets, and each of those is the product of at least eight or nine processes; but they are not supplied in boxes, which would cost more than the pens. The larger industries, subdivided to a remarkable extent, are: (1) the gun trade, the manufacture of all sorts of 'small arms,' military and sporting, not only in hundreds of smaller manufactories, but in the small arms and the Government factories, on the Springfield and Enfield systems, which employ many hundreds of men, and are supplied with the most elaborate and costly machinery; (2) the brass-foundry trades, including about five hundred manufactories, and employing ten thousand artisans in the almost innumerable varieties in which brass is used; (3) the jewellery trade, also of almost infinite variety, from the costliest gold and silver work down to the cheapest productions, and employing about sixteen thousand workers, and, like the gun trade, concentrated in one special quarter of the town, where every signboard shows some subdivision, down even to wedding-rings; (4) the electro-plate trade, which is rivalled only by Sheffield, and employs more than two thousand in the various departments of the manufacture of articles, and the separate works which in many cases 'plate for the trade'; (5) the button trade, including all sorts of buttons—pearl, bone, glass, metal, and cloth-covered—and employing six thousand workers, and one of the oldest and most important trades; (6) the steel pen trade, carried on by nineteen firms, employing more than three thousand six hundred girls and five hundred men and women in the machine-work, and cutting up sixteen to eighteen tons of steel, producing eight tons of pens, every week—furnishing, in fact, the largest part of the pens of the world. These are the principal trades, and also the oldest; but during the last forty years other trades have been established, and have extended to vast works. The Mint of London did not supply the whole of the bronze coinage, and the old firm of James Watt and Co. (Soho Foundry) supplied bronze and copper coin from 1860 to 1866 weighing 3,317 tons, a million of pieces being struck and packed in one day; and R. Heaton and Sons also supplied a similar quantity, and in 1872 silver blanks, to be 'coined' in the London Mint, to the nominal value of £1,000,000, in less than six months. The use of hydraulic power for lifting and pressing and cutting has enormously grown in thirty years. The Cornwall Works (Tangyes, Limited) now employs more than two thousand workmen, and produces enormous quantities of hydraulic presses, lifts, etc., for all parts of the world. Two other remarkable examples of the usefulness of the modern elaborate machinery are found in the automatic machine, first invented by James Watt as an amusement in his later life. In his 'classic garret' at Heathfield, near Birmingham, he adapted the familiar draughtsman's 'pantograph' (for enlarging or reducing a drawing), to be used by a rotary tool in the place of a pencil, so as to cut out a copy of any medal in relief, and finally to copy busts by merely mechanical action. This plan was tried later to produce gun-stocks and gun furniture at Springfield (Mass.), and afterwards at Enfield, and the Small Arms Company, Birmingham, with brilliant success. When the demand for guns diminished, the machinery was soon readjusted for bicycle and tricycle fittings; and in another manufactory similar machinery was turned to profit on the works of peace in the manufacture of sewing-machines, and afterwards of bicycle and tricycle fittings, most of which could be readily, accurately, and cheaply produced by the automatic machinery which the octogenarian James Watt had invented and used for the reproduction of works of art. Another curious example of the newer trades of the town is that of metallic bedsteads. In 1849 there were only four makers in the neighbourhood, producing about 400 bedsteads a week; in 1865 their number had increased to twenty, making 6,000 a week; and now, within a fifteen-mile radius (partly in Staffordshire), there are forty makers, and a supply of 30,000 bedsteads every week, produced by about five hundred workmen only, since comparatively little 'hand-labour' is required. Another remarkable local industry is the glass trade in its various departments, from plate-glass and lighthouses down to chandeliers and table-glass, as produced in the famous works of Chance Brothers, F. and C. Osler, and other manufacturers, who employ some fifteen hundred skilled workers, some of whom are experts in dolls' eyes, and others in the artificial eyes which are now produced with singular success. The Assay Office (the local 'hall-mark' of the gold and silver trades) showed 101,012 assays of 97,618 ounces of gold and 888,391 ounces of silver in 1885 (respectively 120,019 and 142,148 in 1876), showing that Birmingham produces a very large quantity of gold and silver ware, and that its genuine art-work in jewellery is supplied and valued throughout the world.

The civic and social growth of Birmingham has been remarkable, not only since the enfranchisement of the town in 1832 and the incorporation charter in 1838, when a great stimulus swept through all classes; but 'the hardware village' developed into an important town full of life and vigour, and a new era began. The responsibilities of self-government were soon felt, and even from the very first many prominent inhabitants took an active part in public work. The Town Council attracted many of the ablest men, the burgesses took greater interest in the election of representatives, and the Birmingham Town Council has won a fame as one of the foremost of the new municipalities; and the full story of its rise and progress, given in two excellent volumes by Mr. J. Thackray Bunce, and printed for the Corporation, has attracted many inquiries, even from the United States, to examine the history and working of so famous and successful an example of high-class local government, and so striking a proof of the soundness of the representative principle in the good government of a large town. Not only has the machinery of government been carefully divided and skilfully worked, but the general tone of life has been elevated and improved, the standard of town life has been raised, and private as well as public men have grown more generous, and in eleven years (1870-1881) £714,000 was given for educational and public purposes, independently of annual subscriptions, and of bequests and other gifts of £150,000.

Warwick as a town has many attractions, but the Castle is the most important. The Church of St. Mary has not only the grand Beauchamp Chapel and its famous tombs, but also some interesting historical memorials in the church itself, such as the monument to Sir Fulke Grevil, the 'Friend of Sir Phillip Sidney.' The Leicester Hospital, too, founded by Elizabeth's favourite, is full of interest as a relic of old times. *Alcester* has more claims to notice than space allows, as a Roman station and a picturesque place. *Atherstone* has similar claims, and *Mancetter*, nearly adjoining, is on the line of Watling Street, and has also relics of the Roman times. *Nuneaton* is an important town, and once had a priory, founded in Stephen's reign, but of which little now remains. Ribbon-weaving is the chief industry at Nuneaton, and hats are largely made at Atherstone. *Sutton Coldfield* is a royal borough, and has recently had a charter of incorporation. It is a pleasant town, and close to a fine park, given, with many privileges, by Bishop Vesey, *alias* Harman, as already described under his name. *Kenilworth* is a long line of road, broken by the terrace of the Abbey Hill, from which the Priory (in which some further traces of the Norman church have recently been discovered) and a fine view of the Castle can be seen. All through the county there are 'pleasant places' and picturesque villages of great interest, but with no special history, and whose 'simple annals' cannot even be condensed within the limits of these pages; but *Henley-in-Arden*, one of the oldest and most picturesque of the small towns, deserves a few words. It is first noticed in the time of Henry II., when a mill was granted to the monks of Wootten-Wawen by Henry de Montfort. After the Battle of Evesham the town decayed and was damaged by fire, but it was restored and revived. It has the remains of a very fine market-cross, but although the exquisitely carved capital remains, the figures are almost worn away by time and weather. The 'town' is a long street, with very fine old half-timbered houses, and near the main road to Stratford is the little church of Beaudesert, whose Norman window is one of the county treasures. A recently-sold record shows that the Shakespeare Company of Players performed at Henley-in-Arden in 1615, the year before the poet's death. A few miles nearer to Stratford is the church of *Wootten-Wawen*, which still preserves some old books, attached to shelves by chains. Mr. John Hannett, the author of the charming volume 'The Forest of Arden,' now out of print and scarce, although an octogenarian, recently issued some 'Notes Illustrative of the Early Government of the Old Town of Henley-in-Arden, with an Appendix of the Charities;' but the full story of the old town has never yet been told, and a careful examination of some recently-sold documents might throw much light on the history of Henley-in-Arden.

LEAMINGTON (or Leamington Priors, as distinguished from Leamington Hastings) is too well known to be omitted from the record of important towns. Although not much known as an ancient town, its lands were noted in Domesday Book as 'two hides' in extent—probably two hundred and forty acres—and valued at four pounds a year. Its sub-name, 'Priors' (now rarely used), arose from its having been granted to the 'Priors' of Kenilworth. At the Conquest it belonged to Turchill, the Saxon Earl of Warwick, but was taken from his son, after the Conquest, and given to a Norman Baron, Roger de Montmorency, afterwards Earl of Shrewsbury. During the next hundred years it had various owners, and *circa* 1166 the son of the first and famous Geoffrey de Clinton gave the manor, church and mill to the Priors of Kenilworth. At the Dissolution it was granted by Elizabeth (in 1564) to Ambrose Dudley, Earl of Warwick, and afterwards to various owners—a large portion to the Aylesford family. Its famous 'springs' were known and valued as early as 1586, and were noticed by Camden, Dugdale, Speed and Fuller, but it was not till 1784 that the 'waters' gained extensive fame. Fuller, in his usual facetious style, described these as 'two twin springs, as different in taste and operation as Jacob and Esau in disposition.' The waters had been analyzed by Guidot in 1698, and recommended by Dr. Short in 1740 and Dr. Rutty in 1757. They were held to be valuable in scorbutic cases, and even in cases of hydrophobia. A 'dipper' was appointed, and the virtues of the 'waters' puffed in the advertisements of the day. It was claimed that between 1778 and 1786 one hundred and nineteen persons were cured who had been bitten by mad dogs! About 1784 the virtues of the 'waters' were more seriously praised by Dr. Kerr of Northampton, and Dr. Johnstone of Birmingham, and two humble but public-spirited inhabitants of Leamington—Benjamin Satchwell and William Abbott—undertook to provide such buildings as were necessary for the use of the waters as curative means. The town grew rapidly, and became a very fashionable resort, almost rivalling Bath and Cheltenham, and although changes of fashion as to 'spas' may have affected its further progress, it is still a famous 'health resort.' The Leamington waters—springs and baths on an extended scale—are chalybeate, sulphurous and saline, useful alike for drinking or bathing, so that all sorts of invalids resort to the pleasant and prosperous town, and the many historic places—Warwick, Kenilworth, Stratford-on-Avon, Coventry and others, all within a few miles of Leamington. The county has other but less famous 'springs'; at Ilmington, chalybeate; at Newnham Regis, also chalybeate; at Southam, at Bishopton, near Stratford, but none so important as those of Leamington.

STRATFORD-ON-AVON is too generally known to need much description. It has not merely the grand old church on the banks of the Avon, where Shakespeare's remains repose, and a chancel and Clopton Chapel of singular interest and beauty, but a fine fifteenth-century Gild Chapel, an old Grammar School, almost unaltered since his school-days, and the hall beneath it in which he saw his first play in his childhood, when his father was Bailiff and entertained the Queen's and the Earl of Worcester's 'Players' in 1569. Stratford has many other attractions besides its Shakespearian scenes—the home of the Ardens at Wilmcote, and of the Hathaways at Shottery, of the Lucys at Charlecote, and of the Cloptons at Clopton, and many picturesque old houses of the sixteenth century, which have been recently 'restored' by the removal of the plaster and the discovery of the fine half-timber fronts and quaint old windows of Shakespeare's days. The Birthplace of Shakespeare, 'restored' to its size and form of four centuries ago, and with its museum crowded with memorials of the poet and his times and its priceless treasures of old deeds and drawings and rare and unique books, the modern Memorial Buildings (thanks to the munificence of Mr. C. E. Flower), with a fine theatre and art gallery, and library full of valuable Shakespeare literature, and affording the finest view of the Avon and the church, form unrivalled attractions, to which must be added the charms of the many picturesque villages all round the town, which well repay a pilgrimage by those who care to study the 'local colour' of the pleasant country in which Shakespeare passed his earliest and his latest years.

BIBLIOGRAPHY OF WARWICKSHIRE.

[This is not given as a complete list, but only as a reference to the titles of works used in the foregoing pages, and as a guide to those who may wish for further details.]

AGRICULTURE OF WARWICKSHIRE - - 1815
(By A. Murray, from 'Agricultural Surveys,' vol. xxxii.)

AGRICULTURE OF WARWICKSHIRE - - 1794
(Curious contemporary account of Farms, Crops, etc., by J. Wedge.)

BADDESLEY CLINTON: ITS MANOR, CHURCH, AND
HALL - - - - - - 1885
(By Rev. Henry Norris, 37 pp. ; a rare and excellent History from Private Papers of the Ferrers Family and their Ancient Home.)

BREWER'S COUNTY OF WARWICK, WITH PLATES 1814
('Beauties of England and Wales,' vol. xv.)

BIOGRAPHY OF THE LUCY FAMILY - - 1862
(By Mrs. M. E. Lucy; a History of the Family, with some Original Facts from Manuscripts.)

BOTANIST'S GUIDE TO WARWICKSHIRE - - 1810
(By W. G. Perry ; good, useful little work.)

BOTANY OF SUTTON PARK - - - 1876
(By J. E. Bagnall, A.L.S.; valuable account of many years of careful and scientific observations.)

CASTLES: WARWICK, KENILWORTH, MAXTOKE,
  ETC. - - - - - - 1887
  (By G. T. Clarke, in his great work, 2 vols., on
  'Mediæval Military Architecture in England.')
CHURCHES OF WARWICKSHIRE - - 1847-48
  (Two handsome volumes, with Tinted Lithograph
  Plates by A. E. Everitt; Text by M. H. Bloxam and
  W. Staunton.)
CHURCH BELLS OF WARWICKSHIRE - - 1882
  (Original and valuable account and description of
  Bells and Inscriptions.)
CIVIL WARS IN WARWICKSHIRE - - - 1876
  (Pamphlet, 15 pp., of minute and careful History, with
  Extracts from MSS. and Bibliography of Local Civil
  War Tracts.)
COINAGE OF COVENTRY - - - - 1886
  (By W. A. Cotton; History of Coinage from the Mint
  at Coventry, *ante* Edward IV.)
CORPORATION OF BIRMINGHAM, HISTORY OF - 1878
  (By J. Thackray Bunce, F.S.S.; two volumes—I. 368 pp.,
  and II. 582 pp.—full Municipal History, with Statistics,
  Reports of the Growth and Progress of a New Munici-
  pality, and a Sketch of the 'Earlier Government of the
  Town.' The work is 'Published by the Corporation'
  as a record of its work.)
COVENTRY CHARTERS, DEEDS, SEALS, AND MER-
  CHANT MARKS - - - - - 1871
  (By John Fetherston; Pamphlet Catalogue after the
  Treasures had been examined and arranged, describing
  Documents from Henry II.; Autograph of Richard III.;
  Leet Book, Henry V.; Holy Trinity Gild Book from
  thirteenth century, etc.)
COX'S MAGNA BRITANNIA (WARWICKSHIRE) - 1720
  (One of the double-column quarto volumes, with full
  and useful details from Dugdale, and with some few
  additions.)
DIRECTORY OF WARWICKSHIRE - - - 1828
  (By Pigott and Co.; early and accurate Record of all
  Towns and Principal Places.)

19

DOMESDAY BOOK OF WARWICKSHIRE - - 1862
(Photozincograph of Original MS., with Introduction, and History of Domesday Book.)

DOMESDAY BOOK OF WARWICKSHIRE - circa 1880
(Folio copy of Text, with W. Reader's Translation and Notes by E. P. Shirley.)

DOMESDAY BOOK OF WARWICKSHIRE - - 1783
(Record Commissioners' Report.)

DOMESDAY BOOK OF WARWICKSHIRE - - 1835
(Translated into English by W. Reader, Coventry.)

DUGDALE'S (SIR W.) ANTIQUITIES, 2 VOLS. - 1730
(Edited by Dr. Thomas, and chiefly remarkable for the copies of inscriptions after 1656, and with some corrections of Dugdale's edition.)

DUGDALE'S (SIR W.) ANTIQUITIES - - 1765
(A reprint of the edition of 1656, at Coventry, with most of the original plates by Hollar, as in the previous editions.)

DUGDALE'S (SIR W.) ANTIQUITIES - - 1656
(This first edition is valuable as a careful record of Genealogies, Pedigrees and Lands, with many Views and Plans of Towns, Maps of Hundreds, etc., and Etchings of Tombs, Monuments, and the Dresses of Monastic Orders.)

DUGDALE (SIR W.), LIFE OF - - - 1827
(By Wm. Hamper, F.S.A.; a well-known and highly valued work, with Correspondence and Notes from family archives at Merevale. Hamper's own copy, with 600 extra plates and cuttings, is now in Reference Library, Birmingham.)

DUGDALE'S WARWICKSHIRE, ILLUSTRATIONS FOR.
(A fine collection formed by the Earl of Aylesford, circa 1821 to illustrate Dugdale, is now in the Reference Library, Birmingham. It includes Portraits by Vertue and others, 174; Churches, water-colour and sepia drawings, 310; Castles, Mansions, etc., water-colour, 422, paged for insertion in volumes, but now arranged alphabetically.)

DUGDALE'S WARWICKSHIRE - - - 1817
(Abridged, but with later authorities, with many additions on Agriculture, Commerce, Mines, and Manufactures.)

ECCLESIASTICAL ANTIQUITIES OF WARWICKSHIRE - - - - - - 1877
(By M. H. Bloxam; valuable and useful history from personal knowledge and research.)

EDGE-HILL, THE BATTLE AND BATTLE-FIELD - 1886
(By G. A. Walford; account of Battle of Kineton, or Edge-Hill, with Plans of Battle.)

EPITOME OF THE COUNTY WARWICKSHIRE - 1835
(By Thomas Sharp; full, careful, and useful Summary of Places, arranged Alphabetically, from all the best authorities.)

ETHNOLOGY OF WARWICKSHIRE - - - 1837
(By George Jabet; a valuable Paper read to Archæological Section of Midland Institute.)

FLORA OF WARWICKSHIRE - - 1887, etc.
(By J. E. Bagnall, A.L.S.; Results of many years careful study and large knowledge; have appeared in the 'Midland Naturalist,' and will shortly be issued in a volume with plates.)

FOREST OF ARDEN: TOWNS, VILLAGES, AND HAMLETS - - - - - 1863
(By John Hannett 320 pp., with Map of 'Forest,' many excellent Woodcuts and charming Narrative; long out of print and scarce.)

FRIENDS (QUAKERS) IN WARWICKSHIRE - 1873
(Memoirs of Quaker History and Biographies, by William White.)

GEOGRAPHY OF WARWICKSHIRE AND ADJACENT COUNTIES, BY J. W. BURRAGE - - -. 1872

GEOGRAPHY OF WARWICKSHIRE FOR THE 'NEW CODE' - - - - - - 1875
(By W. G. Fretton, F.S.A.; useful little pamphlet, summing up all the most important facts.)

GLEANINGS IN WARWICKSHIRE, ETC. - - 1805
(By S. J. Pratt, from his 'Gleanings'; very curious and interesting Contemporary History and Descriptions of Social and Industrial Life, by J. Morfitt, as to Birmingham and the County generally.)

GRAPHIC ILLUSTRATIONS OF WARWICKSHIRE - 1829
(Illustrations by Cox, Westall, Harding, De Wint, etc., and Text by Dr. Blair.)

GRAPHIC ILLUSTRATIONS OF WARWICKSHIRE - 1862
(Transfers from the original plates and text, entirely new, by James Jaffray.)

HISTORIC WARWICKSHIRE - - - 1875
(By J. Tom Burgess. Memoirs of Principal Events, Gunpowder Plot, etc.)

HISTORY OF COUNTY WARWICKSHIRE - - 1830
(4to. volume, with fine line engravings—views—and careful and useful Summary of History.)

HISTORY AND DIRECTORY OF WARWICKSHIRE - 1830
(By William West; a large volume, with very full and elaborate History of Places and People, with copies of Old Records, a few Etchings of Towns, and a minute Directory of all parts of the County.)

HISTORY AND DIRECTORY OF WARWICKSHIRE - 1866
(By Morris; principally a Directory, but with much useful history.)

HISTORY AND DIRECTORY OF WARWICKSHIRE 1850-74
(By White and Co.; also chiefly Directory of Names, but History, Topography, Geology, and Industries very useful and carefully compiled.)

HOAR STONES; OR, ANCIENT PILLARS OF MEMORIAL - - - - - - 1820
(By W. Hamper; History of Memorial Stones [Hoar-Stones, Hare-Stones, Maen-Hir] in all parts of Great Britain. A unique and curious booklet.)

INDEPENDENCY IN WARWICKSHIRE - - 1855
(By Sibree and Caston; a History of the Independent (Congregational) Chapels and their Ministers.)

KENILWORTH CASTLE - - - - 1872
(By Rev. E. H. Knowles ; a quarto volume with many Plates and Plans illustrating the Military and General Architecture of the Castle ; an original, learned and valuable work.)

LEAMINGTON SPRINGS AND WATERS - - 1828
(An early pamphlet on the newly-found value of the Leamington Springs, by Dr. C. Loudon.)

LEAMINGTON PRIORS, HISTORY OF, TO 1842 - 1842
(By Robert Hopper; History of Leamington Waters, Analysis, Uses, etc.)

LOWER ETTINGTON, MANOR-HOUSE AND CHURCH - - - - - - 1880
(By Evelyn P. Shirley; privately printed History of Ettington, or Eatington, the Home of the Shirleys.)

MEN AND NAMES OF OLD BIRMINGHAM - 1864

MIDLAND ANTIQUARY - - - - 1882-85
(By W. Fowler Carter ; four volumes of original papers on Genealogy and Archæology of Midland Counties, excellently indexed.)

MILITARY ARCHITECTURE OF KENILWORTH, WARWICK, AND MAXTOKE CASTLES - - 1859
(By G. T. Robinson, 56 pp., with valuable History and Descriptions.)

MONUMENTAL BRASSES OF WARWICKSHIRE - 1889
(By E. W. Badger, M.A. ; a monograph which won the Darwin Medal : a series of 'rubbings' of every 'brass' with descriptions.)

NOTES ON HENLEY-IN-ARDEN - - - 1886
(Pamphlet, 14 pp., with History of the Early Government of the 'Old Town,' and Account of its Charities, by John Hannett.)

'OLD CROWN' HOUSE, BIRMINGHAM, HISTORY AND TRADITIONS OF - - - - 1863
(Two works of more than merely local interest as to Warwickshire and Birmingham, by a learned expert in old lore.)

REVELS AT KENILWORTH IN 1575 (REPRINT) - 1821
(Laneham's Letter to his Fellow-'Mercer' in London, describing the Pageants at Elizabeth's visit.)

SOME ACCOUNT OF RUGBY - - - 1871
(By the late M. H. Bloxam ; a Summary of History, with Personal Memories of Fifty Years.)

STONELEIGH ABBEY - - - - 1850
(By F. C. Colvile ; special and privately printed [fifty copies], with Coloured Plans and a few Family Papers.)

SUTTON COLDFIELD, HISTORY OF FOREST AND CHASE - - - - - - 1860
(Excellent History of the Town, Forest and Neighbouring Hamlets, by Miss Bracken.)

THE HUNT, WARWICKSHIRE - - - 1837
(By 'Venator ;' a record of 'Meets' and 'Runs.')

TOPOGRAPHY OF WARWICKSHIRE - - 1800
(By Cooke ; small but useful volume, with facts not previously given.)

VIEWS ON THE AVON, WARWICKSHIRE - - 1795
(Ireland's 4to. volume, with Aquatint Engravings, but 'history' and details highly imaginative.)

WARWICKSHIRE, DIALECT OF - - - 1865
(Privately printed [ten copies] by J. O. Halliwell-Phillipps, from MS. of Thomas Sharp, burned in 1879.)

WARWICKSHIRE DELINEATED - - - 1810
(Small volume, 12mo., 348 pp., by Francis Smith, of Southam, with very full Summary of History.)

WARWICKSHIRE DIRECTORY, ETC. - - 1848
(Kelly's 'Post-office Directories' all very carefully and completely sum up a mass of historical and contemporary facts not otherwise procurable.)

WARWICKSHIRE, HERALDS' VISITATION IN 1619 1877
(Harleian Society's issue ; useful to Genealogists.)

WARWICKSHIRE, THE MANCETTER MARTYRS - 1842
(By B. Richings ; Lives of Glover, Lewis, and others, with full details.)

WARWICKSHIRE (SOUTH) WORDS - - 1868
(By Mrs. Francis, as to Words used in Tysoe ; from English Dialect Society Series, vol. xii.)

WARWICKSHIRE (SOUTH) WORDS - - 1861
(By John R. Wise, in 'Shakespeare : His Birthplace and its Neighbourhood,' with Glossary of Words.)

WARWICKSHIRE FIELD CLUB (NATURAL HISTORY
AND ARCHÆOLOGY): REPORTS AND TRANSAC-
TIONS - - - - - - 1837-89
(Series of Records of Excursions and Papers on Geology
and Archæology, occasionally with Illustrations.)

WARWICKSHIRE IN BRITTON AND BRAYLEY'S
BEAUTIES OF ENGLAND AND WALES - - 1826
(Warwickshire volume very fully and carefully compiled.)

WARWICKSHIRE OLD HOUSES - - - 1878
(By W. Niven; Architectural Elevations, with brief
descriptions.)

WARWICKSHIRE ANTIQUARIAN MAGAZINE 1862-72
(Specially Warwickshire; copies of Black Book of
Warwick, numerous woodcuts of 'Arms' and Genea-
logies, edited by John Fetherston.)

WARWICKSHIRE FAMILY TOPOGRAPHER - - 1835
(By Samuel Tymms; brief, but orderly and excellent
Survey of Historical Facts.)

WARWICKSHIRE ARMS AND LINEAGES - - 1866
(By F. W. Kittermaster, with woodcuts of Arms.)

WARWICKSHIRE AND STAFFORDSHIRE - - 1870
(By Langford and Macintosh, 2 vols., 4to., with plates.)

WARWICKSHIRE PORTRAITS - - - 1848
(Catalogue of Engraved Portraits, by J. Merridew;
very careful, useful, and scarce.)

WORTHIES OF WARWICKSHIRE - - - 1870
(4to. volume, 900 pp., edited by F. S. Colvile, and
with Special Biographies of Worthies from 1500 to
1800 by numerous contributors.)

WARWICKSHIRE MAPS.

[FULL details need not be given as to maps, but all those mentioned include the whole county of Warwick, and sometimes parts of adjoining counties, and are named in the order of date. The earliest map in which Birmingham and other parts of Warwickshire are clearly shown is that of *circa* 1286-1300, now in the Bodleian Library, and which was photozincographed (and coloured afterwards) by the Ordnance Office in 1875. It is remarkable that the only Warwickshire town shown is Birmingham, Coventry and Warwick even not being marked.]

Saxton, 1576 and 1603; Janson, 1600; Overton, 1603; Speede, 1610; Blome, 1670; Ogilby, 1675; Moll, 1680; Bowen, 1700; Beighton, 1725; Jefferies, 1740; Badeslade, 1741; Kitchin, 1750; Sayer, 1750; Yates, 1787; anonymous, 1795; Smith, 1818; Dix, 1820; Greenwood, 1821; Neele, 1840; Walker, 1840; Crutchley, 1849; White, 1850; Merridew, 1850; and many others, including, of course, the Ordnance Survey on the original one-inch and the recent six-inch scale.

Many of those named have special merits as to details, and the list is compiled partly from the writer's own collection and partly from that in the Reference Library, Birmingham, which also contains a large number of manuscripts, Civil War tracts, pamphlets, views, portraits, etc., illustrating the history and topography of Warwickshire.

INDEX.

ACTORS :
  Burbage, Richard, 135
  Greene, Thomas, 137
  Shakespeare, William, 137
Alcester, 283
Anglo-Saxon graves, 91
Anglo-Saxon remains, 59
Antiquaries :
  Archer, Sir S., 118
  Bloxam, M. H., 131
  Dugdale, Sir W., 120
  Ferrers, Henry, 124
  Hamper, William, 125
  Hunt, W. O., 130
  Sharp, Thomas, 127
  Staunton, William, 126
  Wheler, R. B., 128
Archæology :
  Earthworks and tumuli, 61
  Place-names, 63
  Roman roads and camps, 55
Arden, Forest of, 3
Artists :
  Allen, J. B., 138
  Barber, J. V., 138
  Brandard, R., 138
  Cox, David, 139
  Creswick, Thomas, 139
  Eginton, Francis, 140
  Eginton, Francis, jun., 141
  Garner, Thomas, 142
  Goodyear, Joseph, 142
  Green, Valentine, 142
  Haughton, Matthew, 143
  Haughton, Moses, 143
  Humphreys, H. Noel, 143
  Lines, Samuel, 144
  Pye, John, 145
  Radclyffe, William, 145

Artists—*continued*.
  Willmore, J. T., 146
  Wyon, Thomas, jun., 146
Authors :
  Addison, Joseph, 147
  Carte, Thomas, 148
  Cary, Henry F., 149
  Cave, Edward, 148
  ' Eliot, George ' (Mrs. Cross), 149
  Field, Rev. W., 152
  Galton, Mary Ann, 153
  Holland, Philemon, 154
  Holyoke family, 155
  Hutton, William, 157
  Hutton, Catherine, 158
  Landor, W. S., 159
  Noble, Mark, 160
  Parr, Dr. S., 162
  Priestley, Dr., 162
  Rous, John, 163

Beauchamp Chapel, 98
Beauchamp tombs, 101
Beauchamp Grevill tomb, 103
Bibliography of Warwickshire, 288-295
Birmingham :
  Artisans' Dwellings Act, 272
  Boulton, Watt and Murdock, 269
  Castle, 1154, 265
  Civic and social growth, 282
  Court Leet till 1854, 271
  Domesday times, 265
  Early chapel, 1383, 266
  Educational buildings and progress, 275
  Fairs, 1309, 265
  First Municipal School of Art, 273
  First Priory, 1285, 266
  Free Libraries, 274

Birmingham—*continued.*
　Generous donors, 273
　Gild of Holy Cross, 1382, 266
　Grammar School, 1550, 267
　Growth of a 'Free Town,' 268
　Incorporated, 1838, 271
　Leland's visit, 1538, 267
　Political history, 278
　Rapid growth of the town, 272
　Riots of 1791, 271
　Rupert's 'Burning Love,' 1642, 268
　Soho works, 269
　The 'Soho Circle,' 270
　Varied industries, 279
Bishops:
　Bird, John, 164
　Butler, S., 165
　Compton, Henry, 165
　Smalbroke, Richard, 167
　Sumner, J. B., 167
　Vesey, alias Harman, 168
　Willes, Edward, 171

Castles:
　Astley, 235
　Brandon, 84, 235, 237
　Caludon, 84, 235, 237,
　Coventry, 238
　Kenilworth, 79, 232, 246
　Maxtoke, 81, 233
　Tamworth, 83, 234
　Warwick, 73, 80, 231
Churches:
　Early, 77
　Lost, ruined, or desecrated, 112
Coventry:
　Anglo-Saxon charter, 261
　Ford's Hospital, 256
　Grey Friars, 257
　Industrial history, 259
　Leofric and Godiva, 264
　Parliaments, 253
　Ribbons, watches, etc., 259
　Royal visits, 253
　St. Mary's Hall, 256
　St. Michael's Church, 255
　The Charterhouse, 257

Danish traces, 72
Deer-parks:
　Arbury, 251
　Arrow, 251
　Aston, 251
　Charlecote, 250
　Clopton, 251
　Compton Wynyates, 250

Deer-parks—*continued.*
　Eatington, 250
　Fulbroke, 250
　Kenilworth, 249
　Maxtoke, 251
　Merevale, 251
　Packington, 251
　Shuckburgh, 250
　Stoneleigh, 250
　Sutton Coldfield, 249
　Warwick, 249
　Wedgenock, 249
　Weston, 250
Dialect:
　Dialect in Shakespeare, 224
　Dialect of Tysoe, 227
　Glossary of 1820, 221
　Glossary of 1861, 221
　Leicestershire parallels, 221
　Pronunciation, 221

Edge Hill, battle of, 9
Etocetum, 2

Famous houses:
　Arbury, 244
　Baddesley Clinton, 88, 236
　Charlecote, 241
　Clopton, 242
　Combe Abbey, 88, 240
　Compton Wynyates, 86, 236
　Coughton, 245
　Eatington, 243
　Guy's Cliff, 241
　Kingsbury, 246
　Merevale, 243
　Pooley, 246
　Ragley, 245
　Stoneleigh, 242
　Warwick Priory, 241
　Weston, 247
　Wormleighton, 247
Feldon, 3
Folk-lore:
　Curious customs, 217
　Fairy-lore, 220
　Local history of, 211
　Superstitions, 212
　Witchcraft, 215
　Wroth-money, 217

General worthies:
　Aitken, W. C., 207
　Arnold, Thomas, 203
　Cartwright, Thomas, 204
　Catesby, Robert, 204

General worthies—*continued*.
  Chamberlain, J. H., 207
  Croft, William, 204
  Dawson, George, 205
  Hill, Thomas Wright, 208
  Linwood, Mary, 209
  Thomas, William, 209
Geology, 30
  Coal, 35
  Glacial, 40
  Keuper red marls, 37
  Liassic area, 38
  New Red Sandstone, 33
  Marls, 33
  Permian, 36
  Physiography, 31
  Rocks, 33, 35
Gunpowder plot, 7, 204

Henley-in-Arden, 284

Industrial worthies :
  Boulton, Matthew, 199
  Murdock, William, 201
  Thomason, Edward, 202
  Watt, James, 201

Judges :
  Anderson, Edmund, 172
  Willes, John, 172
  Wilmot, J. E., 172

Kenilworth Castle, 79
  Priory, 284
  Revels, 233
  Siege of, 5
  Walter Scott's visit, 233

Leamington, 285
Leamington waters, 285
Legends :
  Godiva and Leofric, 19
  Guy and Phyllis, 17
  Long Compton and Augustine, 21
  Polesworth and St. Edith, 21

Maps, 296
Maps, tapestry, *circa* 1570, 247
Martyrs :
  Glover, Robert, 174
  Lewis, Mrs., 175
  Palmer, Julius, 175
  Rogers, John, 173
Military architecture, 77
Mineral springs, 285

Norman survey, 73
Norman castles, 73
Nuneaton, 283

Physicians :
  Ash, John, 176
  Cooke, James, 177
  Grew, Nehemiah, 178
  Hall, John, 179
  Hector, Edmund, 180
  Johnstone, Edward, 181
  Johnstone, John, 181
  Pearson, Richard, 182
  Willughby, Francis, 184
  Withering, William, 183
Poets :
  Drayton, Michael, 186
  Freeth, John, 188
  Huckell, John, 189
  Jago, Richard, 190
  Jordan, John, 190
  Shakespeare, William, 191
  Somervile, William, 197
  Warner, William, 198

Reform agitation, 15
Roads, 24
  British, 53
  Fosse-way, 57
  Roman, 2, 54
Rollright stones, 22, 90

Sacheverell, Dr., 14
Saxon and Danish remains, 69
Sepulchral monuments, 90-94
Sepulchral brasses, 95
Sepulchral memorials, 99
Shakespeare and Stratford, 193
  in London, 195
  Handwriting, 195
  Portraits, 108
Stratford-on-Avon :
  Birthplace and New Place, 286
  Church, 105, 286
  Gild Chapel, 286
  Grammar School, 286
  Memorial theatre, 287
  Shakespeare's bust, 108-111
  Shakespeare's monument, 109
  Shakespeare's grave, 106
  Shakespeare's daughters, 107
  Shakespeare's portraits, 108
Sutton Coldfield, 283

Tamworth Castle, 83
Temple Balsall, hall and church, 239

Warwick:
  Castle, 73, 80, 83
  St. Mary's Church, 98, 103
  Beauchamp Chapel, 98
  Beauchamp Chapel tombs, 101
  Woodland, 3

Zoology and Botany:
  Algæ, 51
  Beasts, birds and reptiles, 45
  Ferns, 49
  Fishes and molluscs, 47

Elliot Stock, Paternoster Row, London.

www.ingramcontent.com/pod-product-compliance
Lightning Source LLC
Chambersburg PA
CBHW021955220426
43663CB00007B/820